Beyond the Mor

At the Interface

An *At the Interface* research and publications project.
http://www.inter-disciplinary.net/at-the-interface/

The Evil Hub
'Monsters and the Monstrous'

2013

Beyond the Monstrous:

Reading from the Cultural Imaginary

Edited by

Janice Zehentbauer and Eva Gledhill

Inter-Disciplinary Press

Oxford, United Kingdom

http://www.inter-disciplinary.net/publishing/id-press/

The *Inter-Disciplinary Press* is part of *Inter-Disciplinary.Net* – a global network for research and publishing. The *Inter-Disciplinary Press* aims to promote and encourage the kind of work which is collaborative, innovative, imaginative, and which provides an exemplar for inter-disciplinary and multi-disciplinary publishing.

British Library Cataloguing in Publication Data. A catalogue record for this book is available from the British Library.

Inter-Disciplinary Press, Priory House, 149B Wroslyn Road, Freeland, Oxfordshire. OX29 8HR, United Kingdom.
+44 (0)1993 882087

ISBN: 978-1-84888-181-5
First published in the United Kingdom in Paperback format in 2013. First Edition.

Table of Contents

Introduction: Reading beyond the Monstrous

Janice Zehentbauer

Monsters have always simultaneously haunted and enthralled human beings. From Greek myths of metamorphoses to American southern-gothic tales, monsters stalk our imagination—but we often call them forth, as well. 'I have never seen a greater monster or miracle than myself,'[1] Michel de Montaigne observes in his essays, which also include ruminations upon fear and the imagination, of cannibalism and all of the marvels of the New World, elements deemed marvellous by a sixteenth-century French thinker. Yet, as the Montaigne quotation reveals, and as the chapters in this book demonstrate, fascination with the monstrous is not limited to place and time—although, paradoxically, cultural artefacts (ranging from text and cinema to architecture and art) that represent or examine the 'monstrous' articulate anxieties (latent or otherwise) of the place and time in which they were (are) produced. Montaigne effectively highlights another paradox inherent in many concepts of the monstrous: the monstrous is a construction of humankind, but it is an embodiment of humankind as well.

'Monstrosity' is a notoriously difficult category to define, even if one actually wanted to do so, for it is the nature of 'monstrosity' to transgress and to morph and to become something 'other than,' 'in addition to,' or 'more than.' Contemporary cultural critic Jeffrey Jerome Cohen argues, 'the monster signifies something other than itself: it is always a displacement, always inhabits the gaps between the time of upheaval that created it and the moment into which it is to be received, to be born again.'[2] As Montaigne's observation reminds us, however, the monstrous is not always figured as 'Other;' that is, the monstrous is not only a projection of fears, but an internalization as well. Tensions between social constructions and searches for 'individual' identity shape part of the discourse of humanity and monstrosity.

The chapters in this book are drawn from the 9th *Global Conference: Monsters and the Monstrous*, held by Inter-Disciplinary.Net at Mansfield College, Oxford, in early September 2011. The range of papers presented by delegates from around the globe demonstrated that fascination with monsters continues to flourish. The chapters included in this volume, *Beyond the Monstrous*, examine constructions of monsters, from a variety of historical, interdisciplinary, and cultural perspectives. Chapters range from sixteenth and seventeenth-century European treatments of the monstrous, to post-industrial Japan, to the contemporary popular culture's fascination with The *Twilight* Saga.

While chapters are grouped into categories of similarity, the categories are not discrete; like monstrosity itself, these dialogues elude containment. Themes and arguments in one chapter resonate and echo throughout other chapters, as the authors engage in an on-going dialogue.

The first section introduces the construction of 'Monstrous Women.' The chapters scrutinize various roles occupied by women in history throughout the world, ranging from widowhood, to sexual threat, to motherhood. In the first chapter entitled 'Monsters in the Shadows: Brahmin Widows in Twentieth-Century India,' Sarah Rangaratnam draws attention to a marginalized group of women in the caste system of India by juxtaposing two media which feature the plight of widows: Deepa Mehta's film *Water* (2005) and Padma Viswanathan's novel *The Toss of a Lemon* (2008). Both works demonstrate the ways in which widows are cast out of the Brahmin society because they are no longer considered valuable, particularly in relation to a man. Indeed, widows are shunned and become scape-goated figures that are physically and ritualistically isolated from their Hindu communities. As Rangaratnam's steady analysis reveals, such isolation renders identity and spiritual crises for the widows, since social dictates demonize them simultaneously as sexual deviants, models of the Hindu faith, and ill omens.

We remain in the realm of the socially constructed female monster in Michael E. Crandol's chapter about Japanese horror film, or 'J-horror,' in 'Sympathy for the She-Devil: Poison Women and Vengeful Ghosts in the Films of Nakagawa Nobuo.' Crandol points out that contemporary international success of films such as *Ringu* ('The Ring,' 1998) and *Ju-on* ('The Grudge,' 2002) has drawn audiences to re-view the influential twentieth-century Japanese director, Nakagawa Nobuo (1905-84). After a brief review of Nobuo's *œuvre*, of which the horror genre is only a part, Crandol focuses upon two particular films: the kabuki horror *Tōkaidō Yotsuya kaidan*, and *Dokufu Takahashi Oden* ('Poison Woman Takahashi Oden,' 'A Wicked Woman'). The former film features the vengeful ghost of an ill-treated woman, Oiwa, while the latter depicts the story of a notorious female criminal of the Meiji era (1868-1912). Crandol points out that the same actress, Wakasugi Kazuko, plays the role of a martyr in the one film and a villain in the other; he uses this point to argue that these seemingly opposite roles unsettle the boundaries of motherhood, female sexuality, and monstrosity.

Belinda Calderone turns our attention from twentieth-century popular culture to genres that comprised popular culture in early modern Europe: fairy tales, broadsheets, and pamphlets. In 'The Monster Inside Me: Unnatural Births in Early Modern Italian and French Fairy Tales,' Calderone examines that ways in which fairy tales and popular beliefs informed one another regarding the depictions of 'unnatural' progeny, and the mothers who birthed such progeny (mothers who were also, ultimately, marked as monstrous). Calderone reads literary tales by Giovan Francesco Straparola, Giambattista Basile and Marie-Catherine d'Aulnoy, as well as popular publications such as broadsheets, to reveal the widespread fascination with monstrous births, the most popular being animal-human hybrids. As Whitney Dirks-Schuster will observe in a chapter in this volume, fascination with monstrosity parallels a fascination with sexuality; Calderone's argument focuses upon ideas about female sexuality, and the ways in which medical and popular discourses sought to contain it to ensure 'natural' offspring.

As the title of the second section indicates, the second group examines themes of adolescence, liminality, and age. Drawing upon the psychological study of the 'Wolf-Man' by Freud, and the theoretical frameworks of Gilles Deleuze and Félix Guattari, as well as those of Slavoj Žižek, Steven Rita-Proctor analyses the cultural imaginary's figure of the werewolf in his chapter 'Narrativizing Sexual Deviance as both Symptom and Fantasy: The Perverse Sexuality of the Wolf-Child.' Rita-Procter examines a range of twentieth-century cultural texts, including among others the movie that features Michael Landon's performance in *I Was a Teenage Werewolf* (1957) to Michael Jackson's landmark music video "Thriller" (1983) to a brief discussion of the character Jacob Black in Stephenie Meyer's *Twilight* series. Rita-Procter reads against traditional literary and cinematic representations of werewolves as symbols of libido and violence. Rita-Procter stresses that figures of lycanthropy are not external to a community, but are symptomatic of domestic communities themselves. He points out that a werewolf narrative's key scene is the moment of metamorphosis, a liminal moment, which for Rita-Procter signifies the tumult of adolescence, particularly male adolescence, and the ways in which communities demonize the sexuality of young men.

Simon Bacon continues the theme of male adolescence, performance, and liminality in his chapter 'The Lost Boys?! Monstrous Youth of the Cinematic Teenage Vampire.' Bacon offers a brief survey of conceptions of the teenager, as fashioned by American cinematography. He then moves to an analysis of the 1980s film *The Lost Boys*, by Joel Schumacher, and the *Twilight* novels and films. Bacon notes that the1980s, with its intense focus upon films for teenaged-audiences, was also the decade that spawned adolescent-centric vampire movies. For Bacon, *The Lost Boys* is symptomatic of the decade's preoccupation with definitions (and transmutations) of family and gender, and finds that the film, for all its emphasis upon rebellious and wayward youth, contains a conservative core. Bacon argues that while the vampiric youth of the 80s repeatedly perform stereotypical rebellious acts without thought, the vampires of Meyer's *Twilight* series 20 years later are much more knowing in their performativity; he points out that Edward Cullen is much more aware than his 80s forebears about his performance not only as a vampire, but as a teenager. Bacon concludes that Edward's presence renders the *Twilight* series more subversive than the 80s film which overtly advertises rebellion while covertly championing conservative values.

The chapter that rounds out this section, Monica Dufault's 'Mirror, Mirror on the Wall: Youth, Age and the Monstrosity of Beauty in the *Twilight* Saga,' explores further a notion already present in Bacon's argument—that vampires and other monstrous figures have become increasingly youth-centric in the late twentieth-century and early twenty-first century cultural imagination. For Dufault, *aging* constitutes the monstrous in the *Twilight* series. Dufault argues that Meyer's novels solidify, indeed calcify, the divide between youth and age; this divide, for Dufault, is a facet of North American popular culture's obsession with youth and beauty. While Bella's decision to become a vampire is presented in the novels as an individual's 'choice,' Dufault contends that Bella actually buys in to the social ideal that a 'self' is forever young and beautiful. Dufault finds Bella's choice particularly insidious, for it enforces the idea that a woman's mature sexuality must be spurned and rendered monstrous.

The third section comprises examination of the monstrous 'beyond gender.' As with Calderone's focus, Whitney Dirks-Schuster draws our attention to Western, early modern's fascination with monsters in the chapter, 'Print Culture and the Monstrous Hermaphrodite in Early Modern England.' Dirks-Schuster investigates the popularity of ambiguous sexuality in seventeen-century England, using a range of print sources, including pseudo-scholarly sex manuals, articles about real-life hermaphrodites, and broadside ballads. Dirks-Schuster argues that the hermaphrodite body was offered as viewing material, not only for doctors, but also for public spectacle. In addition to providing potential definitions of a hermaphrodite, drawn from seventeenth-century medical documents as well as contemporary social studies about human sexuality ('potential' definitions, because, as the writer notes, defining hermaphrodite is problematic), Dirks-Schuster provides statistics that demonstrate inter-sexed humans were not particularly rare in early modern England. Dirks-Schuster's archaeological study of texts reveals that the perceived transgression of gender boundaries which troubled mid-wives, physicians, parents alike, rendered the hermaphrodite one of the most 'consumed' figures in England.

Rowan Roux continues the discussion of hermaphrodites in 'Monstrous Hermaphrodites: Jeffrey Eugenide's *Middlesex*, the Intersexed Individual and the *Bildungsroman*.' Eugenide's 2003 novel explores the experience of inter-sexed individual Calliope Stephanides, who is born with 5-alpha-reductase-deficiency syndrome; designated female at birth and raised as such, Calliope discovers that s/he is biologically male. After situating the novel in historical, sociological, and medical debates regarding hermaphrodites, Roux examines not only the challenges faced by Calliope, but also the problematic discourses that attempt to determine intersexed individuals. Ultimately Roux demonstrates that the designation 'monster,' actually enables Calliope to unsettle and reveal gender performances, and to realize that ambiguous sexuality is a facet of the human condition.

The third section concludes with a return to Japanese cinematography with Steven A. Nardi and Munehito Moro's discussion of the original *Gojira*, in 'Who Mourns for Godzilla? *Gojira* and De-Asianization of Post-War Japan.' While the film might be viewed by some as a camp horror classic, Nardi and Munehito emphasize that upon its release in 1954, the film terrified audiences whose most recent, searing national memories were the horrors of the atomic bombings, and the atrocities of World War II. Nardi and Munehito argue that the film manifests anxieties regarding Japan's role in the war, its pre-war imperialistic ambitions and subsequent collapse, and its emergent industrial expansion. The authors analyse the creation of *Gojira* and the concept of monstrosity by invoking the Derridean notion of the supplement, finding the nation's ideological reorganization in the post-war era forced its citizens to reinterpret and adopt new modes of political citizenship, only after moving through a period of mourning the past.

The fourth section turns attention to questions of what constitute identity, of individual selves as well as of collective nationhoods. Post-war Japan is the continued focus in Norihiko Tsuneishi's 'Spectres of Capitalism: Ghostly Labour and the Topography of Ruin in Post-Industrial Japan.' Tsuneishi moves beyond text and screen to read geographical monuments and industrial spaces that shape and haunt the cultural imaginary. Specifically, Tsuneishi examines Hashima, one of the islands off the coast of Nagasaki in Japan; a former site of coal-mining industrial activity and colonial subjectivity, the place is now abandoned. However, as Tsuneishi demonstrates, the ruined ferroconcrete edifices which comprise what is known as 'Gunkanjima' (Battleship Island) have become have become a national landmark. Employing Bahktin's theories of the grotesque, Tsuneishi figures the island and its remnants as a grotesque body, offering a persuasive analysis of the ethical ramifications of memorializing as a national landmark a site that also carries echoes of capitalist denigrations of humanity.

The section then shifts from monumental, monstrous landscape to American renderings of history in 'Monsters and Survivors in Oates's Jewish American Saga' by Maria Luisa Pascual-Garrido. This chapter specifically focuses upon Joyce Carol Oates's *The Gravedigger's Daughter* (2007), a chronicle of a Jewish, immigrant family fleeing Nazi Germany. Pascual-Garrido offers a brief survey of Gothic literature to situate Oates' novel, finding that Gothic-inspired narratives appear around times of cultural crises. Pascual-Garrido suggests that Gothic-postmodernist narrative strategies, as exemplified by Oates' novel, signify a response to contemporary anxieties regarding terrorism, for example, in the post-9/11 era. In this analysis, Pascual-Garrido explores the tensions between social constructions of marginalized figures, and a young woman's struggle for individual agency and identity within such a context.

In the final chapter of this volume, 'Grave Tales, Monstrous Realities,' Louise Katz examines the nature of narrative and story-telling, and the strategies through which humans imagine and recreate the realities in which they live. Like Pascual-Garrido, Katz explores the marginalized figure of the Jew, but she also incorporates the debates of Israeli-Palestinian political perspectives into her argument. Katz contends that marginalized figures are condemned to spectral, partial realities in the cultural imagination. Using the theoretical concept of Foucault's heterotopia—the designation of liminal and transitional spaces—Katz investigates the ways in which Jewish people have been figured 'monstrous' (such as the Jew-as-vampire), and the ways in which Palestinian people have been rendered into what she identifies as a 'new kind of ghost.' Katz shares a concern articulated by Norihiko Tsuneishi regarding the ethics of nationhood: monuments may marginalize rather than memorialize, creating spectres out of the living as well as the dead.

Ultimately this book contributes to historical, ethical, and aesthetical discourses of the monstrous, moving beyond traditional conceptions of what constitute the macabre. May these chapters haunt and hold sway over all.

Notes

[1] Michel de Montaigne, *The Complete Essays*, ed. and trans. M. A. Screech (Penguin: London, UK, 1993), 1162.
[2] Jeffrey Jerome Cohen, 'Monster Culture: (Seven Theses),' in *Monster Theory: Reading Culture*, ed. Jeffrey Jerome Cohen (Minneapolis, MN: University of Minnesota Press, 1996), 4. Cohen's idea here is influenced by the Derridean concept of 'supplement;' a similar idea will be echoed in this volume by authors Steven Nardi and Munehito Moro.

Bibliography

Cohen, Jeffrey Jerome. 'Monster Culture: (Seven Theses).' *Monster Theory: Reading Culture*, edited by Jeffrey Jerome Cohen. Minneapolis, MN: University of Minnesota Press, 1964.

de Montaigne, Michel. *The Complete Essays*. Translated and edited by M. A. Screech. Penguin: London, 1993.

Part I

Monstrous Women

Monsters in the Shadows: Brahmin Widows in Twentieth-Century India

Sarah Rangaratnam

Abstract
In the Indian cultural imaginary of the twentieth century, widows were constructed as physical and spiritual monsters as a way of validating the inhumane treatment that they were forced to sustain. Indian society cited religious reasons for such marginalization, but it has become clear that money, or want of it, was the underlying cause. This chapter will discuss high-caste, Brahmin widows from both ends of the financial spectrum, as they are represented in two works set in early twentieth century India: Deepa Mehta's film *Water* and Padma Viswanathan's novel *The Toss of a Lemon*, and will draw comparisons to constructions of widows in the cultural imaginary of early modern Europe. Physically, the widows of both *Water* and *The Toss of a Lemon* are branded as monsters according to the dictates of the Hindu religion – their heads are shaved, they are dressed in a 'uniform' of white, they are forced into seclusion and they are refused any physical contact. Spiritually, these women are demonized in three conflicting ways: they are simultaneously represented as sexual deviants, as celibate paragons of the Hindu faith, and as dangerous bad omens. This paper will also explore how the widows manage their own personal conflicts between faith and conscience in a time of such great political and social transformation. As their identity and their religious rituals are so powerfully connected, when change finally arrives, the widows are not relieved, but are instead left desperately wondering who they are. The women depicted in *Water* and *The Toss of a Lemon* are representative of a large population of widows who were regularly demonized and socially alienated in India at the turn of the century. There are estimated to be over 30 million such widows in India today, still struggling under the monstrous identity constructed for them by society.

Key Words: Widows, India, caste, women, monsters, Hindu, brahmin.

*****

In Indian culture, sons are kept close to home and considered valuable assets, as they can provide financial support to the family, and can inherit land. Daughters, on the other hand, are not attributed equal value. In fact, before 2005, women in most states in India were not legally permitted to inherit property.[1] A girl is raised with the sole purpose of becoming a part of her future husband's household. Sivakami, Padma Viswanathan's protagonist in *The Toss of a Lemon,* comments:

> Everyone says you raise a girl for someone else – you pay for her wedding and then the fruits of your investment are enjoyed by

> others. She is the wealth that leaves your family. A boy is the wealth that stays.[2]

Although they were paid less than their male counterparts, daughters in low-income and lower class families did often work outside the home and contribute to the household finances. However, women in higher caste families were usually prevented from such outside work, and were kept in isolation at home in what is known as 'purdah'. Being able to afford to keep their women at home was traditionally indicative of a family's wealth and status, and is a practice that continues to this day.[3] There was another benefit to keeping women in *purdah*. Having them secluded and close at hand was a way to exert sexual control and ensure purity of lineage. This was of particular importance for upper caste families which had bloodlines to maintain.

Prohibiting women from contributing to the family income has a major downside: it is expensive. Historically, there have been many instances of families which could not afford such practices, but which did not want to compromise their social status in their communities by allowing their daughters to work. The resulting solution was to marry them off as early as possible – as children, preferably – if the parents could afford a dowry. Families who could not afford dowries for their daughters often resorted to drastic measures, including abandonment and female infanticide. Alarmingly, both do still occur in India today.[4]

While a woman who had not yet married was a liability to her parents, a widow was legally the responsibility of her in-laws. If she had no sons to continue their bloodline or inherit the property, she no longer had any connection to them. She was a stranger in their home, and a family already struggling to make ends meet often could not afford to (or did not want to) support her. In the lower castes, widows did sometimes remarry, or were able to find work to support themselves. However, as families in the upper echelons of society were intent on maintaining their status in the community, whether or not they actually had the wealth to support it, widows, as all women, were prevented from leaving the home in search of work, or a new husband. Many families were more willing to 'delete' a member of the household than jeopardize their status in the community by breaking *purdah*. To achieve this, they would abandon their widowed daughters-in-law at ashrams where they were housed in seclusion, forever out of sight and forgotten by their families, and usually in dire conditions. To excuse the lack of food, shelter and other basic necessities in these ashrams, the widows were made to believe that the ancient Hindu scriptures dictated for them a life of self-deprecation. To justify the rejection and abandonment by their families, Hindu society used religion and superstition to construct the widow as monstrous and dangerous in the community.

> SHAKUNTALA. Why are we widows sent here? There must be a reason for it.
>
> NARAYAN. One less mouth to feed, four saris saved, one bed, and a corner is saved in the family home. There is no other reason why you are here. Disguised as religion, it's just about money.[5]

Deepa Mehta's film *Water* focuses on a group of upper-class Brahmin widows forced to live in an ashram in India in the 1930s. It deals with several issues surrounding the fate of these women, from their early beginnings as child brides to their rejection by their families, and finally, to living in the state of self-deprecation that they believe was dictated by the ancient Hindu scriptures. Set during the time of Gandhi's rise in popularity and amidst the resulting political changes, this film sheds light on the effects of those changes on Hindu religious beliefs and the treatment of the widow in Indian society. Mehta considers the effects of poverty on morality – how economics will push a society to marginalize and abandon its most vulnerable, and how hunger can affect ethical values within those marginalized groups. Mehta also attempts to explore how the widows themselves manage their own personal conflicts between faith and conscience in this time of great social change.

The widows in *Water* have been abandoned, having had no sons or heirs to their husbands' property, and therefore no connection to their in-laws. However, their difficulties did not end there. Although Hindu society found ways to marginalize widows in general, these women were particularly vulnerable to demonization because they were childless. In a place and time when a woman's sole purpose was to produce and raise heirs, a childless woman was a problem. She was not living up to her role in the family and in her community. Perhaps she was not worshipping enough, or in the right way. Perhaps she was being punished for wrongdoing in this, or in a former, life. Perhaps she was not giving her husband enough opportunity. Her in-laws would become concerned. Was there something wrong with her? Was she defective? When motherhood was considered the norm for a woman of childbearing age in twentieth century India, it is not surprising then that a childless woman would be considered deviant and would therefore be demonized in her community.[6]

But what happens to a widow who does have children?

Viswanathan's *The Toss of a Lemon* is inspired by stories told to the author by her grandmother of the family history. The central character is Sivakami, a child bride who becomes a widow with young children when she is only eighteen years old. Of her two children, the youngest, Vairum, is a boy, and Sivakami spends the rest of her life in the role of protector of his inheritance. As Vairum's guardian, Sivakami and his older sister are allowed to reside in her late husband's home, but they live modestly in order to safeguard his inheritance. Much care is also taken to protect the family's status, for maintaining Vairum's future social standing. The novel further deals with Sivakami's strict adherence to the rules of her Hindu faith, especially those imposed by her upper class, Brahmin caste, and follows her and her family from 1892 to the 1950s. During this time, India acquires independence from Britain, and the ensuing political and social changes leave Sivakami to struggle with her faith and her identity.

In the Indian cultural imaginary, the widow was constructed as a physical and spiritual monster as a way of validating the inhuman treatment that she was forced to sustain. Indian society has cited religious reasons for such marginalization, but it has become clear that money alone, or want of it, has been the underlying cause. Through Mehta's camera lens, and Viswanathan's prose, we will look at three conflicting ways in which these women have been demonized. They have been simultaneously represented as sexual deviants, as celibate paragons of the Hindu faith, and as dangerous bad omens.

1. A Sexual Deviant

As the conditions in the ashrams were often so poor, many widows resorted to prostitution in order to survive: 'With limited means for survival in a distant unrelated world, it was natural that impoverishment would follow and morality would be at stake'.[7] The ashram in *Water* is dependent upon Kalyani's success as a prostitute, and she is regularly sent out to the homes of local Brahmin men for this purpose. The men feel it is their right to exploit her sexually, but they also have few other options. In such a strict social hierarchy, contact with a woman of a lower caste would be detrimental to their status, but women of their own caste would generally be kept in *purdah*, and therefore would be unavailable. The widows, on the other hand, although impoverished, are still part of the Brahmin caste, are available in the evening under the cover of darkness, and are therefore considered acceptable candidates for sexual exploitation by these men.

As widows had few means of supporting themselves, Indian society assumed that those who were living on their own, even those barely subsisting, were resorting to prostitution to do so, whether or not they actually engaged in the practice. In Indian patriarchal culture, any single woman was considered a potential temptress for men in her community, and therefore a sexual liability for her family. She needed to be reined in and controlled in order to protect the lineage. This was especially important to upper class families, who felt they had bloodlines to maintain. Widows were particularly depicted as sexually deviant, since they had escaped the watchful eyes of their husbands or fathers.

This characterization of widows as sexually promiscuous is reminiscent of the attitudes of early modern Europe. Belinda Calderone's chapter on monstrous births in early modern fairy tales begins a discussion about the perceptions of women's sexuality in that period, and can be expanded to look at how widows fared in the cultural imaginary of the early moderns. As early modern women were expected to be either married or about to be married,[8] widows defied categorization, and early modern men were fearful of the potential dangers of these women existing outside of patriarchal control. It was unfathomable that a woman would be able to resist the sexual advances of unsuitable men on her own accord, and illegitimate children were a threat to bloodlines as well as finances. This obsession with the 'dangers' of widowhood is evidenced in the abundance of widow comportment manuals produced in Europe during that period such as *Book on a Widow's Life* (1491) by Girolamo Savonarola, *Concerning the Life that a Lady who is a Widow Should Live*_(1524), by Giovanni Giorgio Trissino of Vicenza, Juan Luis Vives' *Instruction of a Christian Woman* (1523) and Erasmus' *The Christian Widow* (1529), all of which encouraged a life of solemnity, chastity and dedication to the church. The later French fairy tales of the seventeenth century reflect popular agreement with these practices, an example being the character of the good widow in Marie-Catherine D'Aulnoy's 'Princesse Belle Etoile', who is admired for her adherence to a life of self-deprecation.[9]

One way to exert control over a woman's sexuality was to render her unattractive. Early modern widows in the western world were expected to wear black, unadorned clothing, and to cover their hair. Similarly, Brahmin widows of twentieth century India were expected to remove all jewellery, wear nothing but a white sari and, perhaps most traumatizing, have their heads shaved. This defeminisation, although described as an almost peaceful event in *The Toss of a Lemon* was, in reality, akin to rape for many widows. As one widow wrote:

> The greatest of all miseries, the culmination of the enormities of custom is the forcible shaving of a brahmin and other high caste widows. The cruel and pernicious custom is horrid beyond conception. [The widow] is simply helpless; she must submit to that cruel inhuman operation. She often faints, she is dumbfounded, tears flow in a flood... but nobody cares. Her caste people think they have achieved a great success as soon as she is disfigured. What demonical work.[10]

In *Water*, Kalyani is allowed to forego shaving her head, as her physical beauty is necessary for the ashram's survival. Nevertheless, when it is discovered that Kalyani hopes to remarry, Madhu Didi, the ashram's head matron, violently hacks away at her hair with scissors to punish her. She hopes to keep her from attracting another husband, as the ashram cannot afford to lose Kalyani's income.

Hindu custom, however, did not recognize an economic goal for this enforced 'ugliness'. Rather, it was believed to be necessary to ensure that the widow would remain chaste and faithful to her dead husband, so that she might be rewarded in the afterlife for her celibacy. Altering her outward appearance in this way also ensured that her widow status was physically apparent to all who saw her. It was the easiest way to alert the community of the perceived threat: a single woman without a husband or father to control her. It branded her as requiring strict surveillance by the community at large.

According to Edward Harper in his article 'Ritual Pollution as an Integrator of Caste and Religion', other members of upper caste Indian society often believed widows required the strict religious rituals in order to keep themselves in check. He quotes one man as saying, 'They do these pure things to prevent their doing bad things; to keep themselves [their sexual desires] in control.'[11] This attitude is redolent of the characterization of widows as 'lusty' in early modern Europe. As women in that period were generally considered to be a dangerous mix of sensuality and weak-mindedness, these particular women, having no husbands to satisfy their sexual desires, nor fathers to keep them in line, were viewed as a threat. Patriarchal society's fear of the widow's uncontrolled sexuality manifested in a stereotype: she was made out to be a lusty, promiscuous, even insatiable, sexual deviant. The proliferation of folktales in early modern Europe that represent the widow in this manner reflects this deeply held societal concern with widows and their sexual identities. One such folk tale is Jean de la Fontaine's 'La Matrone d'Ephèse,' published as part of his *Contes et nouvelles en vers* (1664), and which was actually a re-write of *The Widow of Ephesus* first told by the Roman Petronius in the first century. The story, therefore, was nothing new: a widow, at first vowing eternal devotion to her recently deceased husband, quickly forgets him upon meeting a dashing young soldier at his grave. In La Fontaine's version, however, the soldier is not so much dashing as, well, breathing. Feeling sorry for her, he offers her something to eat, upon which the widow immediately seduces him in the crypt itself.[12] The popularity of La Fontaine's version of the tale reflects societal perceptions of widows as sexually insatiable, with the popular thought being that, as these women had experienced sexual intercourse during their marriage they were now unable to control their desire for it, unlike virgins whose sexual urges had not yet been awakened by a husband. This sexual insatiability was cited as a further reason for the strict control of widows in early modern Europe.

Although the reasons officially given for preventing Indian widows from engaging in any romantic affairs were usually religious, families had a much more immediate reason to concern themselves with a widow's sexuality: maintaining social status. The Hindu caste system, which has been in place for thousands of years, has, until recent times, governed all aspects of a person's life. Caste determined where a person lived, who he or she could marry, and his or her potential career choices. People are born into their caste, and social mobility is inconceivable. Brahmins were at the top of the hierarchy both socially and spiritually. The widows in *Water* and *The Toss of a Lemon* belonged to this group.

In Hindu society of the twentieth century, the only real 'sin' that was punishable by outcasting, that is, excommunication from one's caste, was the act of sexual contact with a member of a lower caste. Outcasting, however, did not just apply to the person who was excommunicated, but their entire family was affected by association. As such, it was rare for family members to accuse each other of such actions, and without solid proof, it was almost never worth the effort to point fingers to other unrelated persons within the caste either (which explains why men were almost never outcaste for such behaviour). However, if a widow had a child after her husband died, as it was impossible to prove who the father may have been, she was typically punished by outcasting.[13] The backlash therefore greatly affected her family members both socially and, before land reforms in the mid-twentieth century, this meant economically as well.

Therefore, maintaining purity of blood, social status and economic prosperity, especially in a strict social ranking system such as that which was in place in India, was likely the reason for the Brahmin family's desire to depict their widows as sexual deviants. There was a hope that rendering a widow 'ugly', and branding her as dangerous, would reduce the risk of illegitimate children, which were solid proof of a romantic affair, and grounds for outcasting.

2. A Paragon of the Hindu Faith

During the time of independence, India underwent great political and social change that threatened the ancient Hindu laws involving caste and social status. In a time when women's roles were changing, and a western way of life threatened to move in on the home and family, the Brahmin widow was set up as an example of the perfect traditional, spiritual Hindu woman:

> The spotlessly white, pale and barren widow represented pureness of Indian tradition. In the colonized world of the last century, when western education, freedom and that way of life was penetrating fast, the spiritual superiority of the past tradition of India was put forward against the modernity of the colonizer. Throughout the period after the ban of sati, widows were still considered to bear the mantle of 'inner identity of the east' in its pure and non-corrupt form unlike the women of home. The imagery of the women of home underwent a radical change that the widows did not.[14]

Water is set on the Ganges: India's holy river and site of several of the country's widow ashrams. The cleansing property of water is an obvious recurring theme: the widows bathe in the river and rejoice in the rain. The water represents life, renewal, and ultimately for Kalyani, death.

But, traditionally, for Brahmins, the water also offered religious purification. Being of the highest caste, Brahmins were considered to be the closest to the gods. Lower castes worshipped Brahmins and Brahmins, in turn worshipped the gods.

According to custom, in order to worship, Brahmins had to be in a pure, or *madi*, state. To achieve *madi* they had to take a ritual bath in the morning, and avoid contact with anyone or anything *mailigë* (neutral) or *muttuchettu* (polluted) during daylight hours.[15]

> KALYANI. Learn to live like a lotus, untouched by the filthy water it grows in.[16]

Once Brahmins achieved *madi*, they had to follow strict rules to avoid being 'defiled' throughout the day. Physical contact of any kind with a person of another caste, or with a Brahmin who is not *madi*, was strictly forbidden. Also prohibited were the following: speaking to, eating with or making eye contact with someone who was not *madi*; eating food prepared by someone who was not *madi*, and generally touching anything that may have been touched by someone who is not *madi*. Only Brahmins may be *madi*, therefore any person of another caste was considered potentially defiling. Over time, in order to make it easier to avoid other castes, and therefore to lessen the risk of ritual pollution, Brahmins began to live together in segregated Brahmin quarters in villages.

> The barber cleans up and departs with the dignity of those who do the work the world despises. The locks he gathered will be sold as hairpieces. Sivakami bolts the courtyard and garden doors, then douses herself with buckets of cold water. Barbers are untouchables and she has been temporarily reduced to his status. The water makes her an untouchable of another kind. From now on, she will be madi, maintain a state of preternatural purity from dark to dark, so that no one may touch her after her pre-sunrise bath until the sun sets. And she will be as invisible as any untouchable in the Brahmin quarter, going to her river bath in the pre-dawn dark, returning before light so as to spare her neighbours the sight of a widow. Such a bad omen.[17]

The widow, perhaps turning to her faith for guidance following her husband's death, but more likely as a result of the social pressures discussed earlier, would often develop quite orthodox adherence to these religious rituals. To do so, Sivakami retreats to her kitchen, partly to stay out of the sight of others, and partly because it is where she will best be able to maintain *madi*. She is 'so pure as to be an outcaste'.[18]

But, despite her near invisibility, her strict adherence to Brahmin traditions earns Sivakami a certain respect among the women in her community as a 'paragon of Brahmin widowhood'.[19] Her behaviour is much like that of Catherine de Medici, perhaps early modern France's most famous widow. When Catherine was given the regency by the members of Privy Council in 1560, they had their reservations. After all, it was unheard of for a woman, and a foreigner at that, to be given so much power in France – especially a woman without a husband or father to guide her decisions. France was on the brink of religious war between Catholics and Protestants, and the nobility was crumbling. Catherine spent the rest of her life fighting to maintain control and, in an attempt to do so, she constructed an image of herself as an authoritative figure through portraiture.

Catherine de Medici's portraits, commissioned and performed by her, were in accordance with the comportment manuals and institutional exhortations of Renaissance patriarchal society. Catherine presented herself as a modern Artemisia – solemn, faithful and chaste – in an attempt to thwart potential concerns over the threat of a flighty, disloyal, overly sensual woman in power.[20] Although she was successful in her quest for authority, her desexualized image gained her a reputation for extreme cruelty and wickedness, while her male advisors and peers received much less, if any, criticism for their participation in her government

If Catherine's goal had been to use her widowhood to gain some political strength for herself, it was clearly not without its downside. She continued to struggle with the common paradox: a regency headed by a woman is considered a weak monarchy, but a woman heading a regency is considered unnaturally, even dangerously, powerful. Furthermore, her physical use of mourning served as a reminder to all of her widowhood and her continued status as an uncontrolled single female. As such, despite her solemn, modest portraits, rumours of Catherine's sexual promiscuity and immoral actions spread and persisted.

Sivakami, while shunned by society, is at the same time seen as the standard of purity that all others should try to emulate. To maintain *madi*, however, she gives up all physical contact with her young, grieving, children during daylight hours. Her son, Vairum, is particularly broken by this withdrawal, and lashes out in protest.

> Then he walked slowly past her, dragging his hand across the back of her thighs. She didn't have the heart to reprimand him. She went to take a second bath, after which Vairum strolled past and slapped her knee. She bathed again. An hour before sunset, he rubbed her head.[21]

Vairum's sabotage of Sivakami's *madi* was the first step in his rejection of Brahmin traditions, a confrontation that continues between them throughout the novel.

Although Sivakami does have the respect of some of her neighbours, and is able, until her son inherits his home, to live independently and manage the property, she would be an exception to the standard of treatment of widows in her time. In Sivakami's region of South India, Havik Brahmins, a specific subcaste of

Brahmins, referred to a widow who maintained *madi* and who followed orthodox religious practices as *prãni* – which literally means 'animal'.[22] These women, if not abandoned at ashrams, were sometimes allowed to stay with the family, but were treated as near slaves. They were referred to as 'it', made to work long and difficult hours, kept under close surveillance and were given, grudgingly, very little to eat. This treatment came regardless of their age (some as young as 8 years old), and from both their natal families and their in-laws. In general, widows were not believed to be entitled to any better. Uma Chakravarti studied essays written by young Brahmin widows themselves in the early part of the twentieth century:

> The abject and powerless situation of the high caste widow was continually reiterated through everyday expressions of power such as routine subjection to verbal 'lashings', denial of adequate food, surveillance, performance of drudge labour and even physical assaults….
>
> There are repeated references to the widows as 'burdens'; widows were made to feel that by their continued existence they were eating into the resources which 'belonged' to others and which the widows were not entitled to.[23]

Sivakami's circumstances may be far better than the norm, but she continues to struggle with her family in order to maintain that independence and to hold on to her home. When her husband died, his property, as is customary, was passed on to his son. Sivakami continues to live in the home with the children, but it is only as Vairum's guardian, and the property is considered to be in her safekeeping only until Vairum comes of age. In the meantime, she is perpetually at odds with her in-laws, who attempt to take advantage of her and claim back the property that they feel is rightfully theirs. When Varium does come of age, Sivakami has no real claim to the property, and she is completely dependent on him for her welfare. She feels that she is a guest in his home, and lives in constant fear that he could send her out at any time.

3. A Danger to Others

A widow in India was traditionally seen as a bad omen. Society shunned her to contain her bad luck, and prevent her from endangering others. No matter what the actual cause of her husband's death, she was seen as responsible for it.

> Now that her husband is truly gone, Sivakami feels an odd eagerness for the ceremonies that will brand her a widow. A woman whose husband dies before her is, in some cosmic karmic

> way, responsible for his death, and must be contained. The best way to do this is to make her unattractive…[24]

Throughout the novel, Sivakami does her best to stay out of sight of her neighbours in the Bramin quarter, as she believes she will bring them bad luck. She only leaves her home to bathe in the morning, and does so early enough so that she is able to do it unseen. But this self-policing is further enforced by a community that purposely avoids her out of fear of the bad omen that they believe she represents. In Indian society, which was rife with superstition, it was believed that husbands died because their wives brought them bad luck. These widowed women were then considered bad luck charms, and their presence was avoided at any auspicious occasion, for fear of an unlucky outcome. Unwilling to risk a possible jinx on the wedding couple, families especially prohibited widows from attending marriages (even of their own children, as in Sivakami's case). In *Water*, Shakuntala is reprimanded by a young priest for coming too close: 'Watch it! Don't let your shadow touch the bride!' In general, a Brahmin widow was expected to be invisible in her community so that she would not spread her bad luck around.

> The cotton of her saris grows thick and soft with washing. She draws the end over her head, sheltering her scalp from the sun or stray looks: white reflects all sunlight, any incidental looks glance off her. Bad omen.[25]

To stay out of sight, Sivakami spends most of her widowhood within the confines of the kitchen. There are, however, times when she is even further removed from the rest of society, and that is when she menstruates. Brahmin women were sequestered outside of the house while they were bleeding, so as to not pollute the *madi* occupants within. Menstruating women were temporarily reduced to 'untouchable' status – considered too impure to be in the vicinity of others. The result is an awkward few days every month during which Sivakami must hide on the back porch, in some cases yelling instructions through a crack in the door, while a neighbour takes over the management of the household.

> Menstruation always makes Sivakami feel strange, though she merely trades one kind of untouchability for another. Where she is normally too pure to be touched, not to mention a potent reminder of feminine destructive power, for these three days she is too impure to be touched, and a potent reminder of feminine procreative power.[26]

Again we may draw comparisons to early modern Europe when considering superstitious perceptions of women, sexuality and power. Where Calderone discusses early modern superstitions concerning a woman's procreative power – monstrous births as punishment for the sins of the mother – Indian culture of the twentieth century held fast to beliefs that a woman's sins would lead to the death of her husband and the suffering of her children. Throughout the novel, Sivakami maintains that she is the cause of her husband's death, and the undoing of her family.

Thus the monstrous image of the widow was constructed in twentieth century India. She was so powerful as to be dangerous: if she is not contained, she will seduce men and bear bastard children, or she will kill your sons with her bad luck. On the other hand, widows who maintained *madi* were considered too pure and holy to even be looked upon or, paradoxically, referred to as 'animals' and treated with scorn.

Both *Water* and *The Toss of a Lemon*, however, deal with another issue: the political and social changes that were happening during India's independence were threatening the caste system, which had been in place for thousands of years. Lower castes, which had been at a disadvantage for so long, were beginning to rise up and demand fair treatment and equality in government and society. Some liberal-minded members of the Brahmin caste, including Narayan in *Water* and Vairum in *The Toss of a Lemon,* were champions of the cause, and supported a dismantling of the ancient system. The widows themselves, however, are not in this category, and are guilty of perpetuating the monstrous image of the other, 'lower', castes.

Although the widows of these works are victims of alienation and segregation from other Brahmins, they in turn choose to avoid members of other castes. Believing that these 'lower' castes are dirty and unholy, the widows themselves avoid contact with them in order to secure for themselves a better place in the afterlife. This is apparent in *Water* when Shakuntala prepares the prayer site each day by sprinkling it with water she collects from the river. Brahmins would carry water with them in a vessel, and sprinkle it on the ground ahead of them as they walked, so as to not step on earth that had been defiled by others.[27] The widows in *Water* also keep themselves apart from Kalyani, to protect themselves from her impurity. She does not eat with them or pray with them: 'With her uncut hair and her clients. Eating with Kalyani would pollute our food.'[28]

Of course, the caste system was only one force at work. We cannot forget the patriarchal aspect of Indian society and the Hindu faith. The widows in *Water* may be from upper caste Brahmin families, but they were mostly illiterate and, like most other women in their caste, would have likely been kept in seclusion even before their widowhood.

> Sivakami must also walk the fields, though she cannot actually walk the fields: were she truly to walk in public view, she would be risking their social position in an attempt to maintain their

> economic grip. Any respectable Brahmin matron keeps largely out of sight if her family can afford that modesty; a widow must be kept entirely hidden, so as not to expose her shame at her condition.[29]

Shakuntala is at least able to read, but even she is unaware of what has been happening in the outside world, and is surprised to learn that there is even a law allowing widow remarriage – a law which had been passed over 75 years before. Faith, social structure and way of life were inseparable, and so strongly enforced in Indian patriarchal society, that these women may not have been able to even conceive of another way of life. Furthermore, as in Chuyia's case, many were married and widowed as very young children, knowing no other life than that of a widow.

> MADHU DIDI. A wife is part of her husband while he is alive. And when husbands die, God help us, wives also half die. So how can a half-dead woman feel pain?
>
> CHUYIA. Because she is half alive? I don't want to be a stupid widow![30]

The widows in *Water* truly believed that they needed to ensure their own purity in order to be closer to the gods, and rewarded in the afterlife. And what was that ultimate reward?

> SHAKUNTALA. God willing, she'll be reborn as a man.[31]

However, despite the forces working against her, Shakuntala does begin to struggle with the disparity between her conscience and her faith. When Kalyani commits suicide, and Chuyia is raped, Shakuntala finally sees the disconnect between her faith and the politics of religion. She leaves Chuyia with Narayan and Gandhi, hopeful that she will be saved from further atrocities in the name of religion and caste.

In *The Toss of a Lemon*, the dismantling of the caste system leaves Sivakami grasping for her sense of self. Devoting over forty years to maintaining her *madi* state, and raising her children and grandchildren in keeping with traditional Brahmin Hindu beliefs, Sivakami's identity and religious rituals are powerfully connected. As she feels the caste system, and all she has known, come crashing down around her, she is lost.

In the absence of her dead husband, Sivakami has spent her lifetime in complete dedication to his memory, and to raising her son, Vairum, his heir. Legally, and spiritually, she exists only for him. So, when Vairum turns away from tradition, and the only way of life Sivakami has ever known, she sees her life unravel before her. Vairum's interest in social reform begins when he is a youth, but the climax is reached when an elderly Sivakami joins him and his wife in their new home in the city, and she discovers that he has been allowing non-Brahmins to enter the apartment.

> The first time it happens, she is convulsed with disgust; she has cooked this food and Vairum and Vani are sitting together with three of those people, in plain view of those people, polluted by their gaze. She never shows herself in front of guests, Brahmin or non-Brahmin; the cook serves. But she glimpsed them as they entered – dark-skinned, evidently wealthy – and could hear them, using inflections and terms foreign to Brahmins, and imagined them eating the food she had prepared. She crouches in the door between the kitchen and puja room, feeling ill. The crowning insult is when they cut through the kitchen to the courtyard to wash their hands – they enter the kitchen! On the way back to the sitting room, they stop to compliment her lavishly on the food, mortifying her with their lack of manners.[32]

Fearing for his spiritual well-being, but aware that, being *only* a woman, and a widow at that, she is bound to his decision on the matter, Sivakami meekly asks Vairum to reconsider his association with non-Brahmins, to a disastrous end. Disgusted with his mother's continued prejudices, Vairum sends her to find her own way home. Terrified, lost, and travelling alone on busy trains full of potential 'pollutants' all around her, Sivakami comes close to suicide. It is only the knowledge that her granddaughter lives close by that brings Sivakami back from the brink. She finds the local Brahmin quarter and her granddaughter's Brahmin house. There, she takes a ritual bath and, in doing so, reinstates *madi* and her identity.

Although the widows in these works are certainly victims of demonization and 'monstrous' socio-cultural constructs, they do participate in creating the perception through their own support of the cultural and religious beliefs that perpetuate the image. The widows' obsession with purity, both racial and religious, is the force preventing them from accepting the social and political changes in India that would ultimately benefit them.

In his dialectic of *idem* (sameness) and *ipse* (selfhood), Ricoeur explains,

> ...the identity of a person or a community is made up of these identifications with values, norms, ideals, models and heroes, *in* which the person or the community recognizes itself. Recognizing oneself *in*, contributes to recognizing oneself by.[33]

As an orthodox Brahmin widow through most of the novel, Sivakami's *idem* and *ipse* largely overlap. But, when she is removed from her familiar Brahmin community and transplanted into that busy Indian train station, *idem* and *ipse* separate, and she is forced to consider her selfhood without the support of sameness.

The identity crisis is devastating. Having had the strict rules of widowhood forced upon her at such a young age, and having spent so many years in complete devotion to those traditions, Sivakami cannot find her *ipse* without the *idem*. Her reaction is to cling even more tightly to her Brahmin customs. Her loyalty to this *idem* is so tragic because she never realizes that it is from this group in particular that she has been ostracized all along. The community with which she identifies herself is the one that has constructed and represented her as a monster all these years.

> Janaki watches her grandmother. She has never seen her angry like this. *Her convictions are what sustained her*, Janaki thinks. *How dare Vairum Mama try to challenge her on her beliefs? They are the reason she is alive.*[34]

Regardless of her faith, the world is changing around her and Sivakami is forced to acknowledge it. In a final scene, Vairum returns to claim his family home, and brings with him an outsider: Bharati, a woman from the Devadasi caste of prostitutes who, we have learned, is the illegitimate daughter of his sister's husband. From the kitchen doorway, Sivakami witnesses Bharati enter the home, and eat with the family:

> Somehow, though, they are all present to witness the first fistful of rice Bharati lifts from the leaf to her mouth.
> There – there.
> The house is defiled.[35]

Her shock at what her son has done to his home causes Sivakami to suffer a stroke, but in the moments before she collapses, she continues to link this disastrous event to the bad luck she believes she has brought to the family. She sees herself as the cause of her husband's death, and reasons that she is therefore responsible for the family's social downfall as well. Sivakami is unable, or unwilling, to admit that the social changes around her are inevitable and driven by politics. She continues to cling not to her faith, but to the superstitions imposed by Hindu society. She thinks that she, either through bad behaviour in a former life, or an unlucky horoscope, or by somehow lacking in her ritual purity, has caused the undoing of her family.

The women depicted in *Water* and *The Toss of a Lemon* are representative of a large population of widows who were demonized and socially alienated in India at the turn of the century. Broken and demoralized, many relied on their convictions, their faith and their Hindu culture to keep them going. But with the societal changes in India over the past century, the basis on which these widows might have formed their own identities has been pulled out from under them. There are estimated to be over 30 million such widows in India today, still struggling under the monstrous identity constructed for them by society.

Notes

[1] T. K. Viswanathan, Hindu Succession (Ammendment) Act 2005, *Human Rights Law Network*, 15 September 2005. Viewed 27 September 2011. http://hrln.org/admin/issue/subpdf/HSA_Amendment_2005.pdf.
[2] Padma Viswanathan, *The Toss of a Lemon* (Toronto: Random House, 2008), 31.
[3] Elisabeth Bumiller, *May You Be the Mother of a Hundred Sons: A Journey among the Women of India* (New Delhi: Penguin Books India, 1991), 80.
[4] Ibid., 104-112.
[5] Deepa Mehta, *Water* (Mongrel Media, 2005).
[6] Catherine Kohler Riessman, 'Stigma and Everyday Resistance Practices: Childless Women in South India.' *Gender & Society* 14.4 (February, 2000): 111-135.
[7] Swati Ghosh, 'Bengali Widows of Varanasi'. *Economic and Political Weekly* 35.14 (Apr. 1-7, 2000): 1151.
[8] The Law's Resolution of Women's Rights, published in 1632 by an anonymous author, said of women: 'All of them are understood either married or to be married; … the common law shaketh hand with Divinity', quoted in Henderson, 72.
[9] D'Aulnoy, 110.
[10] Quoted in Uma Chakravarti, 'Social Pariahs and Domestic Drudges: Widowhood among Nineteenth Century Poona Brahmins.' *Social Scientist* 21.9/11 (1993): 130-158. *JSTOR*. Viewed 11 February 2010. 140.
[11] Edward Harper, 'Ritual Pollution as an Integrator of Caste and Religion' *The Journal of Asian Studies* 23 (1964): 151-197. *JSTOR*. Viewed February 16 2010.
[12] de La Fonataine, Jean, 'La Matrone d'Ephèse,' *La Fontaine's Bawdy: Of Libertines, Louts, and Lechers*, trans. Norman R. Shapiro (Princeton: Princeton University Press, 1992), 230-243.
[13] Ibid., 172.
[14] Swati Ghosh, 'Bengali Widows of Varanasi.' *Economic and Political Weekly* 35.14 (Apr. 1-7, 2000): 1152.
[15] Edward B. Harper, 'Ritual Pollution as an Integrator of Caste and Religion,' *The Journal of Asian Studies* 23 (1964): 151-197.

[16] Mehta, *Water*.
[17] Padma Viswanathan, *The Toss of a Lemon*, 65.
[18] Ibid., 66.
[19] Ibid., 135.
[20] Katherine Crawford, *Perilous Performances: Gender and Regency in Early Modern France* (Cambridge, MA: Harvard University Press, 2004).
[21] Ibid., 122.
[22] Harper, 'Ritual Pollution', 176.
[23] Chakravarti, 'Social Pariahs and Domestic Drudges', 131 – 133.
[24] Padma Viswanathan, *The Toss of a Lemon*, 64.
[25] Ibid., 73.
[26] Ibid., 160.
[27] Harper, 'Ritual Pollution', 154.
[28] Mehta, *Water*.
[29] Padma Viswanathan, *The Toss of a Lemon*, 41- 42.
[30] Mehta, *Water*.
[31] Ibid.
[32] Padma Viswanathan, *The Toss of a Lemon*, 540.
[33] Paul Ricoeur, *Oneself as Another*, trans. Kathleen Blamey (Chicago: The University of Chicago Press, 1992), 121.
[34] Padma Viswanathan, *The Toss of a Lemon*, 521.
[35] Ibid., 609.

Bibliography

Agarwal, Bina. 'Landmark Step to Gender Equality.' *The Hindu*, 25 September 2005. Viewed 28 April 2010. http://www.thehindu.com/thehindu/mag/2005/09/25/stories/2005925005010 0.htm.

Bean, Susan S. 'Toward a Semiotics of "Purity" and "Pollution" in India.' *American Ethnologist* 8.3 (1981): 575- 595.

Bouwsma, William J. 'Anxiety and the Formation of Early Modern Culture.' *After the Reformation: Essays in Honour of J. H. Hexter*, edited by Barbara C. Malament, 215-246. Philadelphia: University of Pennsylvania Press, 1980.

Bumiller, Elisabeth. *May You Be the Mother of a Hundred Sons: A Journey Among the Women of India*. New Delhi: Penguin Books India, 1991.

Chakravarti, Uma. 'Social Pariahs and Domestic Drudges: Widowhood among Nineteenth Century Poona Brahmins.' *Social Scientist* 21.9/11 (1993): 130-158.

Crawford, Katherine. *Perilous Performances: Gender and Regency in Early Modern France*. Cambridge, Mass.: Harvard University Press, 2004.

D'Aulnoy, Marie-Catherine. *Contes, Tome II*. Champaign, IL: Project Gutenberg, 2006. Viewed 01 August 2010.
http://www.gutenberg.org/catalog/world/readfile?fk_files=1512075&pageno=1.

Douglas, Mary. *Purity and Danger: An Analysis of Concepts of Pollution and Taboo*. London: Routledge, 1978.

Erasmus, Desideratus. *Erasmus on Women*, edited by Erika Rummel. Toronto: University of Toronto Press, 1996.

Ghosh, Swati. 'Bengali Widows of Varanasi.' *Economic and Political Weekly* 35.14 (Apr. 2000): 1151-1153.

Harper, Edward B. 'Ritual Pollution as an Integrator of Caste and Religion.' *The Journal of Asian Studies* 23 (1964): 151-197.

Henderson, Katherine U. and Barbara F. McManus. *Half-Humankind: Contexts and Texts of the Controversy about Women in England, 1540-1640*. Urbana: Illinois University Press, 1985.

Kohler Riessman, Catherine. 'Stigma and Everyday Resistance Practices: Childless Women in South India'. *Gender & Society* 14.4. (February, 2000): 111-135. Viewed 30 April 2010.
http://www2.bc.edu/~riessman/pdf/Stigma%20and%20everyday%20resistance%20practices.pdf.

Lanza, Janine M. *From Wives to Widows in Early Modern Paris: Gender, Economy and Law*. Burlington, VT: Ashgate, 2007.

La Fontaine, Jean de. 'La Matrone d'Ephèse.' *La Fontaine's Bawdy: Of Libertines, Louts, and Lechers*. Translated by Norman R. Shapiro. Princeton: Princeton University Press, 1992.

Levy, Allison. 'Framing Widows: Mourning, Gender and Portraiture in Early Modern Florence.' *Widowhood and Visual Culture in Early Modern Europe*, edited by Allison Levy, 211-231. Burlington, VT: Ashgate, 2003.

Ricoeur, Paul. *Oneself as Another*. Translated by Kathleen Blamey. Chicago: The University of Chicago Press, 1992.

Seiffert, Lewis C. *Fairy Tales, Sexuality, and Gender in France 1690-1715: Nostalgic Utopias*. Cambridge: Cambridge University Press, 1996.

Viswanathan, Padma. *The Toss of a Lemon*. Toronto: Random House, 2008.

Viswanathan, T. K., Hindu Succession (Ammendment) Act 2005, *Human Rights Law Network*, 15 September 2005. Viewed 27 September 2011. http://hrln.org/admin/issue/subpdf/HSA_Amendment_2005.pdf.

Vives, Juan Luis. *The Education of a Christian Woman: A Sixteenth Century Manual*. Translated and edited by Charles Fantazzi. Chicago: University of Chicago Press, 2000.

Warner, Marina. *From the Beast to the Blonde: On Fairy Tales and Their Tellers*. London: Vintage, 1995.

Water. Dir. Deepa Mehta. With Lisa Ray, John Abraham, Seema Biswas and Sarala. Mongrel Media, 2005.

Sarah Rangaratnam is a graduate student based in Ontario, Canada with degrees in Translation and Comparative Literature from York University and Brock University, Canada. Her current research focuses on the representation of widows in the arts across cultures and time periods.

Sympathy for the She-Devil: Poison Women and Vengeful Ghosts in the Films of Nakagawa Nobuo

Michael E. Crandol

Abstract
Nakagawa Nobuo (1905-84) is best known as the first major director of Japanese horror movies, with films such as *Tōkaidō Yotsuya kaidan* ('The Ghost Story of Yotsuya,' 1959) and *Jigoku* ('Hell,' 1960) often cited as major influences by the directors of Japan's later international horror successes like *Ringu* ('The Ring,' 1998) and *Ju-on* ('The Grudge,' 2002). One year before completing his acclaimed adaptation of the Edo period (1600-1868) kabuki horror classic *Tōkaidō Yotsuya kaidan*, Nakagawa directed the historical melodrama *Dokufu Takahashi Oden* ('Poison Woman Takahashi Oden,' a.k.a. 'A Wicked Woman'), based on fictionalized accounts of a famous real-life female criminal from the Meiji era (1868-1912). Despite major dissimilarities in the source material, *Dokufu Takahashi Oden* and *Tōkaidō Yotsuya kaidan* share a surprising number of formal and thematic points in common. Nakagawa uses the same actress, Wakasugi Kazuko, to portray Takahashi Oden and *Yotsuya kaidan*'s famous female *onryō* (vengeful ghost), Oiwa. Moreover, the two films structure Oden's and Oiwa's tragic character arcs among quite similar thematic lines, building both women's narratives around a pivotal moment of monstrous transformation. While Oiwa returns from the grave as a hideous spirit intent upon revenging herself on her unfaithful husband, Oden becomes a living monster driven by the cruelties of society to swear vengeance upon the men who wronged her. By seizing upon a similar sense of nostalgia surrounding two quite different female characters from popular 19th century fiction, Nakagawa blurs the boundaries between horror and melodrama, creating a pair of complementary films in which the injustices of a patriarchal society give birth to monstrous feminine avengers.

Key Words: Japan, ghosts, poison women, Nakagawa Nobuo, Takahashi Oden, *Yotsuya kaidan*, Oiwa, horror movies, monstrous feminine.

*****

The global success in the past decade of Japanese horror films such as *Ringu*, *Pulse*, and *Ju-on: The Grudge*, has sparked unprecedented interest in the history of Japanese horror cinema. The creators of 'J-Horror,' as the films which followed in the trail blazed by *Ringu* would come to be known, are quick to give credit to the work of director Nakagawa Nobuo as a major source of inspiration. Nakagawa was a venerable genre filmmaker with more than 100 pictures to his credit by the time of his death in relative anonymity in 1984. Although he worked in virtually every genre imaginable, it is his eight or so seminal excursions into the realm of cinematic horror that have single-handedly secured the director's legacy. The bulk of these were produced between 1957 and 1960 at the Shintōhō studios under tight deadlines and shoestring budgets, culminating in his critically lauded adaptation of the 19th-century kabuki classic *Tōkaidō Yotsuya kaidan* ('The Ghost Story of Yotsuya') in 1959, and his avant-garde evocation of Buddhist hells, *Jigoku*, in 1960. Nakagawa's concise, tightly plotted re-imaginings of Edo Period (1600-1868) ghost stories or *kaidan* – as well as some original, contemporary horror stories – pioneered the film grammar of modern Japanese horror cinema and laid much of the groundwork for the later international successes of J-Horror.

A seeming anomaly in Nakagawa's oeuvre during this period is 1958's *Dokufu Takahashi Oden* ('Poison Woman Takahashi Oden,' a.k.a. 'A Wicked Woman'). At a time when Nakagawa was concentrating his attention almost entirely on tales of supernatural horror, a movie about Takahashi Oden, the Meiji era's (1868-1912) most notorious female criminal or *dokufu* (lit. 'poison woman'), may appear an odd filmmaking choice. It is true that Shintōhō was in the business of making quickly produced exploitation films for a fast profit, and lurid crime dramas were as much the studio's stock-in-trade as B-grade horror films. However, the picture's many thematic similarities with Nakagawa's *kaidan* adaptations of the same period, notably *Kaidan Kasane ga fuchi* (1957) and *Yotsuya kaidan*, are too striking to ignore. For the role of Oden, Nakagawa casts actress Wakasugi Kazuko, who portrayed the *onryō* ('vengeful ghost') Orui in the previous year's *Kasane ga fuchi* and would go on to appear as Oiwa, Japan's most infamous *onryō*, in *Yotsuya kaidan*. More significantly, Nakagawa constructs Oden's transformation from sympathetic anti-heroine to wrathful demon along much the same trajectory that would mark Oiwa's daemonification in the following year's *Yotsuya kaidan*. While Oiwa has been portrayed as an innocent victim (if terrifying ghost) ever since her debut on the kabuki stage in 1825, the original Meiji-era newspaper serials of Takahashi Oden's exploits painted her as an intrinsic 'bad seed' whose evil behaviour is genetically predetermined.[1] Although not a literal demon, the *dokufu* was a far more fearsome threat than the otherworldly *onryō*, whose behaviour was restricted to haunting those who wronged her in life. Yet Nakagawa conceives Oden and Oiwa as kindred spirits, iconic ghouls from the popular fiction of bygone eras, wronged women wreaking vengeance upon their male tormentors. By the 1950s their shared status as legendary female monsters lurking in a romanticized Japanese past may have at least partially overshadowed the vast differences in the original conceptions of their characters. More importantly, the relative freedom-within-boundaries Nakagawa enjoyed under the Shintōhō studio system allowed the director to bring his own thematic concerns regarding victimized women and monstrous transformation to bear, re-imagining the late-Edo *onryō* of kabuki and popular fiction and the Meiji *dokufu* of newspaper serial notoriety as quite similar creatures.

1. Wronged Women and Wrong Women

Kabuki playwright Tsuruya Nanboku IV created the quintessential Japanese ghost in the character of Oiwa, the doomed heroine of *Tōkaidō Yotsuya kaidan*. With her long unkempt hair, grotesquely distorted face, tattered white robe and bloody fingernails, Oiwa's ghostly visage continues to haunt contemporary Japanese horror films in the form of *Ringu's* Sadako and *Ju-on's* Kayako. Whereas these modern-day *onryō* have turned their rage on humanity at large, however, Oiwa's grudge remains ruthlessly fixed on the ones responsible for her suffering. Terrifying as she may be to behold, Oiwa is a justifiably karmic monster.

Nakagawa's *Yotsuya kaidan* remains largely faithful to the plot of the original kabuki play. Both the play and Nakagawa's film follow the misfortune of Tamiya Oiwa, who is poisoned, disfigured, and indirectly murdered by her samurai husband Iemon, only to return from the grave as a hideous spirit hell-bent on revenge. In life Oiwa is the model 'good wife' and epitomizes the virtue of the samurai class, remaining loyal to her husband despite his cruel indifference to her and their newborn son. Yet once the extent of Iemon's treachery is made plain, Oiwa's spurned virtue gives birth to palpable rage. With her dying breath Oiwa curses her faithless husband, and a horrific female monster arises from the ashes of the mutilated and cast aside Edo feminine ideal. Oiwa's hideous ghost returns to make good on her curse, and both Nanboku and Nakagawa present their audience with a gruesome and disturbing haunting as Oiwa's spirit causes the deaths of Iemon and all of those complicit in her demise. Exploited and abused while alive, she can find redress only in death and monstrous transformation.

Nakagawa's take on Takahashi Oden, meanwhile, bears little resemblance to the historical criminal or the contemporary fictionalized accounts of her exploits. Little is known about the real Oden, who became the last woman in Japan to be executed by beheading on January 31, 1879 after being convicted of murdering her lover in a Tokyo inn. Rumours soon spread that she had also previously murdered her husband, who died several years before. The same year of her execution novelist Kanagaki Rōbun began writing a fictionalized serial of Oden's life in the newspaper *Kanayomi shinbun*, *'Takahashi Oden yasha monogatari'* ('The Tale of the Demon Takahashi Oden'). Rōbun's tale presents Oden as a sexual deviant whose insatiable lust for men compels her toward an unrepentant life of crime. Born out of wedlock to a gambler and a prostitute, Oden's wicked nature is genetically predetermined. As a child Oden fistfights with the boys and as an adult is driven by uncontrollable sexual urges that lead to the murder of her husband and subsequent lovers.[2] In stark contrast to the sympathetic *onryō* whose once ideal feminine temper is mutilated and twisted into an incarnation of horrifying yet justified hatred, Rōbun's Oden simply is born evil.

The conception of the poison woman as an intrinsically wicked female monster played upon the specific fears and anxieties of her day. Much like the demonized Brahmin widows of *Water* and *The Toss of a Lemon* discussed in the previous chapter, the roots of this monstrous feminine archetype can be located largely in fears of unrestrained female sexuality and the perceived dangers it poses to traditional social structures. Rōbun's Oden took advantage of new civil freedoms guaranteed to women by the recently established Meiji government to threaten society at an unstable, changing moment. If the utter powerlessness of women in Edo society ensured wronged women's only option for justice was transformation after death into a vengeful spirit, the more 'fair and open' society of the Meiji left itself dangerously vulnerable to unchecked female aggression.[3] Nanboku's Oiwa was the ghost of murdered traditions, the 'good woman' ruined beyond hope of recovery. Robun's Oden, meanwhile, was the spectre of a terrifying future in which traditions had been cast aside and the 'bad woman' let loose to destroy society. Yet apart from their roles as feminine monsters of popular fiction whose stories express societal fears, vast differences remained in the original conceptions of these characters. But by the postwar era both the *onryō* and the *dokufu* had become nostalgic figures, icons of a shared, romanticized Japanese past. The time was right for Nakagawa Nobuo to remake Takahashi Oden in Tamiya Oiwa's image.

2. The Monstrous and the Maternal

Nakagawa's *kaidan* films of the late 1950s have been identified as part of a global zeitgeist of gothic horror at the movies.[4] For many international fans of horror cinema, the words '1950s' and 'Japan' conjure images of Godzilla and other giant monsters (*kaijū*) spawned by the atomic age. However, as Steven Nardi and Moro Munehito demonstrate in their look at Godzilla elsewhere in this volume, Godzilla and his *kaijū* ilk speak directly to both anxieties and hopes about the future. Nakagawa's period ghost stories play on much of the same apprehensions about modernity; but their nostalgic recreations of the past foregrounds what might be irretrievably lost over what promises (and fears) the future might hold. More specifically, Nakagawa's work from this period can be seen as a part of an international trend in low-budget horror films of the postwar era to evoke an idyllic 19th-century past under attack by supernatural or quasi-supernatural monsters. Terence Fisher's adaptations of *Dracula*, *Frankenstein*, and other classics of Victorian gothic literature for the British Hammer Film Productions and Roger Corman's Edgar Allan Poe cycle for American International Pictures are all roughly contemporaneous with Nakagawa's retellings of Edo Period *kaidan* at Shintōhō, and serve much the same purpose for their respective audiences. Primarily conceived to shock and frighten filmgoers, all of these pictures nonetheless exhibit tremendous nostalgia for the preceding century.

Yet for all of their thematic affinities with the Corman Poe films and Hammer horror movies,[5] the actual circumstances behind the production of Nakagawa's Shintōhō pictures more closely resembles that of the Val Lewton horror films produced at RKO Pictures in the 1940s. A producer in RKO's B-unit, Lewton was famously given prescribed horror movie titles from the studio executives, along with a miniscule budget and a short deadline, but was otherwise free to craft his pictures however he saw fit.[6] Nakagawa appears to have enjoyed this same 'freedom within boundaries' at Shintōhō. Although the studio had originally been founded by defecting directors from Tōhō seeking artistic freedom, in 1955 Shintōhō was taken over by Okura Mitsugu, a former theatre owner more interested in producing crowd-pleasing genre pictures for fast profit. After Mōri Masaki, one of the studio's contract directors, scored a box office hit with his version of *Yotsuya kaidan* in 1957, Okura implemented a policy of producing at least two horror films per year, a mandate that stood until the studio's collapse in late 1960.[7] That Nakagawa's best work coincides exactly with this period is significant. Although his star actress, Wakasugi Kazuko, has suggested that 'had he worked for a different studio, like Kurosawa Akira, where he would have access to more money, Nakagawa would have become a world-famous director,'[8] it is unlikely that his legacy as the father of the Japanese horror movie could have been secured anywhere except at Okura's Shintōhō. Nakagawa does not appear to have been particularly interested in horror prior to 1957,[9] and it seems likely that without Okura's insistence he might never have tried his hand at the genre. He was of course not the only director the studio put to work on horror movies, and several of his fellow Shintōhō directors also produced many fine example of *kaidan eiga* contemporaneously with Nakagawa. Okura's supervision resulted in Shintōhō becoming synonymous with period horror films, recalling Hollywood film historian Thomas Schatz's declaration that 'the chief architects of a studio's style were its executives.'[10]

Yet this in no way diminishes Nakagawa's own artistic contribution to his pictures, which regularly exhibit a uniqueness of vision and formal excellence a step above that of his fellow directors' efforts. Interviews with Nakagawa's cast and crew reveal that the director was largely free to interpret his assigned projects in whatever way he pleased, to the extent that even a crime drama like *Dokufu Takahashi Oden* might mirror the themes of wronged women, monstrous transformation and vengeance more typical of *kaidan* narratives. Discussing the conclusion of both *Tōkaidō Yotsuya kaidan* and *Dokufu Takahashi Oden*, Wakasugi recalls that the final shots of both films did not appear in the shooting scripts and were improvised by Nakagawa on-set.[11] As will be discussed below, these two concluding shots are key moments that not only solidify the internal logic of their onscreen world(s), but underscore the ways in which the director has repositioned the *dokufu* Takahashi Oden vis-à-vis the *onryō* Tamiya Oiwa.

Although concerned exclusively with the director's horror films, film scholar Colette Balmain provides evidence that *Dokufu Takahashi Oden* belongs to the same cinematic world as Nakagawa's *kaidan* adaptations. Holding up *Yotsuya kaidan* as the exemplar Japanese horror movie from the period, Balmain identifies what she sees as the defining motifs of the postwar *kaidan* movie: 'doomed love, adulterous affairs, and female avengers.'[12] Tellingly, these three features also figure prominently in *Dokufu Takahashi Oden*. The first two had also been components of the *dokufu* serials since the Meiji era, although the sympathies lay with the poison woman's male victims rather than the *dokufu* herself. But in introducing the female avenger motif into Oden's story, Nakagawa shifts the sympathies to his antiheroine, who becomes a pitiable monster of vengeance, a victim of evil male machinations much like the *onryō* of his *kaidan* pictures.

Another key element Balmain finds in Nakagawa's horror films that significantly also appears in *Dokufu Takahashi Oden* is what she calls 'the valorisation of the maternal.'[13] *Yotsuya kaidan's* Oiwa is not only a model wife, she is a model mother, and her unwavering devotion to her infant son becomes an essential component of her ultimate salvation in Nakagawa's version. In *Dokufu Takahashi Oden*, Oden's relationship with her young daughter offers similar hope for redemption. Under Nakagawa's lens, the *onryō* and the *dokufu* become two sides of the same coin. Tragic figures of ruined femininity, they transform into monsters of vengeance whose chances for final redemption lie in the bond between mother and child. In this way both films partially resonate with the *haha-mono* or 'mother pictures' that were in vogue during the postwar era. In these films, typified by Kinoshita Keisuke's *Nihon no higeki* ('A Japanese Tragedy,' 1953), the suffering mother figure stood in for a battered and beaten-down Japan, and her attempts to maintain the traditional family structure represented the nation's last hope for salvation.[14] In *Nihon no higeki*, the death of the mother is the final tragedy, but in adapting the *haha-mono* to the horror and crime genres, Nakagawa goes one step further. For Oiwa and Oden, death (be it literal or figural) is only the beginning.

For the role of Oden, Nakagawa cast Wakasugi Kazuko, who had just finished playing the vengeful ghost in the previous year's *Kaidan Kasane ga fuchi*, and who would go on to portray Oiwa one year later in *Yotsuya kadian*. In fact, the idea of constructing Oden's story along the thematic lines of a traditional *kaidan* narrative may have been suggested by Wakasugi's performance in *Kasane ga fuchi*. Based on Enchō Sanyūtei's *Shinkei Kasane ga fuchi* – a work in turn influenced by Nanboku's *Yotsuya kaidan* – the film clearly anticipates Nakagawa's later *kaidan* movie masterpiece; yet key elements from *Kasane ga fuchi* would reappear in *Dokufu Takahashi Oden* as well. Shinkichi, an orphaned child of samurai stock brought up as a merchant's apprentice, begins an affair with Orui, an older *shamisen* instructor whose father was murdered by Shinkichi's own father in cold blood decades earlier. Despite Shinkichi's pledge of fidelity to Orui, his heart truly lies with Ohisa, the beautiful daughter of Shinkichi's adoptive parents. Orui's jealousy and suspicion of Shinkichi and Ohisa are enflamed by Omura, a stock villain character of Nakagawa's invention who has designs on Orui; also significant is her dead father's curse, which manifests itself in a disfiguring facial scar much like Oiwa's in *Yotsuya kaidan*. When Shinkichi finally abandons the woman he vowed to remain faithful to and elopes with Ohisa, the distraught Orui kills herself, only to return as an *onryō* which soon destroys Shinkichi and Ohisa, as well as the villainous Omura.

The parallels with *Yotsuya kaidan* are plain. Although the creation of the Mephistophelian Omura mitigates some of our contempt for Shinkichi, he nonetheless comes off as a cowardly version of Iemon. Forsaking the woman he swore to love exclusively, Shinkichi slinks off with hardly an explanation, only to be plagued by the demon he unwittingly creates. But beyond the physical and circumstantial similarities, the character of Orui departs from the Oiwa template in significant ways and marks her as a transitional figure between the victimized Oiwa and the self-destructive Oden. Like Oiwa, Orui finds herself manipulated, disfigured, and forsaken by various male tormentors, primarily her husband. Yet Orui possesses an overbearing and fiercely jealous streak that stands at great odds with Oiwa's 'good submissive woman' temperament. In contrast to Oiwa's resigned devotion to Iemon despite his mounting offences, Orui is not afraid to speak her mind. When her elderly maidservant discovers Shinkichi's father murdered Orui's father, she begs her mistress to break off the relationship. Orui angrily retorts, 'I don't want to hear it! I'll do as I like!' – only to be stricken by her father's disfiguring curse. Orui is also the one responsible for goading the weak-willed Shinkichi into the relationship in the first place despite his plain feelings for Ohisa. Although clearly a wronged woman turned *onryō* avenger in the Oiwa tradition, Orui's sexually aggressive nature also plays a hand in causing the ensuing tragedy. The film playfully hints at the 'bad girl' side of her personality early on when Orui is shown in a semi-nude state to the tune of throaty saxophone music, evoking the femme fatales of Hollywood film noir. As Oden would do in *Dokufu Takahashi Oden*, Orui wields her sexuality as a defensive weapon, seducing Shinkichi to deflect Omura's unwanted advances, and in both heroines' cases the successful seduction ultimately fails to avert the inevitable tragedy. Both a 'wronged woman' and a 'wrong woman,' *Kadian Kasane ga fuchi's onryō* antiheroine represents an important step towards Nakagawa's re-imagining of *Dokufu Takahashi Oden's* titular antiheroine the following year.

When we first meet Oden in the film's opening sequence she is already a criminal, evading the police with uncanny speed and cunning that suggests thematic affinities with the supernatural. But Nakagawa quickly humanizes his protagonist, as we soon learn that Oden turned to a life of crime after leaving her first husband Jinjuro – who 'drank, gambled, and whored everything away.' Her second marriage to Takahashi Ryonosuke offers no solace; Ryonosuke is an upright man but has become bedridden with consumption, and Oden has resorted to thievery to support her sick husband. The thankless Ryonosuke, who has grown suspicious of his wife's frequent and unexplained absences from home, angrily accuses her of sleeping around and threatens to take her life. Like Oiwa in *Yotsuya kaidan,* Oden remains with and cares for a husband who rewards her devotion with verbal and physical abuse. But if she strives to be the traditional 'good wife' in the Oiwa mould, the headstrong and impetuous Oden goes about it in 'bad girl' fashion. Despite her refusal to abandon Ryonosuke, his accusations of infidelity are not unfounded. Oden has in fact entered into an extramarital affair with Namikawa Kazuma, a naive young police officer who catches Oden in an act of thievery only to be seduced into complicity by Oden's charms. Kazuma rejects his 'good girl' sweetheart Kozue for a woman who is clearly using him for her own ends, and by the climax of the picture devolves into a despondent, useless drunk unable to come to grips with the reality of his situation. Oden meanwhile becomes involved with an unnamed crime boss, who rapes her and then forces her to become an accomplice in his human trafficking operation.

Nakagawa's filming style emphasizes that, despite her cunning and ultimately self-destructive nature, Oden is essentially a victim who is reacting in the only way she knows how to the cruel misfortunes of her life. The camera frequently frames her in long, high-angle shots that reinforce her powerlessness against the forces of the larger world closing in around her. The high-angle shot was a favourite of several Shintōhō directors, including Mōri Masaki, who regularly employed the technique in his *kaidan* pictures, albeit without the careful mise-en-scene that Nakagawa brought to his own work. In one especially masterful setup, Nakagawa films a conversation between Oden and Ryonosuke by placing his camera above the tattered roof of their decrepit Tokyo dwelling. The tight composition of the shot allows Oden just enough room at the bottom of the frame to partially emerge from the shack and hang some meagre laundry out to dry, while Ryonosuke, huddled inside, is visible through a large hole in the roof. Both characters are essentially trapped on all sides by the dire circumstances of their living situation. But these high-angle shots occur most often when Oden is leaving home to engage in some illegal activity, framed by barren tree branches that suggest claws reaching out for the tiny figure slinking out into the night.

Despite the mounting gravity of Oden's crimes, Nakagawa holds out hope for his heroine's redemption in the form of her daughter from her previous marriage, Omitsu. A chance meeting with her first husband early in the picture reveals Oden left behind her newborn child when she abandoned the deadbeat Jinjuro, a matter of agonizing regret for Oden which Jinjuro exploits to extort drinking money from his ex-wife on the pretext that the girl needs medical attention. Oden's guilt over leaving Omitsu and her continuing concern for the child's well-being keeps the audience's sympathies squarely with Oden, who is no longer the heartless murderess of the Meiji serials but a conflicted mother figure.

Image 1: High-Angle Shots in *Dokufu Takahashi Oden*

Nakagawa builds audience sympathy for Oiwa in much the same way in *Yotsuya kaidan* by emphasizing Oiwa's maternal sense of duty to her newborn son. In Nakagawa's version Oiwa refuses to be parted with her child even in death, lamenting, 'You poor child! How could I leave you with a man like Iemon? Die with your mother! *I could never enter paradise if I left you behind!*' With her dying breath Oiwa's body falls on the child, presumably smothering him. Although such action might seem reprehensible out of context, in the world of *Yotsuya kaidan* the act represents an oddly touching (if disturbing) valorisation of the maternal, and her dedication to the child provides the means for her final salvation. Oden's relationship with her own child proves more problematic. Although she exhibits tremendous love for her daughter, Oden's prior abandonment of the child represents an irreconcilable failure to live up to her maternal obligations, a point which will come back to haunt her.

Perhaps the most explicit parallel between Nakagawa's versions of Oiwa and Oden – apart from Wakasugi's portrayal of both characters – is their moment of monstrous transformation (literal in Oiwa's case, figurative in Oden's). Along with implications of female empowerment through death and daemonification, Nakagawa makes his own concerns with parent-child relationships critical in the creation of the *onryō/dokufu* monster. The pivotal scene in *Dokufu Takahashi Oden* occurs when Oden discovers that the money she has given Jinjuro to take care of their daughter was squandered on booze, resulting in the malnourished child's death. To this point in the film Oden has remained an essentially decent woman, forced by cruel circumstance and evil men to commit increasingly serious crimes, but the last vestiges of her morality die with her child. After learning of Omitsu's passing, Oden not only embraces her life of crime, she devotes herself wholeheartedly to bringing about the demise of her male tormenters.

Nakagawa strikingly stages Oden's figurative death scene almost exactly in the manner he would film Oiwa's literal death scene in *Yotsuya kaidan.* In a dingy

Tokyo hovel, Wakasugi as Oden learns of her daughter's passing and falls to her knees, staring in shock at Omitsu's memorial tablet, assuming a pose almost identical to the one she strikes in *Yotsuya kaidan* when Oiwa discovers she has been poisoned, staring in shocked horror at her own disfigured reflection in her mirror. The mise-en-scene is virtually identical in both films. Nakagawa places his camera at a 'dog's-eye view,'[15] a low angle that puts the camera in a straight-on position from Wakasugi, who is on her hands and knees on the floor in a 90-degree profile shot. In the far left of the frame stands the object that confirms her imminent destruction (the memorial tablet/mirror), and in the presence of which she can only react in disbelieving horror. Behind her crouches an elderly servant figure (an elderly neighbour woman in *Oden*; the masseur Takuetsu in *Yotsuya*), whose expression mirrors the audience's own expected sense of empathy for Wakasugi's character. As Oden, she makes explicit that any hope of escaping her life of crime died with her daughter, telling the memorial tablet, 'I was going to take you away, where we could be respectable, just the two of us. *Forgive me for not being a mother to you.*' Oden's statement represents a notable inversion of Oiwa's ultimate pledge of motherhood to her son, in which Oiwa refuses to let death separate parent and child.

Following their heartfelt declarations to their respective children, Oiwa and Oden go on to the moment of monstrous transformation. 'Iemon, you heartless and cold-blooded brute, do you think I will leave you with this debt unpaid?!' Oiwa shrieks in her final moments, swearing otherworldly vengeance upon the husband and the father. When next we see Oiwa, she has become the monstrous feminine *onryō*, empowered by death to exact her revenge on those who wronged her – and her child – in life. Her ghost first appears to Iemon on his wedding night to his new bride, Oume. All traces of Oiwa's long-suffering devotion to her heartless husband have vanished, and the literal death of the 'good wife' is externalized by the once beautiful Oiwa's ghastly, blood-splattered visage. In a cinematic flourish that demonstrates Nakagawa's flair for horror, the dichotomy between the submissive samurai 'good wife' and the vengeance-driven *onryō* is illustrated in a single terrifying take. The docile Oume smiles at her new husband before lying back on the marriage bed, dropping out of the frame. Menacing *dorodoro* drum music then announces the presence of Oiwa's wrathful ghost, who rises up into the frame from Oume's position. Her words to Iemon make explicit her dying curse and establish Oiwa in her *onryō* form as a transformed monstrous feminine avenger: 'Iemon, how could you give me poison to drink? I will visit my hatred upon you – be sure of that!...I will make an end to the blood of the Tamiya line!'

Images 2 and 3: Moments of Transformation in *Tōkaidō Yotsuya kaidan* (above) and *Dokufu Takahashi Oden*

Oden's moment of transformation, while not a literal metamorphosis, hinges upon an identical vow of retribution upon the husband and father, 'I swear the man who did this to us will pay for it!' Afterwards Oden immediately becomes the monster of vengeance that Oiwa does. The next shot moves the action forward one year, removing the setting from Tokyo to Yokohama and re-introducing a drastically changed Oden who has at last wholly embraced her criminal lifestyle. As the head madam of a Chinese-themed gambling parlour/brothel, she has traded her traditional kimono and Japanese coiffure for a slinky cheongsam outfit, her back emblazoned with a fierce *oni* demon tattoo. Such tattoos carry blatant associations with the criminal underworld in Japanese culture, but Oden's has an added significance. An image of the female demon *hannya*, Oden's bodily emblem serves as a literal symbol of the female monster she has become. Even Wakasugi's performance has changed, and gone are Nakagawa's frequent close-ups of Oden's tormented and conflicted face as she laments the circumstances that force her to commit her crimes. Now Oden appears to enjoy her work, and her smug and confident attitude as she gambles with her disreputable patrons and plots the murder of her enemies recalls the truly monstrous Oden of Rōbun's serial. Like Oiwa, Nakagawa's Oden must undergo the death of the 'good woman' if she wishes to have her revenge, a point underlined late in the film when she exclaims to the heartbroken Kazuma, 'The Oden you knew is dead!'

Kazuma is not the only man who has been emotionally ruined by Oden. Jinjuro too turns up in Yokohama, and after the death of Omitsu seems to have had a change of heart. Playing right into Oden's hands, the despondent Jinjuro swears to make up for his past mistakes by doing whatever Oden asks of him. This is the moment Oden has been plotting ever since the death of her child, as she wreaks her vengeance not only on her former husband, but the villainous crime boss as well. Convincing Jinjuro that he can make amends with her by killing the man who embroiled her in a life of crime, Oden then alerts the boss to the impending attack, hoping the two will finish each other off. As Jinjuro and the crime boss struggle in Oden's boudoir, Oden shoots both of them dead, exclaiming, 'You can all go to hell!'

The 'monster' Oden completes her vendetta, yet Nakagawa denies her the final peace in death he ultimately grants Oiwa. Once Oiwa's curse finally succeeds in bringing about Iemon's demise, Nakagawa concludes his version of *Yotsuya kaidan* with a shot of Oiwa's ghost – no longer hideously deformed, but beautiful as she once was – seemingly at peace with her infant son. Oden, meanwhile, cannot be allowed to truly die. As the cops raid the gambling den in the aftermath of the double-murder, Oden attempts suicide but finds herself thwarted at the last second. 'Let me die! Please let me die!' she pleads as the police wrest the sword from her hands. In sharp contrast to *Yotsuya kaidan's* final shot of the once-wrathful *onryō* finally at rest, *Dokufu Takahashi Oden* ends with Oden in handcuffs, despondently gazing out a train window as she is being transported back to Tokyo to face punishment for her crimes.

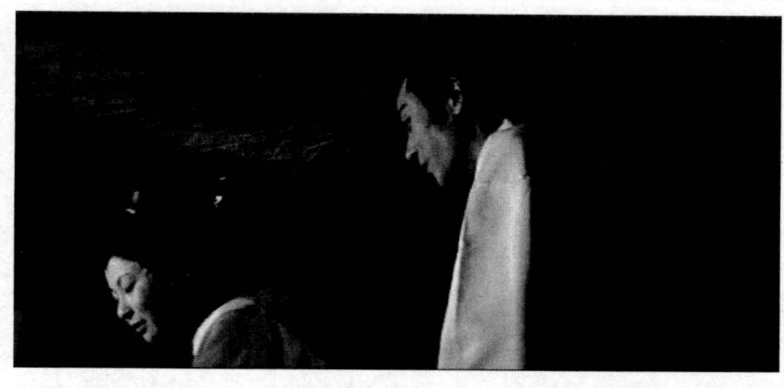

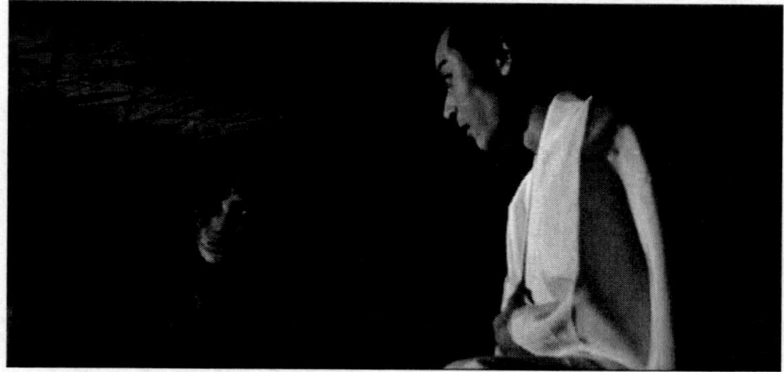

Images 4 and 5: Oiwa's Ghost First Appears to Iemon in *Tōkaidō Yotsuya kaidan*, taking the place of his new bride Oume

Image 6: Oden before Omitsu's Death...

Image 7: ...and after (*Dokufu Takahashi Oden*)

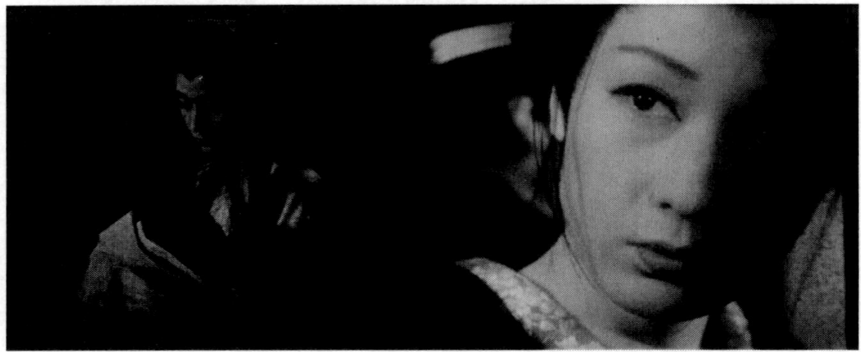

Image 8: Contrasting Denouements: *Tōkaidō Yotsuya kaidan* (left) and *Dokufu Takahashi Oden*

Nakagawa significantly chooses to end his film here, rather than go on to address Oden's trial and execution. Despite their similarities, it seems Oden has made a mistake that Oiwa has not, a mistake that condemns her to live on in suffering rather than enjoy the repose of the grave that Oiwa finally attains. The differences in their ultimate fates may have to do with genre conventions; after all, Oden is a criminal (one of Japan's most infamous), and crime dramas typically end with the criminal brought to justice. In this way Nakagawa's take on Takahashi Oden resonates with the original Meiji serials, which were in large part cautionary tales about the consequences of a dissolute lifestyle.[16] As for Oiwa, her vengeance possesses an air of legitimacy lacking in Oden's case. As an *onryō*, Oiwa participates in the traditional Buddhist karmic system; ghosts are supposed to haunt those who wronged them in life. Her revenge is thusly 'authorized' in a way Oden's is not, and Oden must be made to answer for her illegal transgressions. Although Nakagawa constructs Oiwa's and Oden's character arcs along quite similar trajectories, the conventions of two ultimately distinct genres – the ghost story and the crime drama – suggest different fates for their respective monsters.

The two films' contrasting denouements do not contradict the internal logic of Nakagawa's filmic universe, however. A subtle yet crucial difference in the 'valorisation of the maternal' as represented in *Yotsuya kaidan* and *Dokufu Takahashi Oden* explains Oden's final damnation, which stems from her failure as a mother. Had she not lost her child, she would not have lost her essential humanity, which Oiwa retains even after becoming a hideous *onryō*, as evidenced by the closing shot of mother and son at peace. Oden's fatal mistake lies in allowing death to separate the parent from the child, something Oiwa explicitly avoids by taking her child with her to the land beyond. Although the child's death is the catalyst for everything that comes after, *Dokufu Takahasi Oden* significantly makes no explicit reference to Omitsu after Oden's transformation – the child passes utterly beyond the diegesis of the film. Oiwa's baby, meanwhile, continues to be a conspicuous presence during the final horrific act of *Yotsuya kaidan.* At the climax of the film, Iemon has shut himself up in a mountain temple in an effort to escape the ghost of his wife. Standing in front of a Buddhist altar, Iemon watches in horror as the golden statue recedes into the darkness, to be replaced by the image of the mosquito net he had earlier threatened to pawn despite Oiwa's pleas that, without it, their child would be eaten alive. We then hear the wail of their child, which acts as a sound bridge to the next shot, revealing the ghost of Oiwa still clutching the baby in her arms. Nakagawa then alternates between several shots of an increasingly panicked Iemon and the now blood-red mosquito net, descending upon him from above while Oiwa shrieks his name. Although Oiwa's rage remains the driving force behind the haunting, its manifestation as the mosquito foregrounds the continued presence of the child in the film's diegesis.

Nanboku's original kabuki script pays little attention to the child, who survives his mother's death only to be devoured in a stage direction by the ghost of another of Iemon's victims.[17] The play ends with no mention of the *onryō*'s ultimate fate, but Nakagawa's Oiwa still has a child to care for, which proves the final salvation of a monster almost utterly consumed by rage and vengeance, hence the final shot of mother and child together and at peace. As a living monster, Oden can no longer protect her dead child, and reflexively the deceased Omitsu cannot redeem her mother. Without the ties of love between parent and child, nothing remains to prevent Oden from completely embracing her dissolute lifestyle. The *onryō* Oiwa is a monster *and* a mother, but the *dokufu* Oden tragically becomes just a monster. In light of Oden's fate, Oiwa's dying declaration to her child, 'I could never enter paradise if I left you behind,' rings especially true.

Nakagawa's Oiwa and Oden thusly stand in striking opposition to much of Western horror cinema's monstrous mothers, who frequently are monstrous precisely because of the threat they pose to their own offspring. Drawing on the work of Julie Kristeva, Barbara Creed famously theorizes the horror movie mother as an embodiment of the abject in her essay, 'Horror and the Monstrous-Feminine.' Because all individuals have experienced abjection in their earliest attempts to free themselves from dependency on the figure of the mother, Creed sees a distinguishing feature of horror film as the construction of the maternal as abject, an issue rendered doubly horrifying by the mother's desire to retain a hold over her child:

> ...we can see abjection at work in the horror text where the child struggles to break away from the mother, representative of the archaic maternal figure...constructed as the monstrous-feminine. By refusing to relinquish her hold on her child, she prevents it from taking up its proper place in relation to the Symbolic.[18]

Creed clearly has a certain strain of horror film in mind (*Psycho*, *Carrie*, *The Birds*) in regard to the monstrous-feminine, although she does argue that confrontation with the abject – so often symbolized by the mother – is 'the central ideological project of the popular horror film.'[19] Yet Nakagawa's monstrous mothers are very much the inverse of this formulation. A 'refusal to relinquish a hold on her child' in fact *preserves* Oiwa's humanity despite her horrific transformation, and perhaps the most horrific tragedy of *Dokufu Takahashi Oden* lies in the title character's fatal mistake of doing just that – losing her hold on the child she was meant to save and thusly becoming unable to save herself from damnation. If, as Belinda Calderone examines in 'The Monster Inside Me' later in this volume, the act of birth often made women into monsters in European folk and fairy tale traditions, in Nakagawa's world motherhood has the ability to make monsters back into women.

A more general link between parenthood (paternal as well as maternal) and salvation manifests again and again in Nakagawa's oeuvre. The motif also plays a central role in his best-known film abroad, *Jigoku*, which is about a young man named Shirō suffering the torments of the various Buddhist hells. Discovering his girlfriend Yukiko had died while carrying his child, Shirō embarks on a frantic search throughout Hell for his unborn daughter. Nakagawa implies the reunion of parent and child will somehow procure salvation, as other characters mock Shirō, 'Think you can escape from Hell? Just try it!' – whereupon the unborn baby's cries are heard in the distance. Although the film never makes the exact relevance of the child explicit, its affinities with Buddhist salvation are implied by several shots of the baby floating downriver on a lotus blossom, which the damned Shirō fruitlessly chases after but never quite manages to reach.

Jigoku's sensational subject matter and lurid atmosphere make it typical of Nakagawa's Shintōhō output, but the film's unrelentingly dark and dour contemporary setting and purposely unappealing characters stand at odds with the sympathetic heroines and nostalgic recreations of 19th-century Japan seen in *Dokufu Takahashi Oden* and the director's *kaidan* films. Yet *Jigoku's* vaguely defined yet pervading obsession with Shirō's unborn daughter illustrates that Nakagawa finds the relationship between parenthood and salvation of ongoing significance in his work. *Jigoku* concludes indeterminately, with father and daughter stuck on opposite ends of the wheel of fate, the parent desperately trying to reach the child. Sitting handcuffed in the train car, Oden's own deceased daughter – and the mother's salvation – lay decidedly out of reach.

3. Conclusion

Nakagawa revisited the female criminal subgenre in 1960's *Onna shikeishū no datsugoku* ('Death Row Woman'), a contemporary crime drama whose strikingly dissimilarity to both *Dokufu Takahashi Oden* and *Yotsuya kaidan* reveals just how closely the Edo *onryō* and the Meiji *dokufu* were linked in Nakagawa's eyes. One might expect *Dokufu Takahashi Oden* would have much more in common with *Onna shikeishū no datsugoku* than with Nakagawa's *kaidan* pictures, but apart from an appearance by Wakasugi Kazuko in a small role as a hardened criminal, the two films share surprisingly little common ground. *Onna shikeishū no datsugoku's* protagonist, unlike Oden, is falsely accused of murder and remains a thoroughly 'good girl' throughout the picture, valiantly fighting to clear her name. Although she too loses her young child to illness, issues of maternity and redemption fail to figure into the plot. The scene in which the heroine Kyoko (whose name means 'pure child') learns of her son's death leads to no moment of sworn vengeance and monstrous transformation. Parenthood plays no role in Kyoko's salvation, not because Nakagawa is inconsistent in his attitude, but because his thoroughly righteous heroine was never in danger of losing her soul in the first place. A modern and virtuous Japanese woman, Kyoko has little in common with such legendary monsters of the past as Oiwa and Oden.

In conclusion, by Nakagawa's day the fundamental differences of two quite distinct female monsters, the *onryō* and the *dokufu*, had been blurred by the passing of time. The Edo ghost of the discarded 'good wife' and the Meiji female sexual predator were now both nostalgic ghouls from a romanticized past, and – in Nakagawa's films at least – more sisters than strangers. Free to explore his own personal themes within the nominal boundaries of assigned genre projects, Nakagawa conceives both Oiwa and Oden as victimized mothers who undergo death (literal or figural) and monstrous transformation as a means of empowerment to enact vengeance upon their male tormentors. But Oiwa remains a maternal figure, refusing to abandon her child even in death. Although, as an *onryō*, she becomes a disfigured and horrific perversion of femininity, Oiwa's unbroken link with her child preserves a crucial vestige of her former ideal womanhood. Thus Nakagawa's *Yotsuya kaidan* ends with mother and child together and at peace; Oiwa's spirit is granted repose in true death. Oden, however, forsakes her ideal femininity and thereby loses her chance at salvation along with her daughter. Utterly renouncing all traces of the 'good woman,' Oden is denied the release of true death. Despite the many parallels Nakagawa draws between the *onryō* and the *dokufu*, the contrasting denouements of *Yotsuya kaidan* and *Dokufu Takahashi Oden* reinforce the fundamental difference in the traditional conceptions of their characters. Oiwa remains the ghost of a lost, idealized past, the 'good woman' cast aside. Oden too has become a monster from the past, but she continues to function ultimately as a spectre of an immoral future where the 'good woman' has ceased to exist.

Notes

[1] Christine Marran, *Poison Woman: Figuring Female Transgression in Modern Japanese Culture* (Minneapolis: University of Minnesota, 2007), 9.
[2] Ibid.
[3] Ibid., 56-64.
[4] Colette Balmain, *Introduction to Japanese Horror Film* (Edinburgh: Edinburgh University, 2008), 51.
[5] In particular Terence Fisher's *The Curse of Frankenstein* (1957) may have been an influence on Nakagawa's later Shintōhō efforts. See Osawa Jō, 'Shintōhō no obake eiga to Tōkaidō Yotsuya kaidan: jyanru no fukkatsu to kakushin,' in *Kaiki to gensō e no kairō*, ed. Uchiyama Kazuki (Tokyo: Shinwasha, 2008), 78.
[6] *Val Lewton: The Man in the Shadows*, Turner Classic Movies, 2007, DVD.
[7] Osawa, 'Shintōhō no obake eiga to Tōkaidō Yotsuya kaidan', 75-76.
[8] Suzuki Kensuke, ed., *Jigoku de yōi hai!: Nakagawa Nobuo, kaidan/kyōfu eiga no gyōka* (Tokyo: Wides, 2000), 30.
[9] In 1949 Nakagawa directed the fantasy/comedy *Enoken no Tobisuke bōken ryokō*, which included some tongue-in-cheek horror imagery, and in 1956 his period film *Utsunomiya no tenjō* incorporated *kaidan* elements into a mostly mundane samurai picture, but his first 'true' horror film is generally held to be 1957s *Kaidan Kasane ga fuchi*.
[10] Thomas Schatz, *The Genius of the System: Hollywood Filmmaking in the Studio Era* (Minneapolis: University of Minnesota Press, 2010), 7.
[11] Suzuki, *Jigoku de yōi hai!*, 29.
[12] Balmain, *Introduction to Japanese Horror Film*, 49.
[13] Ibid., 62.
[14] Joseph L. Anderson and Donald Richie, *The Japanese Film: Art and Industry* (Princeton: Princeton University Press, 1982), 188.

[15] This angle is typically associated with the films of Ozu Yasujiro, who employed it regularly in his work.
[16] Marran, *Poison Woman*, 37-39.
[17] Tsuruya Nanboku IV, 'Tōkaidō Yotsuya kaidan,' trans. Mark Oshima, in *Early Modern Japanese Literature*, ed. Shirane Haruo (New York: Columbia, 2002), 871.
[18] Barbara Creed, 'Horror and the Monstrous-Feminine: An Imaginary Abjection,' in *Horror, The* Film *Reader*, ed. Mark Jancovich (New York: Routledge, 2002), 72.
[19] Ibid., 75.

Bibliography

Anderson, Joseph L. and Donald Richie. *The Japanese Film: Art and Industry*. Princeton: Princeton University Press, 1982.

Ayakashi Samurai Horror Tales: Yotsuya Ghost Story. Dir. Imazawa Tetsuo. Geneon, 2006. DVD.

Balmain, Colette. *Introduction to Japanese Horror Film*. Edinburgh: Edinburgh University Press, 2008.

'Building the Inferno: Nobuo Nakagawa and the Making of *Jigoku*.' *Jigoku*. Criterion, 2006. DVD.

Creed, Barbara. 'Horror and the Monstrous-Feminine: An Imaginary Abjection.' In *Horror, The* Film *Reader*, edited by Mark Jancovich, 67-76. New York: Routledge, 2002.

Dokufu Takahashi Oden. Dir. Nakagawa Nobuo. Shintōhō, 1958. DVD.

Jigoku. Dir. Nakagawa Nobuo. Shintōhō, 1960. DVD.

Kaidan Kasane ga fuchi. Dir. Nakagawa Nobuo. Shintōhō, 1957. DVD.

Marran, Christine. *Poison Woman: Figuring Female Transgression in Modern Japanese Culture*. Minneapolis: University of Minnesota Press, 2007.

Nihon no higeki. Dir. Kinoshita Keisuke. Shōchiku, 1953. DVD.

Okamoto Kidō. *The Curious Casebook of Inspector Hanshichi: Detective Stories of Old Edo*. Translated by Ian MacDonald. Honolulu: University of Hawaii Press, 2007.

Onna shikeishū no datsugoku. Dir. Nakagawa Nobuo. Shintōhō, 1960. DVD.

Osawa Jō. 'Shintōhō no obake eiga to Tōkaidō Yotsuya kaidan: jyanru no fukkatsu to kakushin.' In *Kaiki to gensō e no kairō: kaidan kara J-horā e*, ed. Uchiyama Kazuki, 68-94. Tokyo: Shinwasha, 2008.

Oshima, Mark. 'Ghosts and Nineteenth-Century Kabuki.' In *Early Modern Japanese Literature: An Anthology 1600-1900*, edited by Shirane Haruo, 843-844. New York: Columbia University Press, 2002.

Schatz, Thomas. *The Genius of the System: Hollywood Filmmaking in the Studio Era.* Minneapolis: University of Minnesota Press, 2010.

Suzuki Kensuke, ed. *Jigoku de yōi hai!: Nakagawa Nobuo, kaidan/kyōfu eiga no gyōka.* Tokyo: Wides, 2000.

Tōkaidō Yotsuya kaidan. Dir. Nakagawa Nobuo. Shintōhō, 1959. DVD.

Tsuruya Nanboku IV. *Tōkaidō Yotsuya kaidan.* Translated by Mark Oshima. In *Early Modern Japanese Literature: An Anthology 1600-1900*, edited by Shirane Haruo, 843-844. New York: Columbia University Press, 2002.

Val Lewton: The Man in the Shadows. Turner Classic Movies, 2007, DVD.

Michael E. Crandol is a graduate student in the Asian Literatures, Cultures, and Media program at the University of Minnesota.

The Monster Inside Me: Unnatural Births in Early Modern Italian and French Fairy Tales

Belinda Calderone

Abstract
Births in early modern Italian and French fairy tales were frequently monstrous. These tales abound with heroines giving birth to serpents, monkey-girls, wild boars and even myrtle branches. Meanwhile, early modern midwives and medical men, still ignorant about the female reproductive system, let their imaginations run positively wild over the many mysteries and abnormalities of childbirth. This paper argues that the early modern European cultural imagination infused the fairy tale genre with frightful depictions of unnatural progeny. The parallels between popular belief and fairy tales are highlighted by examining literary fairy tales alongside cheap publications of the time such as broadsheets and pamphlets. Furthermore, this paper explores the implications for fairy tale mothers who bear monsters. For even within the marvellous space of the fairy tale, giving birth to a monster is still an abnormality. The key fairy tale authors discussed in this paper are Giovan Francesco Straparola, Giambattista Basile and Marie-Catherine d'Aulnoy. From Straparola's snake offspring to d'Aulnoy's fur covered princesses, there is no end to the incredible creatures that can spring from the womb.

Key Words: Fairy tale, monstrous birth, print culture, early modern, Giovan Francesco Straparola, Giambattista Basile, Marie-Catherine d'Aulnoy.

*****

Early modern Italian and French fairy tales abound with monstrous births. Heroines give birth to serpents, monkey-girls, wild boars and even myrtle branches. The female body becomes the very origin of monstrosity. These unnatural births reflect the popular beliefs of their time; early modern midwives and medical men, knowing little of the female reproductive system, let their imaginations run positively wild over the many mysteries and abnormalities of childbirth. The link between these popular beliefs and fairy tales in early modern Europe is clear when we consider two aspects of print culture: cheap popular print and the literary fairy tale. Both were short narratives, one offered to the public as a real story, the other a make-believe tale that mirrored the cultural imagination. It is unsurprising that the prolific popular print which was seen, read and heard daily on European streets found its way into the tales of fairy tale authors. Indeed, their fairy tales – like enchanted mirrors – reflect the nightmarish superstitions of their age.

Fairy tale authors, Giovan Francesco Straparola, Giambattista Basile and Marie-Catherine d'Aulnoy all wrote in a time when monsters and magic were a topic of daily discussion. As Suzanne Magnanini reminds us, 'The literary fairy tale was born at a time when marvels were not relegated to fantastic fictions, but swirled around the courts, academies, churches, and public squares of Europe.'[1] Perhaps the most frightening – and fascinating – of these marvels were monstrous births. According to Valeria Finucci, unnatural birth stories of early modern Europe included 'a baby girl covered with hair as the result of her mother having gazed at a portrait of Saint John in a bearskin hanging over her bed'[2] and 'a baby girl born in 1517 with a frog-like face because her mother had held a frog for the sake of curing a fever and kept holding it during coitus.'[3] Magnanini describes the supposed case of a dog-boy born in 1543 in Avignon. Apparently a woman gave birth to a baby girl who died immediately, then three days later she gave birth again to a dog-boy. It was reported that the mother confessed to having sexual relations with a dog, and that both mother and child were burned to death.[4] These cases reveal that often causes provided for birth abnormalities were deeply rooted in superstition. They also represent the belief that monstrosity arises from the mother's actions or her maternal imagination – that what a woman sees or imagines during pregnancy can imprint itself on the child. Thus women's bodies and minds are identified as the origin of monstrosity, a mysterious place from which all things unnatural can spring. As Marilyn Francus asserts, 'In the West, the image of the fecund female has often been associated with monstrosity.'[5] This reveals an underlying fear of the female body in Western history. In instances of molar pregnancies where an irregularly shaped growth inhabited the uterus instead of a healthy baby, the imagination ran positively wild. Jacques Gélis discusses such accounts which 'gave rise to the weirdest interpretations on behalf of the women who had witnessed the event.'[6] Some of the women claim to have seen mothers 'give birth to a dead animal, rat, mole or tortoise; others saw a living four-footed animal, armed with claws or hooked nails.'[7] Some midwives even maintained that 'there were flying molas which could hang from the ceiling, and that others tried to hide and even re-enter the womb.'[8] In such accounts, the womb becomes a space of potential horror and evil. In the context of these nightmarish stories, monstrous fairy tale births do not seem quite so out of place. In fact, they seem positively mundane!

Physical proof that monstrous births were constantly in the early modern public consciousness exists in the sheer number of unnatural birth stories which inundated the print culture of early modern Europe. Alan W. Bates divides this print culture into two categories: 'scholarly publications such as books, theses and sermons, and popular prints such as broadsides, ballads, chapbooks and advertisements.'[9] It is these popular prints which are of particular interest as they were widely accessible to the general public and so would have infiltrated the public consciousness more easily. Bates reports that monstrous births appeared in these publications in the sixteenth century, first in Italy and then in France.[10] Considering that fairy tales also emerged in sixteenth century Italy, it is unsurprising that their content was influenced by these popular publications. Elizabeth S. Cohen and Thomas V. Cohen discuss the nature of cheap popular print: 'presses churned out cheap editions, poorly printed, badly edited, on flimsy paper, many of them full of dubious information: booklets, broadsheets, ancestral junk mail.'[11] They argue that 'It was this low-end product that found its way into the daily lives of the nonelite.'[12] And so, before the existence of newspapers, it was these 'cheap publications that purveyed news of marvels: floods, earthquakes, monstrous births.'[13] Booklets, broadsheets, and pamphlets were brimming with tales of animal-human hybrids and deformed infants. According to Katharine Park and Lorraine J. Daston, these publications were 'Displayed and recited publicly'[14] and 'appealed through spoken word and image to the illiterate as well as to the reading public.'[15] Broadsheets reporting monstrous births began with a provocative title and a woodcut of the creature.[16] Almost like an early modern version of today's tabloid magazines, this cheap popular literature was intended to shock and horrify the public. Yet, like fairy tales, they were also meant to entertain and to evoke wonder. As such they were frequently exaggerated and sensational. As Bates reports, 'Some ballads suggested a tune to which the verses could be sung, probably by the seller in order to attract customers.'[17] This practice of singing the ballads suggests a storytelling element to these cheap publications. People were, in a sense, performing a tale, which links cheap print to other storytelling mediums like fairy tales. In fact, fairy tales have a rich oral tradition alongside the literary tradition. Authors such as Marie-Catherine d'Aulnoy were known to write a tale down and then perform it to others, bringing the tale to life. The performance element of both fairy tales and cheap print links them together even further.

Dudley Wilson goes so far as to say that cheap print material 'is in fact a literary genre involved with journalism in that it reports incidents.'[18] These popular prints certainly straddled the line between fact and fiction, reality and fantasy. In fact, a 1609 broadsheet from France reads just like a fairy tale. The rather lengthy broadsheet begins with a good man who promises to marry a lady. However, he betrays her by marrying another woman instead. The first lady is furious and seeks revenge, and so she enlists a witch to cast a spell on him. The witch gives him a potion which causes him to become pregnant and give birth to a monster. In the broadsheet the creature is represented as bestial and devil-like. It has the general form of a human but has clawed feet, horns and a tail. The devil-like appearance no doubt reflects the evil act of witchcraft. In the end, the two women behind the wicked plot are discovered. The witch is hanged and the lady is whipped and banished from the town. The punishments are treated with great ceremony and all of the townspeople come to witness the gruelling violence.[19] The monstrosity in this broadsheet lies not only in the offspring, but in the male pregnancy which defies the natural order. This cheap publication makes a striking link between fairy tales and popular culture in early modern Europe. The themes of love, betrayal, witches and spells align it with the fairy tale genre. Just like a fairy tale, this broadsheet is a narrative sold to the public. Many of the magical and monstrous aspects of fairy tales may seem entirely foreign to us today, but in early modern Europe they were simply a reflection of what was being sold to the public as true stories.

Giovan Francesco Straparola, acknowledged as the first European fairy tale author, wrote at a time when print culture was soaring, particularly cheap literature for the masses. In sixteenth-century Venice, Straparola wrote two volumes of tales entitled *Le Piacevoli Notti* (*The Pleasant Nights*). Straparola's tales are far from the sanitised and didactic fairy tales with which contemporary readers would be familiar. His tales abound with trickery, thieving, sexual scandal, mutilation and murder. In Straparola's tales it is not uncommon for heroines to give birth to animals such as pigs and snakes. In Straparola's 'Ancilotto, King of Provino', a young mother, Chiaretta, is tricked into believing that she has given birth to a litter of puppies. She promises her husband, King Ancilotto, three extraordinarily beautiful children, which she successfully produces. However, her sisters conspire with her mother-in-law and midwife to replace the triplets with three mongrel pups. Placing the puppies in the heroine's arms they taunt, 'Look, oh queen, at the work that you've produced! Make sure that you regard it well so that the king can see the fruit of your womb!'[20] When her husband sees the puppies he is horrified. Chiaretta breaks down into tears and desperately denies that the dogs are her offspring, but to no avail. Her husband strips her of her position as queen and gives the following orders: 'she was to wash the pots and pans, and ... she was to be fed the rotten garbage that fell to the dirty, stinking ground.'[21] No blame whatsoever is placed upon the husband and Chiaretta is treated as though she has committed a crime. Eating garbage from the ground is typically animal behaviour, and so giving birth to animal offspring marks her as an animal also. The progeny is treated as a reflection of the mother's body. Thus, the monster status of the offspring marks the mother as monstrous. But we must look at why the puppies are seen as monstrous. An animal in itself is not viewed as a monster; it is only when it comes from a human body or incorporates human body parts that it becomes monstrous. It is human and not human, animal and not animal. It is the familiar yet foreign aspect that is at the root of the monstrosity.

We must also consider the implication of how the monster came to be. Certainly, the maternal imagination was often implicated in monstrous births, as Finucci's examples above indicate. However, mothers were often accused of something much more sinister. In the case of Chiaretta's dog offspring, there is an underlying stain of guilt: that of bestiality. The tale recalls Magnanini's case above of the woman who gave birth to the dog-boy in Avignon after supposedly copulating with a dog. As Magnanini reports, in Straparola's time 'there was no consensus in scientific writings as to whether the coupling of two disparate species could produce offspring.'[22] In the absence of scientific knowledge, people truly believed that a woman could have sexual intercourse with an animal, become pregnant and give birth. This belief is the crux of Straparola's tale, for without it Chiaretta could not be shamed and removed from the throne. As Magnanini reports, in the period when Straparola was writing, there existed a deep 'fear of the disintegration of the boundaries between animals and humans.'[23] She argues that this fear was so great that 'the birth or alleged birth of animal-human hybrids rent the fantastic fabric of the fairy tale.'[24] Boundaries are particularly significant as the concept of monstrosity is closely tied up with the breaching and blurring of borders and boundaries. It is that which disturbs order and normality, and thus evokes anxiety and fear. Magnanini's statement suggests that this fear was so real and intense in early modern Europe that it inevitably permeated the fairy tale genre. Fairy tales were thus infused with heroines who give birth to animals, heroines who disturb the natural order.

The notion of bestiality is even more prominent in Straparola's 'Biancabella and the Snake', in which a queen experiences a monstrous conception and a monstrous birth. The queen, who longs for a child, ventures into the woods one day and is overcome with sleep. While the queen is sleeping, a grass snake crawls beneath her clothes. We are told that the snake 'entered her vagina and carefully made its way into her womb, where it rested quietly. Shortly thereafter, the marquis's wife became pregnant.'[25] The biblical significance of being impregnated by a snake is obvious in constructing the monstrosity of this conception due to associations with the devil. When the queen gives birth she and her midwives are incredibly frightened, for out comes 'a baby girl who had a grass snake wrapped around her neck three times.'[26] And so, the tale describes a literal act of bestiality in which the snake rapes and impregnates the human woman. The snake defies nature in being both the impregnator and the offspring. It instigates the pregnancy and is then birthed from the womb, taking on the roles of both parent and child. The monstrosity in this tale is overwhelming. We see the sexual union between an animal and a human, and then a human giving birth to an animal. This intermingling of human and beast is even more overt when the snake emerges wrapped around the baby girl's neck, almost like a monstrous umbilical cord. The human and animal bodies are entwined, two species acting as one body. The boundaries between animal and human have truly disintegrated in this tale.

These anxieties over the boundaries between human and animal are strongly reflected in early modern cheap print about the monster of Ravenna born in 1512. Reports of this creature spread throughout Europe in the form of pamphlets and broadsheets.[27] Though images and descriptions of the monster vary throughout cheap print, some of the most famous woodcuts generally show a creature that had a human face with a horn on its head, wings instead of arms, a human leg with an eye at its knee, and a second leg that was covered in scales. This creature melds the human body with animal characteristics like horns, wings and scales. The monster of Ravenna is the epitome of hybridity and liminality. In one account, the monster is believed to be the offspring of a nun and friar.[28] And so, a monstrous act – two people who should remain chaste and holy engaging in the unholy act of fornication out of wedlock – produces the monstrous offspring. In a sense, the progeny is a reflection of the 'goodness' or 'wickedness' of the parents. It is clear that fears about hybridity that abound in cheap print about the monster of Ravenna are reflected in both of Straparola's tales.

It is also significant that the monster of Ravenna, though initially drawn with male genitalia, was often later depicted as a hermaphrodite in early modern cheap print. The hermaphroditic body is another which defies boundaries – that of male and female. In fact, Straparola's tales also include a hermaphroditic transformation. In 'Filomena the Hermaphrodite', a young woman is struck by a terrible fever and becomes gravely ill. Her groin swells to become a large ball which causes her great pain. At last the physicians decide to operate and cut into the swelling, at which point a penis emerges. We are told that Filomena has become both man and woman. The tale describes a fever, pain and an eventual incision which brings forth the penis. All of these details evoke images of labour pains and caesarean sections. In a sense, Filomena gives birth to her own hermaphroditic body. She is simultaneously the mother and the monstrous offspring. Interestingly, the fictional narrator of 'Filomena the Hermaphrodite', Signor Antonio Molino, insists that the tale is in fact a true story. Antonio begins the tale by telling his listeners that these events happened 'no great time ago in the city of Salerno'[29] and adds 'in sooth this is no fable.'[30] Later in the tale he reiterates, 'I am now telling you the sober truth in lieu of a fable.'[31] Finally he states that he can confirm the tale with 'the testimony of mine own eyes,'[32] for he saw Filomena after she had transformed into a hermaphrodite. Antonio's repeated assurance of the validity of the tale reflects the construct of popular print culture. The tale is almost like an embellished broadsheet. This is another example of how fairy tales and cheap print overlapped in early modern Europe. For a deeper discussion of the hermaphroditic aspect of the monster of Ravenna and early modern cheap print, see Whitney Dirks-Schuster's chapter, 'Print Culture and the Monstrous Hermaphrodite in Early Modern England.'

In the seventeenth century, Neapolitan courtier, Giambattista Basile, wrote a fairy tale collection entitled *Lo Cunto de li Cunti (The Tale of Tales)*. Basile's tales are vibrant and bawdy. He never shies away from the grittier aspects of life as he happily discusses sex, menstruation and flatulence. Basile's tales include a queen who has a dragon twin, a heroine who is impregnated by eating a dragon's heart and another who is accused of giving birth to a dog. In fact, it is not only animals that can sprout from the womb in Basile's tales, but even shrubbery! In 'The Myrtle' a woman who longs for a child constantly cries, 'Oh, God, if only I could bring something into this world, I wouldn't care if it were a branch of myrtle!'[33] We are told that she 'bothered the heavens so much with these words'[34] that she became pregnant and after nine months, instead of a healthy baby, she gave birth to a branch of myrtle, just as she asked. The tale reminds us that God is ever watchful and has the power to punish humans by causing unnatural births. Basile's tale echoes a 1609 broadsheet which tells of a woman who gives birth to a calf in Geneva. While in labour, the woman experiences terrible pains. The attendants offer to say prayers for her in the hopes of alleviating her pain. However, she exclaims that she would rather die or give birth to a calf than have prayers said for her during her labour. God hears her words and transforms her baby into a calf in her womb and she gives birth to the calf instead of a human baby.[35] Like Basile's tale, this broadsheet reminds us that God has the power to engender monsters in punishment for human sin. Dudley Wilson reminds us that God was believed to be omnipresent, 'an awesome, even a terrible and threatening presence, expressing himself directly through mutilation and disasters.'[36] This popular belief is reflected in the broadsheet and has permeated Basile's tale. Indeed, it is sometimes impossible to tell fairy tales and popular print culture apart. In both texts the mother is the cause of the unnatural offspring; this time it is not the mother's actions which have been sinful, but her words. In both the fairy tale and the broadsheet, the idea of monstrosity is again tied up with the blurring of boundaries. In the broadsheet it is the boundary between human and animal that has been blurred, and in the fairy tale it is human and plant.

Cheap print continued into seventeenth century France, when Marie-Catherine d'Aulnoy was writing and performing fairy tales in Paris salons with her female contemporaries. Lengthy, complex, witty and filled with lavish descriptions, d'Aulnoy's tales deal with real life issues for women of her day such as the misery of forced marriages, sexual scandals and the perils of childbirth. D'Aulnoy wrote two collections of fairy tales, *Les Contes des Fées* (*Tales of the Fairies*) and *Contes Nouveaux ou Les Fées à la Mode* (*New Fairy Tales or Fairies in Fashion*). Like Straparola and Basile, d'Aulnoy was immersed in a world where monstrous births were spoken of daily. Holly Tucker observes that in d'Aulnoy's era, 'pregnancy and childbirth inspired anxiety, wonder, and – most important – tale telling.'[37] Tucker comments on the popular beliefs of d'Aulnoy's era: 'From monsters to cats, there seemed to have been no limit to the astonishing things that could come out of a woman's body.'[38] Stories floating around in French cheap print of the seventeenth century include a monster born with a human face and a body covered in scales, and a chambermaid who gave birth to a hairy monster with a tail after having sexual relations with a monkey.[39] The latter of which is particularly relevant to d'Aulnoy's 'Babiole' which tells of a queen whose baby girl is transformed into a monkey by a cruel fairy. After she gives birth, the baby does not remain human for long, for 'all of a sudden, a marvel occurred! She became a monkey, jumping, running, and skipping about the room.'[40] The queen is horrified by her baby's transformation but above all she laments the reflection of her offspring on herself: 'What will become of me? What a disgrace! All my subjects will think I've given birth to a monster. The king will be horrified by such a child!'[41] Again, this monstrous child taints the mother with the mark of monstrosity. Like the young Chiaretta in Straparola's tale, this queen risks losing her royal status and honour. One of her attendants advises, 'you must tell the king that the princess was stillborn. Then put this ape in a box and let it sink to the bottom of the sea.'[42] Even though the creature is still a rational being on the inside, the queen agrees to this infanticide for the sake of her own honour.

We must look at why the monkey-girl must be erased. What will people think the queen has done? The suspected crime is present in the broadsheet mentioned above: the chambermaid who gives birth to a hairy monster with a tail after having sexual relations with a monkey. The broadsheet warns of the monstrous repercussions that will arise from the sin of bestiality. Since the queen in the tale is married, her supposed sin would be twofold: copulating with a real monkey and committing adultery. And so, the notion of bestiality and the mother's sin has come through into d'Aulnoy's fairy tale. Again, we encounter the notion that a monstrous act produces monstrous offspring. The animal offspring reveals parental sin and taints the mother with the stain of deviant sexuality. In her analysis of 'Babiole', Kathryn A. Hoffman argues that 'D'Aulnoy's tale has more than a hint of bestiality, a suspicion of a deviant slip into a dangerous sexuality. Monkey bodies were particularly suspect of deviant desires.'[43] The slip into a dangerous sexuality that Hoffman mentions is a slip into animal sexuality. A woman who has copulated with an animal has, in a sense, renounced her own humanity and so no longer deserves to be treated as human. Yet she is not truly an animal either; she is a liminal being hovering between two classifications. This blurring of human and animal boundaries in fairy tales provokes no end of anxiety, as it did in reality. Once again, the mother is to blame. The monster has come from her body, so her body must somehow be unnatural and monstrous. This points once again to an underlying fear of women's mysterious bodies in early modern Europe. As in the tales of Straparola and Basile above, d'Aulnoy's tale is concerned with bestiality and animal-human progeny, bringing ideas of hybridity and liminality to the fore. We can see how there was a very real anxiety about something that couldn't be classified which spans the work of all three authors.

As it happens, the monkey-girl is saved from death and given the name Babiole. Little Babiole is adopted by her cousin before she can be drowned and lives as a form of entertainment in her aunt's court. Babiole is dressed up and put on display to speak and play instruments. As Hoffman observes, 'Hairy people, both fictional and real, were caught in practices of display that turned them into liminal beings, caught at the borders of nature and culture, monstrosity and civilization.'[44] Interestingly, once the monster is distanced from the actual birthing process from a human woman, it becomes a marvel, a source of entertainment. This suggests that it is the human origin of the monster that is the most disturbing element, perhaps even more so than the monster itself. It is the idea that the human body can produce something so inhuman that so horrified early modern Europe. Once Babiole's human origins are forgotten, she is simply a foreign other, completely disconnected from the human race and no longer a threat.

Babiole eventually returns to the queen who is once again faced with her monstrous offspring. One of her attendants tells her, 'you must protect your honor. What would the world think if you declared yourself the mother of a monkey infanta?'[45] The shame she feels triumphs once again and she decides to have Babiole locked away where no-one will ever see her. However, after many trials, Babiole eventually becomes human after marrying a prince, at which point her mother can accept her as her child. Marriage has transformed and redeemed the monstrous monkey-girl. The act of entering into a heteronormative existence somehow remoulds Babiole's body into an acceptable shape. This tale is remarkably similar to a fifteen page pamphlet from 1640 mentioned by Hoffman, which tells of Tannakin Skinker, the hog-faced gentlewoman. The pamphlet tells of a baby girl whose face looks like a pig because she was bewitched while in the womb by an irate witch. The mother is told that Tannakin can become human if she marries a gentleman. Apparently a dowry of forty thousand pounds attracted many suitors who wished to attempt the feat.[46] The pamphlet of course ends there. Unfortunately, it cannot report the successful transformation of Tannakin into a human. This pamphlet is overflowing with typical fairy tale themes and so links literary fairy tales and popular print culture together even closer. In the pamphlet, the wish for transformation is overwhelming – a wish that only fairy tales could grant. Being fantasy, fairy tales had free reign to make anything happen, and to make dreams come true, so to speak. The wish for humanisation of the monster is also present in d'Aulnoy's 'The Wild Boar', in which a queen gives birth but 'instead of a handsome prince, a little wild boar was born!'[47] Though her husband wishes to 'have the little monster drowned,'[48] the queen feels pity for the creature and decides to raise him as her son. However, she attempts to humanise him and soften his monstrosity by dressing him in ribbons, jewellery, silk stockings and shoes. She also teaches him to walk on his hind legs and beats him to stop him from grunting. Though the queen allows the wild boar to live, she cannot accept him as he is; she must attempt to coax him from his liminal position between animal and human into the human realm. Like Babiole, he eventually becomes human after marrying, and so order is eventually restored. In fact, in many fairy tales, a monstrous child is transformed into a human at the end – a miraculous blessing that real life mothers could only wish for. And so, the fairy tale provides the happy ending that the booklets, broadsheets and pamphlets cannot. The fairy tale attempts to right the wrongs of popular print and re-establish the boundaries between human and animal, human and monster. Though there are many striking links between the literary fairy tale and popular print, this is the point at which they diverge. While many cheap prints are sensational, exaggerated and fantastical, they are still bound by the construct of a 'real' report. Fairy tales, on the other hand, are limitless.

As we have seen, the early modern European cultural imagination infused the fairy tale genre with frightful depictions of unnatural progeny. A lack of scientific knowledge gave rise to weird and wonderful interpretations of abnormal births. The causes ranged from acts of God, to bestiality, and even the maternal imagination. When monstrous progeny emerged from the womb, it was often the mother who was implicated as the cause, thus marking the mother as a monster also. In fact, the womb was frequently seen as both a mysterious and dangerous space from which evil could potentially spring forth. Women's bodies were thus marked as dark and unknowable, the monstrous alter ego of the male body. The effect of these popular beliefs on fairy tales is shown by the extraordinary connection between popular print and literary fairy tales, two different mediums telling the same narratives. In both genres, monstrosity is closely tied up with hybridity and liminality; creatures that defied the boundaries between human and animal, human and plant, or even male and female. Any offspring which couldn't be classified was destined to be an outsider, excluded from human culture. We have seen that monstrosity is not necessarily what is different, but what is the same but different, familiar and foreign at the same time. The knowledge that humanity can be permeated by and intermingled with nature was a most disturbing concept in early modern Europe. The tales of Straparola, Basile and d'Aulnoy mirrored their cultural environment along with its fears and anxieties over reproduction. However, some fairy tales provided what the booklets, broadsheets and pamphlets could not: the hope of the humanisation of the monster, the reversal of monstrosity. In the fairy tale genre, in which all things are possible, the supposed wrongs of abnormal progeny could be made right. For in the fairy tale realm wild boars can become handsome young men and hairy monkey-girls can be transformed into beautiful maidens once more. Perhaps these fairy tales represent what early modern cultures wished for: the restoration of order and the peace of mind that the monster inside had been kept at bay once more.

Notes

[1] Suzanne Magnanini, *Fairy-Tale Science: Monstrous Generation in the Tales of Straparola and Basile* (Toronto; Buffalo; London: University of Toronto Press, 2008), 4.

[2] Valeria Finucci, 'Maternal Imagination and Monstrous Birth: Tasso's *Gerusalemme Liberta*', in *Generation and Degeneration: Tropes of Reproduction in Literature and History from Antiquity to Early Modern Europe*, ed. Valeria Finucci and Kevin Brownlee (Durham, North Carolina: Duke University Press, 2001), 55.

[3] Ibid.

[4] Magnanini, *Fairy-Tale Science*, 105.

[5] Marilyn Francus, 'The Monstrous Mother: Reproductive Anxiety in Swift and Pope', *ELH* 61, no.4 (1994): 829. Barbara Creed has also examined depictions of the fecund female as monstrous in her book, *The Monstrous-Feminine: Film, Feminism, Psychoanalysis*.

[6] Jacques Gélis, *History of Childbirth: Fertility, Pregnancy and Birth in Early Modern Europe*, trans. Rosemary Morris (Boston: Northeastern University Press, 1991), 259.

[7] Ibid.

[8] Ibid.

[9] Alan W. Bates, *Emblematic Monsters: Unnatural Conceptions and Deformed Births in Early Modern Europe* (Amsterdam; New York: Editions Rodopi B.V., 2005), 43.

[10] Ibid.

[11] Elizabeth S. Cohen and Thomas V. Cohen, *Daily Life in Renaissance Italy* (Westport, Connecticut: Greenwood Press, 2001), 129.

[12] Ibid.

[13] Ibid.

[14] Katharine Park and Lorraine J. Daston, 'Unnatural Conceptions: The Study of Monsters in Sixteenth- and Seventeenth-Century France and England', *Past & Present* 92 (1981): 28-30.

[15] Ibid.

[16] Ibid., 28.

[17] Bates, *Emblematic Monsters*, 43.

[18] Dudley Wilson, *Signs and Portents: Monstrous Births from the Middle Ages to the Enlightenment* (London; New York: Routledge, 1993), 38.

[19] Ibid., 60.

[20] Giovan Francesco Straparola, 'Ancilotto, King of Provino', in *The Great Fairy Tale Tradition: From Straparola and Basile to the Brothers Grimm*, ed. Jack Zipes (New York; London: W.W. Norton & Company, 2001), 222.

[21] Ibid., 223.

[22] Magnanini, *Fairy-Tale Science*, 108.

[23] Ibid., 109-110.

[24] Ibid.

[25] Giovan Francesco Straparola, 'Biancabella and the Snake', in *The Great Fairy Tale Tradition: From Straparola and Basile to the Brothers Grimm*, ed. Jack Zipes (New York; London: W.W. Norton & Company, 2001), 406.

[26] Ibid.

[27] Ottavia Niccoli, *Prophecy and People in Renaissance Italy*, trans. Lydia G. Cochrane (New Jersey: Princeton University Press, 1990), 37.

[28] Ibid., 35.

[29] Giovan Francesco Straparola, 'Filomena the Hermaphrodite', in *The Nights of Straparola*, trans. W. G. Waters. (London: Lawrence and Bullen, 1894), 287.
[30] Ibid.
[31] Ibid., 289.
[32] Ibid.
[33] Giambattista Basile, 'The Myrtle', in *The Tale of Tales, or Entertainment for Little Ones*, ed. Nancy L. Canepa (Detroit: Wayne State University Press, 2007), 53.
[34] Ibid.
[35] Wilson, *Signs and Portents*, 55-56.
[36] Ibid., 3.
[37] Holly Tucker, *Pregnant Fictions: Childbirth and the Fairy Tale in Early-Modern France* (Detroit: Wayne State University Press, 2003), 4.
[38] Ibid., 18.
[39] Wilson, *Signs and Portents*, 56.
[40] Marie-Catherine d'Aulnoy, 'Babiole', in *Beauties, Beasts and Enchantment: Classic French Fairy Tales*, ed. Jack Zipes (New York: New American Library, 1989), 439.
[41] Ibid.
[42] Ibid.
[43] Kathryn A. Hoffmann, 'Of Monkey Girls and a Hog-Faced Gentlewoman: Marvel in Fairy Tales, Fairgrounds, and Cabinets of Curiosities', *Marvels & Tales: Journal of Fairy-Tale Studies* 19.1 (2005): 75.
[44] Ibid., 74.
[45] D'Aulnoy, 'Babiole', 450.
[46] Hoffman, *Of Monkey Girls*, 80.
[47] Marie-Catherine d'Aulnoy, 'The Wild Boar', in *The Great Fairy Tale Tradition: From Straparola and Basile to the Brothers Grimm*, ed. Jack Zipes (New York; London: W.W. Norton & Company, 2001), 58.
[48] Ibid.

Bibliography

Basile, Giambattista. 'The Dragon'. In *The Tale of Tales, or Entertainment for Little Ones*, edited by Nancy L. Canepa, 326-336. Detroit: Wayne State University Press, 2007.

———. 'The Enchanted Doe'. In *The Tale of Tales, or Entertainment for Little Ones*, edited by Nancy L. Canepa, 108-114. Detroit: Wayne State University Press, 2007.

———. 'The Myrtle'. In *The Tale of Tales, or Entertainment for Little Ones*, edited by Nancy L. Canepa, 52-60. Detroit: Wayne State University Press, 2007.

———. 'Penta with the Chopped-Off Hands'. In *The Tale of Tales, or Entertainment for Little Ones*, edited by Nancy L. Canepa, 223-232. Detroit: Wayne State University Press, 2007.

Bates, Alan W. *Emblematic Monsters: Unnatural Conceptions and Deformed Births in Early Modern Europe*. Amsterdam; New York: Editions Rodopi B.V., 2005.

Cohen, Elizabeth S., and Thomas V. Cohen. *Daily Life in Renaissance Italy*. Westport, Connecticut: Greenwood Press, 2001.

Creed, Barbara. *The Monstrous-Feminine: Film, Feminism, Psychoanalysis*. London: Routledge, 1993.

D'Aulnoy, Marie-Catherine. 'Babiole'. In *Beauties, Beasts and Enchantment: Classic French Fairy Tales*, edited by Jack Zipes, 438-458. New York: New American Library, 1989.

———. 'The Wild Boar'. In *The Great Fairy Tale Tradition: From Straparola and Basile to the Brothers Grimm*, edited by Jack Zipes, 57-81. New York; London: W.W. Norton & Company, 2001.

Finucci, Valeria. 'Maternal Imagination and Monstrous Birth: Tasso's *Gerusalemme Liberta*'. In *Generation and Degeneration: Tropes of Reproduction in Literature and History from Antiquity to Early Modern Europe*, edited by Valeria Finucci and Kevin Brownlee, 41-77. Durham, North Carolina: Duke University Press, 2001.

Francus, Marilyn. 'The Monstrous Mother: Reproductive Anxiety in Swift and Pope'. *ELH* 61, no.4 (1994):829-51.

Gélis, Jacques. *History of Childbirth: Fertility, Pregnancy and Birth in Early Modern Europe*. Translated by Rosemary Morris. Boston: Northeastern University Press, 1991.

Hoffmann, Kathryn A. 'Of Monkey Girls and a Hog-Faced Gentlewoman: Marvel in Fairy Tales, Fairgrounds, and Cabinets of Curiosities'. *Marvels & Tales: Journal of Fairy-Tale Studies* 19, no. 1 (2005): 67-85.

Magnanini, Suzanne. *Fairy-Tale Science: Monstrous Generation in the Tales of Straparola and Basile*. Toronto; Buffalo; London: University of Toronto Press, 2008.

Musacchio, Jacqueline Marie. *The Art and Ritual of Childbirth in Renaissance Italy*. New Haven: Yale University Press, 1999.

Niccoli, Ottavia. *Prophecy and People in Renaissance Italy.* Translated by Lydia G. Cochrane. New Jersey: Princeton University Press, 1990.

Park, Katharine, and Lorraine J. Daston. 'Unnatural Conceptions: The Study of Monsters in Sixteenth- and Seventeenth-Century France and England'. *Past & Present*, 92 (1981): 20-54.

Straparola, Giovan Francesco. 'Ancilotto, King of Provino'. In *The Great Fairy Tale Tradition: From Straparola and Basile to the Brothers Grimm*, edited by Jack Zipes, 220-229. New York; London: W.W. Norton & Company, 2001.

———. 'Biancabella and the Snake'. In *The Great Fairy Tale Tradition: From Straparola and Basile to the Brothers Grimm*, edited by Jack Zipes, 406-415. New York; London: W.W. Norton & Company, 2001.

———. 'Filomena the Hermaphrodite.' In *The Nights of Straparola*. Translated by W. G. Waters, 287-290. London: Lawrence and Bullen, 1894.

———. 'The Pig Prince'. In *The Great Fairy Tale Tradition: From Straparola and Basile to the Brothers Grimm*, edited by Jack Zipes, 51-56. New York; London: W.W. Norton & Company, 2001.

Tucker, Holly. *Pregnant Fictions: Childbirth and the Fairy Tale in Early-Modern France*. Detroit: Wayne State University Press, 2003.

Wilson, Dudley. *Signs and Portents: Monstrous Births from the Middle Ages to the Enlightenment*. London; New York: Routledge, 1993.

Belinda Calderone is currently completing her PhD in English at Monash University, Clayton, Australia. While her thesis examines changing representations of motherhood in European fairy tales, her broader research interests include classic and modern fairy tale literature, print history, translation and censorship.

Part II

The Age of Monstrosity: Teens and Beyond

Narrativizing Sexual Deviance as both Symptom and Fantasy: The Perverse Sexuality of the Wolf-Child

Steven Rita-Procter

Abstract
This chapter aims to trace out the underlying socio-cultural motivations for the historical development and propagation of the monstrous narrative – specifically the werewolf figure. That is, it aims to reveal the specific function(s) of the werewolf-figure in contemporary and historical literatures and arts, and to identify the particular social group(s) that the werewolf represents through its the archetypal sexual-deviance and anti-social behaviour. Operating dialectically, it is argued that the werewolf's monstrosity is defined by the antithetical relationship between, on the one hand, those pre-established socially-accepted behaviours and sexual expectations which govern the prevailing social order, and on the other, the extreme transgressions of the monstrous figure which spill over and upset this stability *from within*. It is argued that the treatment of the werewolf in folklore, literature, and the arts is, then, our way of ostracizing or otherwise indignifying those *internal* delinquent offenders which they have come to represent – mainly, the adolescent male. I stress that the werewolf and its male adolescent counterpart are considered 'internal deviants' within the prevailing socio-sexual framework because their respective 'monstrous characteristics' can be considered to be typically inherent products of the social-codification of sexuality within the societies to which they belong; or better still, as *consequences* or *symptoms* of the very sexual classifications against which they are measured.

Key Words: Werewolf, adolescence, teenage, male, sexuality, abstinence, Żižek.

*****

As Andrea Gutenberg writes, '[w]erewolves have been regarded as prime emblems of the marginal, of deviance, and of hybridity, for more than two millennia.'[1] More often than not, literary and cinematic portrayals of werewolves have come to signify the savage, barbaric and transgressive acts which society officially prohibits – particularly excessive violence and sexual indiscretions. Werewolves are almost always typified by predatory, cannibalistic, and sadistic traits that often mirror the social groups that they depict. For instance, werewolf narratives from antiquity portray lycanthropy as a form of punishment imposed upon those individuals who violated the laws of the gods. Likewise, Christian depictions of the werewolf are typically infused with pagan imagery, suggesting a parallel between monstrosity and sin. And even fairy-tales often portray the werewolf as outright paedophiles, rapists, or serial-killers.

These traditional portrayals of the werewolf, however, are *extreme* illustrations of the types of marginal or deviant anti-social behaviour that stand out from the 'norm' because of their *excessively* violent transgressions of the existing social order. Their monstrosity is defined, then, by the dialectical relationship between those pre-established, socially-accepted behaviours which *govern* the social order, and the extreme transgressions which spill over and upset this stability *from within*.

The treatment of the werewolf in folklore, literature, and the arts *is*, then, our way of ostracizing or otherwise indignifying these *internal* delinquent offenders. I stress 'internal' because the abovementioned villains and criminals can be considered to be typically inherent products of the societies within which they exist, or better still, as *consequences* or *symptoms* of the very social order against which they are measured. Paedophiles, rapists, and serial-killers, for instance, are not generally regarded as external threats who assault a community from beyond. Instead, they are typically considered to be unfortunate, and sometimes even inevitable consequences of the ways in which subjectivity and sexuality are constituted within a given social order.

To put it differently, we might say that a society produces the category of the depraved delinquent by virtue of the very *delimitation* of what we consider to be the 'ideal, and sexually-balanced subject' – or at the very least, the establishment of such ideals systematically re-creates the conditions for the possibility of such figures, through the stringent codification and regulation of social norms.[2]

It is these types of *domestic* delinquents that the werewolf figure is typically associated with, as opposed to a foreign intruder who wreaks havoc on a community and then quickly disappears. The representation of foreign intruders in contemporary literature and films, for instance, tend to be embodied by Zombies, as is the case with any number of films from the Nazi-zombie genre. In these films – most notably Jesús Franco Manera's 1983 cult-classic *Bloodsucking Nazi Zombies* – an external threat ambushes a closed community from beyond, but there is a certain sense of solidarity amongst the closed community that is being attacked *in opposition* to the foreign adversary. On the contrary, the werewolf figure classically epitomizes an *internal* deviant within the community itself, who on a surface level is able to adapt and conform to the social and legal conventions, yet at times must yield to his violent and 'perverse' desires.

What makes the werewolf figure the ideal symbol for this type of *domestic* monstrosity is the manner in which the lycanthrope seemingly blends in and assimilates into the social order *by day*, and only by night does he transform into a violent monster. It is, then, the struggle between one's private and public lives that the werewolf figure traditionally represents; particularly the effort to assimilate one's individual carnal desires and urges (no matter how deviant they may be considered according to the prevailing discursive regime) into its often astringent and harsh regulations.

In the werewolf narrative, this struggle is exemplified by the often evocative and climactic scenes of metamorphosis in which, generally, a man transforms into a wolf-like creature. This transformation typically signals the surrendering of oneself to those *abject* desires that are the source of the private/public struggle. Legendary depictions of the werewolf transformation – such as the scene in which David Naughton's character in *An American Werewolf in London* excruciatingly morphs into a repulsive monster – often exaggerate the depiction of the antagonist as the classic outsider with intense sexual or psychological collapses. This, one would assume, is meant to convey to the viewer, or reader that, in one intense moment of self-discovery, the creature is no longer able to curtail their perverse cravings and must, once-and-for-all, abandon the stifling social codes that inhibit their true nature.

This, I would argue, is the reason why the werewolf figure has been employed so often in representing the unique struggles of the young, adolescent male. The distinctive predicaments of the male adolescent all resonate with the 'outsider' traits of the lycanthrope. The natural growth process, intensified social demands, sexual curiosities and urges, the development of an autonomous self-identity, and frequent moral dilemmas all characterize this peculiar phase in a young man's life, and are almost universally accompanied by a general sense of ostracization from one's own family and community.

In Gene Fowler's 1957 film, *I Was a Teenage Werewolf*, Michael Landon plays a typically angry teenager who struggles to fit in at school, and to control his developing passions. Seeking hypnotherapy from a local doctor so that he can 'fit-in' with the other kids his age, he is unfortunately (and somewhat humorously) subjected to an experimental medical procedure that renders him an all-the-more violent werewolf. Only upon this transformation are his seemingly unnatural male, adolescent behaviours and desires codified in explicit binary opposition to the expected adult norms, and he is openly and graphically rendered a mere spectacle of monstrosity.

Similarly, Larry Cohen's 1981 film *Full Moon High*, and Rod Daniel's 1985 hit *Teen Wolf* both portray many of the typical adolescent experiences with the over-the-top flash of werewolf monstrosity. In the latter, Michael J. Fox's character has a larger-than-life nervous breakdown when his voice suddenly deepens, he notices the unexpected and rapid growth of facial and body hair, and the abrupt transformation of the shape of his face and skeleton appear before his very eyes. In an instant, the boy turns into a young man – yet this natural progression is rendered monstrous by exaggerating the reality that, for a very brief time, he does not fit into either of the social categories: child, nor adult. For that especially brief moment, Scott Howard (teen wolf) does not have a social identity. In this way, the state of the adolescent is explicitly portrayed as an abject one; he is the unclassified subject who is always only an exception and who is forever relegated to the interstitial (perhaps luminal) non-space between childhood and adulthood.

In these three films, the protagonist is paradoxically represented as a type of domestic outsider within his own community. The adolescent male is nurtured and is entirely constituted within the social order, yet he does not have a place within its symbolic classifications. As Deleuze and Guattari outline in *A Thousand Plateaus*, the entirety of an individual's life is lived as various lines of flight between the socially constructed opposable terms: man, woman, child, and adult.[3] In this sense, the two dominant creative forces which capriciously assert themselves throughout a subject's life are labelled 'childhood' and 'adulthood' tendencies – 'childhood' referring to those compulsions which incite rebellious, subjugating actions and 'adulthood' tendencies implying those impulses to dominate or hierarchize. There is, however, no mention of 'adolescent' creative energies.[4] For Deleuze and Guattari, then, adolescence is simply the 'intermezzo'; the interstitial distance between binaries.

Similarly, for developmental psychologists 'adolescence' is merely a transitional period; a phase which links the stages of infancy with full subjective-development. As such, the adolescent is neither afforded the wide-ranging freedom and innocence of the child, yet he does not yet possess an individual identity or the fully realized (and controlled/censored) drives of an adult. In this way, adolescence is a period in which the basic sexual drives that constitute our being are no longer in their primary, developmental phases; nor are they fully realized yet, in a social-context.

Moreover, the bodily transformations that take place in each of these cases reduce the boys to the most base and animalistic elements of their former selves. In this sense, the fantastical transformations of the teenage body serves to further disrepute members of that non-class by stripping them of the sexual and social significance of the sophisticated adult-male body, and reducing them to their basic physiological essentials. In this sense, Mikhail Bakhtin's notion of the grotesque body serves well to elucidate the teenage-male werewolf body, through its perverse relation to the typical adult-form.

As Bakhtin writes in *Rabelais and His World*, 'the essential principle of grotesque realism is degradation, that is, the lowering of all that is high, spiritual, ideal, abstract; it is a transfer to the material level, to the sphere of earth and body in their indissoluble unity.'[5] This degradation takes place once the child has entered into the interstitial phase of puberty – at the point in which he begins to assume the basic physical and sexual characteristics of a man, but does not yet possess the symbolic and social standing that these traits hold for members of the higher social class.

This process is reversed, as Sarah Rangaratnam indicates in her chapter 'The Monstrous Widow in Early Twentieth-Century India,' in the case of the widowed Brahmin women in Deepa Mehta's film *Water* (2005) and Padma Viswanathan's novel *The Toss of a Lemon* (2008). In these cases, as Rangaratnam indicates, these women are reduced – by force – to the interstitial, non-categorized space between

'Woman' and 'Man'; their heads are shaved, they are dressed in a 'uniform,' they are forced into seclusion and they are refused any physical or sexual contact in an attempt to *deprive* them of the physical and sexual characteristics of a woman and to strip them of the symbolic and social standing that these traits hold for members of the 'female' social class.

Prior to their violent physical transformations, not only did these women fit into a stable and established social class, but they were also codified as such through their bodily appearances. Yet, the moment the women become 'widowed,' they no longer correspond to the socially codified dialectics of 'single' and 'wed'; and their bodily image is savagely mutilated so as to conform to the 'monstrosity' of her non-status.

The pre-pubescent boy, in a similar sense, is recognizable by his physical appearance and sexual ranking as the dialectical inverse of the full-grown man (and he is classified, socially, as such). In other words, on a purely physiological level, the 'pre-pubescent boy' is categorized by his lack of 'adult-male' physical features, and by the fact that he has not yet – or, at least, is not supposed to have – entered into the symbolic realm of sexual conduct and the reproductive process.

The entire social order for males is demarcated as such by the rankings: infant, child, man, and elderly man, etc. And, not only are these respective rankings defined according to their particular physical and sexual appearances, but also by the ideal and abstract social meanings that these physical and sexual characteristics take on. The typical bodily form of the adult man, then, comes to symbolize the noble, ideal, and abstract virtues of that accepted social order: facial hair, muscle mass, etc. correspond to the virtues of an adult male: sexual virility, power, supposed authority, etc. Particularly, sexuality is regulated by the strict delineation between social categories, and it is thus promoted to a high and dignified status insofar as it is reserved only for members of the 'adult' classes. In that way, sexuality – in its 'mature,' adult manifestation – has been historically linked to reproduction, in its highest and most divine sense.

However, the abject, transitional phase of the adolescent male poses a particular threat to the stability of this social structure in that the high, noble and ideal is lowered down to its most basic, animalistic essential nature. The traditional 'nobility' of certain adult-male traits – body hair, sexuality, muscle mass, etc. – represent the privileges and marks of distinction for only those members of the alleged or self-styled 'uppermost class' in this social hierarchy. Yet, for the pubescent male, these 'noble' symbols of manhood are reduced to their brute, material cores. Sexuality is likewise brought down from its noble form – stripped of any correlation to *eros* or divine notions of procreation – and reduced to its base form; its material and fleshy matter. In its werewolf manifestation, then, the teenage male is depicted as being dominated solely by his primary, bodily needs.

The degradation and materialization of the male body thus violates the established social order, and the grotesque transformation of the werewolf exacerbates this change through its exaggerated depiction of Rabelaisian vulgarity.[6]

Along these lines, teenage sexuality is depicted as base, vulgar, and even immoral in many cases; it is the general period in which masturbation is performed for the first time – at least, in its relation to fantasy – and any quick survey of literature on teenage sexuality reveals a wide array of book-chapters entitled something like: 'introduction to masturbation,' or some such variation. The linkage between the development of sexual identities in male adolescence and the earliest explorations of masturbation are described by Wardell Pomeroy as such:

> It provides a full outlet for fancy, for daydreaming, which is characteristic of adolescence. Fantasy, or daydreaming, is usually an accompaniment of masturbation… This is a really private matter, between the boy and himself.[7]

However, as Żižek notes in *The Plague of Fantasies*:

> For humans, the "zero form" [of sexuality] is *masturbation with fantasizing*… When, in the eighteenth century, masturbation became a moral problem with a distinctly modern twist, what bothered the moralist sexologists was not primarily the non-[re]productive loss of semen but, rather, the "unnatural" way desire is aroused in masturbation – not by a real object but by a fantasized object created by the subject itself. When, for example, Kant condemns this vice as so unnatural that "we consider it indecent even to call it by its proper name," his reasoning goes as follows: "Lust is called unnatural if man is aroused to it, not by its real object, but by his imagination".[8]

In other words, masturbation – in its modern conceptualization – is regarded as the basest version of sexual activity because it divests itself of the need for an Other. It is, thus, the degradation of ideal, *reproductive* sexual conduct, and is therefore seen as reducing all that is divine and splendid about the sexual act to its most animalistic and vulgar essentials. Whereas 'ideal adult-sex' is regulated by a number of social codes and 'acceptable ways of behaving' which inscribe it with its high, spiritual, ideal and abstract qualities, teenage masturbation is regarded as essentially 'grotesque,' insofar as it is the lowering of all that is good. It is, in other words, the transferring of sex to its most material level, 'to the sphere of earth and body,' as Bakhtin would put it.

This theme is depicted in the independent Canadian film *Ginger Snaps* (2000), in which lycanthropy serves, once again, as a metaphor for puberty – only, in this case with specific reference to the female experience. In this film, sexuality is reduced to the most basic, brute, and animalistic manner by a pack of teenage werewolf figures: a crude scene of group-masturbation. However, following the theoretical framework of both Żižek and Bakhtin, this scene rather appropriately represents the 'zero form' of sexuality, and the carnivalesque and grotesque manifestation of what is considered, at least in its high or ideal form, to be decent and good. Furthermore, this scene succeeds in lowering the already base act of masturbation to an even more animalistic level, in that it transfers it from a solitary act of self-gratification to a group or *pack*-activity. In this sense, the brute animalism of the act is awarded even greater symbolic import – and is, perhaps, even more monstrous or grotesque – in that the otherwise intimate act of reproduction is presented as a type of wildly brute and animalistic behaviour.

Michael Jackson's classic music video for his 1983 hit *Thriller* similarly presents the male adolescent experience as overtly monstrous and devoid of any official social-status. Insofar as his primal sexual urges do not correspond to his former needs as a child, nor are they fully developed enough that they can be tempered by the expected social codes of adulthood, the teenage male falls somewhere *between* the two social classes. In the opening sequence, the central character is overcome with sexual desire after the girl with whom he is on a date agrees to see him exclusively. The typically adolescent dilemma of wanting to simply give in to all of his newly discovered sexual urges (while acknowledging that he is expected to temper them and assimilate into the accepted role of an adult) comes to a head when he is confronted by a full moon. It is at this moment that his adolescent status is exposed as utterly monstrous, and upon his own metamorphosis he pursues his victim through the forest in some sort of base, predatory hunt. To this end, his sexual urges correspond to the mature, fully-developed sexuality of an adult male, yet they are reduced to their most primal and animalistic elements. He possesses, in a sense, the basic sexual passions of an adult-male, but lacks the sophistication required to conform to the adult social-roles. Instead, his desires manifest themselves in monstrous acts of self-gratification, symptomatic of the child's tendency towards pleasure-seeking, albeit mixed with the more acute sexuality of an adult figure. We might say, then, that it is in this way that society projects the monstrous werewolf figure onto the pubescent-male, as a means of signifying his degenerate status in comparison to both that of the child and the adult.

On the other hand, however, it is entirely possible to argue that the imagery of the werewolf figure might, in fact, be an edifice that is entirely constituted on the part of the teenage male – that is, as the manner in which the child sees *himself* and his transition into manhood. In such a case, as opposed to the monstrous figure being a description or classification that the rest of society ascribes *to* the teenage male (as a way of ostracizing or otherwise rejecting him from the activities of society), it is entirely possible that the monstrous figure is, in fact, a form of auto-interpretation; a kind of self-portrait on the part of the child, himself. In other words, the monstrous transformation might operate as a symbol of the ways in which the teenage-male views himself at that crucial phase in his life. It is conceivable, in this sense, that the pubescent male associates with the werewolf figure simply because he perceives himself as a sort of monstrous pariah. Again, the bodily transformations of puberty and the awakening of his sexual desires certainly seem foreign and monstrous to the child who first experiences them, and it is reasonable – I think – to say that many of us feel as though we are undergoing some sort of 'monstrous' transformation.

In Freud's famous case-study of Sergei Pankejeff – otherwise known as the 'Wolf Man' – it is argued that the patient suffered from the unfortunate experience of having witnessed his parents having sex at a young age, 'in a posture especially favourable for certain observations.'[9] The resulting neuroses which the patient suffered from manifested themselves, according to Freud, in various nightmarish dreams featuring wolves and wolf-like figures – suggesting that his regrettable early encounter with parental sex corresponded to what he saw as the wild compulsions of a wolf. The association that the child made between sexual acts and desires, and the brute animalism of the wolf-like figure, is perhaps a verification of the fact that the child is unable to adequately make sense of his own developing sexuality and is, instead, forced to reproduce the primal scene in a pathological context. In this way, like Freud's 'Wolf-Man,' the depiction of the pubescent-male as a lycanthrope might be attributable to a misplaced, unconscious projection of one's own primal, sexual urges, which, at that time, find no adequate symbolic meaning and thus manifest themselves in a series of neuroses and/or nightmares.

In his evaluation of this case, Freud argues that, '[the 'primal scene'] which the patient saw his parents adopt – the man upright, and the woman bent down like an animal'[10] was unconsciously supplemented by his sister, who used to torment him with fairy-tale books featuring terrifying images of werewolves. He continues,

> we have already heard that during his anxiety period [stemming from his experience with his parents] his sister used to terrify him with a picture from the fairy-book, in which the wolf was shown standing upright, with one foot forward, with its claws stretched out and its ears pricked… he thought that the attitude of the wolf in this picture might have reminded him of that of his father during the primal scene.[11]

It is possible then, as Freud points out, to assume that our early encounters with werewolf fairy-tales and folklore have become deeply inscribed within our cultural unconscious. It is natural, then, that these pre-figurative impressions inevitably begin to mirror the social structures within which they arise. Today, the werewolf figure (contrary to Freud's single observation) often corresponds to the young adult or adolescent, whereas the related mythological figure of the vampire tends to correspond to adult authority-figures. In this way, the contemporary trend in popular literature and films tend to portray vestiges of the classical fairy-tale werewolf as young, wild teenage types, and the old, pale vampires as their disagreeable parent-figures. Furthermore, the traditional vampire-figure (who tend to live into their 'hundred's,' and are thus already presented as aged) are often depicted as sophisticated, elegant, and refined monsters, usually of classical European ethnicity, whereas the werewolf-figure, on the other hand, is typically portrayed as undeveloped, uncivilized and unruly animals (often of North American, or more often still Native American, heritage). As such, in the uncanny realm of monster mythology it is no surprise that the werewolf-figure is classically represented as slaves of the vampires, or at the very least as their novice apprentices[12] – setting up an ideal opposition for portrayals of the teenage experience.

Perhaps, (we should reluctantly admit) none of these aforementioned portrayals of the teenage-werewolf have reached the acclaim and success of the character of Jacob Black in Stephenie Meyers' The Twilight Saga. In Meyer's popular series, the werewolf is presented as a complex, sensitive and vulnerable creature who struggles to curb his natural aggression, and who suffers from the typical heartache and sorrow associated with male adolescence. Jacob Black at once embodies the carnal and primal desires which pubescent boys clumsily discover, while also coping with the complicated emotional sentiments that go along with a first love, courtship, and sexual awakening. To this end, Meyers' depiction of the werewolf as a sensitive, misunderstood monster accurately represents the monstrosity of the teenage male, and his passage to maturity. Jacob and his Quileute companions represent the marginalization and ostracization of pubescent males who struggle to come to terms with their newfound 'savage' and 'feral' passions. In this way, Meyers' saga reverses the typical transformation of man into wolf, opting instead for the conversion of a bewildered boy into a man.

In the initial volume of the saga, Jacob is portrayed as a typically awkward fifteen-year old, who clearly has a sort of juvenile infatuation with the story's protagonist Bella, yet there is no sense of sexual tension or awareness on his part. At this point in the narrative, Jacob does not yet possess the type of individual identity that is necessary to critically examine the social codes of his Quillette tribe, and he is more than willing to innocently pass-on the warnings of his elders to Bella regarding the Cullen family. This type of passive obedience or conformity to the accepted values and belief-system of his community is characteristic of the childhood phase, and one which his impending adolescence will soon cast doubt upon. In *Twilight*, it is apparent that Jacob plays only a minor role, yet his diminutive stature and childlike nature will serve as key points of contrast against his forthcoming pubescent transformation.

When we next come across Jacob in *New Moon*, the second volume of the Saga, it is apparent that he is no longer the awkward, innocent, scrawny child that we found in *Twilight*. Instead, Jacob Black (portrayed by Taylor Lautner in the film adaptations) is now immediately in the throes of puberty, and similar to the teen heroes in *Teen Wolf, Full Moon High*, and *Thriller*, has begun his testosterone-fuelled physical transformation. He has shed his long hairstyle, opting instead for a conventional crew-cut style – an indication that he, like all teenage boys, has begun to be concerned about what others think of him. This sudden awareness of how others might perceive him points to his progression beyond what Lacan refers to as the primary narcissism of the childhood phase. Jacob, in a sense, has just begun to see himself as an autonomous individual, although his typically adolescent need to fit-in to an exclusive peer group (such as his 'pack' of Quillette brothers) attests to his not yet having fully developed a strong, adult sense of self. Once again, the werewolf protagonist is caught within the transitional non-space between childhood and adulthood.

As Jacob officially joins his exclusive 'pack' of peers, it is revealed to the reader that he possesses a hereditary trait common amongst certain Quillette tribes people that renders him a werewolf – or something quite similar, at least. This well-timed monstrous revelation occurs at about the average age when most adolescent males enter into a disobedient, rebellious, and unreservedly defiant social phase. The typical tensions of pent-up social pressures, sexual frustrations, feelings of being suppressed by authority-figures, and raging upsurges in hormone-levels are typically discharged by the average male teenager with severe, emotional flare-ups. The nonconformity and seditious qualities of such outbursts are rendered all the more monstrous in Meyers' narrative, as the werewolves are portrayed as being notoriously short-tempered, exceedingly violent, and prone to burst into wolf-form whenever incensed.

What sets Jacob Black apart from traditional representations of the teenage werewolf-figure is the emotional complexity, and sexual restraint that he shows. Whereas Michael Landon's character in *I was a Teenage Werewolf* and Michael Jackson's character in *Thriller* have absolutely no control over their sexual desires, and must abandon themselves unequivocally to the throws of their carnal desires, Jacob is somehow able to curtail his cravings. When he initially promises his pack that he will stay away from Bella – in order to 'protect' her from himself – he renders himself all the more monstrous and *especially* inhuman in comparison to his traditional werewolf counterparts. His transformation is not presented as being grotesque in any way, and is, in fact, not even mentioned; it occurs between volumes, and as such is hidden away entirely.

In these ways, perhaps what Jacob represents is the *even more monstrous* nature of today's current adolescents, whose penchant for solitude, abstinence, moderation, and other forms of self-denial are all the more atrocious according to our society's current value-system. Although our stringent codification and regulation of social norms do aim to regulate and temper our natural aggressive and sexual instincts, it is acknowledged, as stated above, *to some extent* that such ideals do in fact systematically re-create the conditions for the possibility of individuals who will violate them through over-indulgence and excessiveness. However, our generation of teenagers' newfound predilections towards absolute denial of their natural sexual urges and suppression of *all* primal or animalistic instincts has produced a breed of exceptionally monstrous monsters, since these teenagers have no definable social classifications; and thus, do not correspond to any of our prevailing social rankings.

Perhaps Nietzsche might provide us with the most acute explanation of the monstrosity of today's male teenager. Had he been around today to read Meyers' hugely successful saga, perhaps he would tell us that Jacob's natural inclinations towards aggression, power, and sexuality are stifled simply because the 'herd mentality' of the adult-classes have codified our social value-system according to a *de*scending, nay-saying morality. And since Jacob and other male adolescents are unable to discharge their natural urges and tendencies externally, perhaps they have become predisposed to internalizing their cravings – thus choosing to inflict their pent-up aggression upon themselves through a denial of their sexuality and naturally aggressive instincts.

Whereas Michael Jackson's *Thriller* might portray an exceptional instance of a social-pariah throwing off the shackles of his society's restrictive value-system and affirming his individual urges and desires in all their horrific glory, Jacob Black instead represents our current generation of male-adolescents' unwillingness to affirm their natural bodily and emotional urges at all. Instead, as today's adolescents' monstrous 'pledges of abstinence' attest to, our teenage werewolves are reduced to pathetically sitting-back and seething over their collective sexual frustrations, while the 'life-affirming' vampires have all the fun.

Notes

[1] Andrea Gutenberg, 'Shape-Shifters from the Wilderness,' in *The Abject of Desire: The Aestheticization of the Unaesthetic in Contemporary Literature and Culture* (Amsterdam: Rodopi Press, 2007), 147.

[2] For instance, Slavøj Żižek – in *The Parallax View* – refers to the ways in which the constitution of the subject and the organization of sexuality within the Catholic Church has 'produced' the conditions for the possibility of the sexual abuse of children by priests. This, he argues, is an internal symptom of the symbolic order within the organization of the Church, itself.

[3] Gilles Deleuze and Felix Guattari, *Thousand Plateaus: Capitalism and Schizophrenia* (Minnesota: University of Minnesota Press, 1987), 227.

[4] Although one would assume that the pair's rhizomatic model of the subject would allow for some sort of admixture or trans-species assemblage of the former two creative forces, which might resemble adolescent behaviours.
[5] Mikhail Bakhtin, *Rabelais and His World*, trans. Helene Iswolsky (Bloomington: Indiana University Press, 2009), 19-20.
[6] In the Bakhtinian sense, however, we might then read the werewolf figure – at least in its teenage-male versions – as a satirical trope. The degradation of the high, noble male figure to its base essence may, in fact, be construed as a satirical criticism of the prevailing social system itself. Perhaps in the spirit of *Don Quixote* or *Candide*, the teenage-male werewolf figure – in all of its repugnant, crass vulgarities – might be read as a way of turning the 'dignified' social order upside-down, and of exposing the underside of the adult male figure in all its grotesque glory.
[7] Wardell Pomeroy, *Boys & Sex* (New York: Dell Publishing. 1968), 32.
[8] Slavøj Żižek, *The Plague of Fantasies* (London: Verso, 2008), 82.
[9] Sigmund Freud, 'The Dream and the Primal Scene', in *Three Case Studies: The 'Wolf Man,' The 'Rat Man,' and the Psychotic Doctor Schreber* (New York: Touchstone Books, 1963), 55.
[10] Ibid., 196.
[11] Ibid.
[12] The *Underworld* film series, directed by Len Wiseman and Patrick Tatopoulos, provide a nice depiction of this classical mythological relationship.

Bibliography

An American Werewolf in London. Dir. John Landis. Perf. David Naughton, Jenny Agutter, and Griffin Dunne. Polygram. 1981. Film.

Bakhtin, Mikhail. *Rabelais and His World.* Translated by Helene Iswolsky. Bloomington: Indiana University Press, 2009.

Bloodsucking Nazi Zombies. Dir. Jesús Franco Manera. Perf. Manuel Gélin, France Lomay, and Jeff Montgomery. Eurociné. 1983. Film.

Deleuze, Gilles and Felix Guattari. *Thousand Plateaus: Capitalism and Schizophrenia*. Minnesota: University of Minnesota Press. 1987.

Freud, Sigmund. 'The Dream and the Primal Scene'. In *Three Case Studies: The 'Wolf Man,' The 'Rat Man,' and the Psychotic Doctor Schreber*. New York: Touchstone Books. 1963.

Full Moon High. Dir. Larry Cohen. Perf. Adam Arkin, Ed McMahon, and Roz Kelly. Filmways Pictures. 1981. Film.

Ginger Snaps. Dir. John Fawcett. Perf. Emily Perkins, Katharine Isabelle, and Kris Lemche. Copperheart. 2000. Film.

Gutenberg, Andrea. 'Shape-Shifters from the Wilderness.' In *The Abject of Desire: The Aestheticization of the Unaesthetic in Contemporary Literature and Culture*, edited by Konstanze Kutzbach and Monika Mueller. Amsterdam: Rodopi Press. 2007.

I Was a Teenage Werewolf. Dir. Gene Fowler. Perf. Michael Landon, Yvonne Fedderson, and Whit Bissell. Sunset Productions. 1957. Film.

Meyers, Stephenie. *Twilight*. New York: Little, Brown Books for Young Readers, 2008.

Meyers, Stephenie. *New Moon*. New York: Little Brown Books for Young Readers, 2008.

Meyers, Stephenie. *Breaking Dawn*. New York: Little Brown Books for Young Readers, 2009.

Pomeroy, Wardell. *Boys & Sex*. New York: Dell Publishing. 1968.

Teen Wolf. Dir. Rod Daniel. Perf. Michael J. Fox, James Hampton, and Susan Ursitti. Wolfkill. 1985. Film.

Thriller. Dir. John Landis. Perf. Michael Jackson, Ola Ray, and Vincent Price. Optimum Productions. 1983.

Żižek, Slavøj. *The Plague of Fantasies*. London: Verso, 2008.

———. *The Parallax View*. Cambridge: MIT Press, 2009.

Steven Rita-Procter is a PhD student in English at York University, Canada. His research focuses on the intersections of trauma, memory studies, and testimony, and he is currently curating an online exhibit of 'testimonial photography' taken by witnesses of the September 11 attacks.

The Lost Boys?! Monstrous Youth of the Cinematic Teenage Vampire

Simon Bacon

Abstract
This chapter will take a comparative look at two representations of monstrous youth, that in *The Lost Boys* directed by Joel Schumacher in 1987, and then from *Twilight* directed by Catherine Hardwicke in 2008. I will argue that whilst both are seen as monstrous, in comparison to human adolescents, the 'vegetarian' revenants of today offer far more possibilities for negotiation to societal constructs of what might constitute a 'normal' child's life. *The Lost Boys*, as part of a larger series of 1980s teenage vampire movies, created alternative versions of boyhood, unlike those propagated by the more normative ideology that underpinned the other teen-vamp movies of this period. Here, the lifestyle of the young vampire, whilst monstrous, is shown as not totally without redemption but alluring and other, and intriguingly subversive. Unlike the monstrous youth in *The Lost Boys*, the vampire Edward Cullen in The Twilight Saga is not the sideshow but the main event. He is not newly turned, as the Lost Boys were, but has been trapped in adolescence for a century. His monstrous youth is seen in his repeated performances of childhood. This re-enactment is a form of eternal recurrence – he has graduated over twenty times – and forms part of what is seen as his inherent monstrosity, but in fact reveals the performativity at the heart of his configuration of youth. Such reflexivity, rather than being a monstrous performance, or mimicking, of youth, in fact allows for a strategic staging of cultural expectation as well as a deconstruction and tactical repositioning of its various parameters. Consequently, his monstrosity reflects back the monstrous character of a society that delimits the potential configurations of identity, not just of youth, but of any minority group within society.

Key Words: Vampire, teenager, childhood, youth, monstrous, film, performance, enactment, society.

*****

1. Introduction: This Thing Called Youth

> All teenagers are monsters. Misunderstood, hated, blamed for the evils of the world. Also, reckless, selfish. With huge appetites as they slowly change from innocent things into something new. Did you know there's a part of the brain, the part that makes plans, considers consequences? It's sort of the part that makes us

> responsible and less destructive. Teenagers don't have that part of the brain.[1]

Youth in itself is often considered a monstrous thing, as often evidenced by the representations of emotionally and hormonally volatile adolescents that have regularly appeared in soap operas, on television and in films. Possibly the 'Brat Pack' films of the 1980s typify this idea in movies such as *The Breakfast Club* (1985) by John Hughes, *St. Elmo's Fire* (1985) by Joel Schumacher and *Pretty in Pink* (1986) by Howard Deutsch, and were watched by disaffected teenagers everywhere.[2] What they show is not so much how monstrous youth is or can be, but that there is such a distinct category as acceptable youth. This category is seen to conform to certain cultural parameters and norms, and expects one who wants to become a responsible adult to obey these socially constructed strictures. As such, the monstrous youth in this chapter is specifically configured as an antithetical term to that category, and intentionally disrupts the normative frameworks of behaviour that society desires of its youth. Perhaps it is not coincidental that it was also in the 1980s that the teenager and the vampire became, almost inextricably, linked, firstly on film and then later in literature as well. The vampire, as an inherently transgressive figure, is specifically configured in this structure as an oppositional force, where its undead nature not only constructs it as not being human but against life, and, therefore, inherently against the heteronormative structure expected of 'living' society. Yet just as the expectations of society change over time, so does the figure of the vampire. To illustrate this and the changing nature of the adolescent that the eternal undead youth embodies I shall consider two films: both from periods of huge popularity in the figure of the vampire but which are separated by over twenty years. The first film is *The Lost Boys* by Joel Schumacher from 1987, and the other – The Twilight Saga, which comprises five films of which I shall concentrate on the first two: *Twilight* (2008) directed by Catherine Hardwicke and *New Moon* (2009) directed by Chris Weitz.[3]

The film, *The Lost Boys*, marks an agreement with but also an opposition to this reading, representing examples of what is not expected of 1980s American youth, whilst simultaneously showing its monstrosity to be both alluring and desirous. The more recent films, *Twilight* and *New Moon*, take this even further, making the vampire an aspirational figure, where its vampiric hero, Edward Cullen, examples the 'perfect' adolescent; he is obedient to both the law of his father and the wider society around him, whilst also loving his siblings and not wanting sex before marriage. However, I contend that it is the knowingness of this performance that makes the modern vampire far more monstrous and transgressive than any of his predecessors.

2. Our Teenagers, Ourselves

> It is as if, to every period of history, there corresponded a privileged age and a particular division of human life: "youth" is the privileged age of the seventeenth century, childhood of the nineteenth, adolescence of the twentieth.[4]

The title of this section is taken from Nina Auerbach's often quoted text *Our Vampires, Ourselves* where she convincingly argues that each age produces the vampire that it needs, and that different times create monsters that particularly reflect the anxieties and concerns of that society, So too, it can be argued, does the image of youth that each period creates. The well-known biographer of childhood, Phillipe Aries, as quoted above, intimates that it is the different ages of youth that gain precedent. Chris Jenks views it slightly differently, and possibly more in line with Auerbach's thinking, when he comments, 'I came to see that our collective images of childhood and our subsequent relations with children could be regarded as indices of the contemporary state of the social structure.'[5] This sees the relationship as one that is more specifically socially-imposed and not necessarily a position of privilege. The recognition of particular categories of childhood becomes a means of containment and control. As Aries himself notes,

> it was recognized that the child was not ready for life, and that he had to be subjected to a special treatment, a sort of quarantine, before he was allowed to join the adults. This new concern about education would gradually install itself in the heart of society and transform it from top to bottom. The family ceased to be simply an institution for the transmission of a name and an estate – it assumed a moral and spiritual function, it moulded bodies and souls.[6]

The classification of childhood and also the teenager then becomes a way to control and contain that which is viewed as somehow dangerous. Why youth should be seen as the focus of social anxiety is indicated by Jenks when he observes,

> In the same way that the "savage" served as the anthropologist's referent for humankind's elementary forms of organization and primitive classifications, thus providing a speculative sense of the primal condition of human being within the socio-cultural process, so also the child is taken to display for adults their own state of once untutored difference, but in a more collapsed form.[7]

Youth, then, becomes what James Kincaid describes as 'a wonderfully hollow category' that can be filled with adult anxiety.[8] 1950s America typified this situation perfectly. Trapped in suburbs and with nothing to do, teenagers became the focus of societal fear and loathing. Films such as *Rebel Without a Cause* (1955) starring James Dean typified this ambivalence and exampled how the teenager was seen as a site of 'confusion, trauma and upheaval [and] instability and transition,'[9] representing what Timothy Shary calls the 'ephebiphobia – fear of teenagers – that was seeping into popular culture and politics.'[10] However, simultaneously with this anxiety, the teenager was also seen as a source of income for the flagging film industry, and it was not long before the two became entwined, as Leerom Medovois notes: 'the youth audience, the exploitation film, and the drive-in venue [were joined] into the coherent strategy of the "teenpic."'[11] This somewhat uneasy balance, then, created films that were meant as teenage entertainment, and yet still exampled forms of societal anxiety. It is not surprising then that they often portrayed somewhat schizophrenic representations of youth with the good versus the bad, and, ultimately, the bad ones coming to no/know good.

We see this in *Rebel Without a Cause* when the troubled teenager, Jim Stark, played by Dean, returns to the family after his friend dies. As such, this became the archetype for many 'teenpic' films that followed manifesting both the bad and uncontainable representations of youth alongside those that were desirable. Of course, the undesirable ones were always trying to tempt the good teenagers over to the dark side, and it was only through resisting this that one could safely enter and be accepted by adult society. The mirroring of the teenager that this produced within films made its coupling with the forces of darkness not just compelling but virtually inevitable, with the ultimate example of a monstrous form of youth flouting parental conventions and sleeping all day and partying all night. In particular this dark reflection of the adolescent and to society itself belongs to the teenage vampire that we see in the 1980s teen-vamp film *The Lost Boys*.

3. Neverland in California

> One thing about living in Santa Carla I never could stomach ...
> all the damn vampires.[12]

The teenage vampire is a relatively new phenomenon in the genre, and did not really come into its own until the teen-vamp explosion of films in the 1980's.[13] From 1985 to 1988, there were six major films released in America featuring the combination of the adolescent and the vampire: *Fright Night* (Holland, 1985); *Once Bitten* (Storm, 1985); *Vamp* (Wenk, 1986); *The Lost Boys* (Schumacher, 1987); *Near Dark* (Bigelow, 1987); *My Best Friend is a Vampire* (Huston, 1987); and *Fright Night II* (Wallace, 1988). In the varying twists and turns of plots these films are all about self-absorbed adults and, consequently, teenagers must take care of themselves. As Pat Gill remarks:

> The result in these films is a world emptied of the family as a resource for coping with growing up. The self-absorbed parents of these films, whether divorced or together, provide no useful knowledge, no understanding of their children's needs or fears, no viable models for negotiating the world, and certainly no protection from that world.[14]

As such, the films are predominantly seen as a Reagan-era attempt to re-establish the values of the 'All American Family' with the newly emergent youth being encouraged to hold the conservative banner high to redress the failures of 60s liberalism. *The Lost Boys* makes this explicit, a point which Sorcha Ni Fhlinn describes:

> The breakdown of the Emerson family in *The Lost Boys* can be largely blamed on the hippie generation, of which the mother, Lucy, is a proud member. In the opening credits of the film, she is crooning to songs such as "Groovin' on a Sunday Afternoon" and when we first meet her hippie father, we notice he is growing marijuana on his windowsill.[15]

In fact, Schumacher's film encapsulates all the concerns of the other films, and so it is time to go to Santa Carla, 'the murder capital of the world.'[16]

When it was released, the movie was advertised with the tag line 'Sleep all day. Party all night. Never grow old. Never die. It's fun to be a vampire.' This immediately intimates what the movie represents as a monstrous youth – irresponsibility that never ends. Laurence Rickels has consequently named the film as 'the Californian syndication of *Peter Pan*, the fantasy of perpetual adolescence,'[17] constructing the opposing views of youth as being the responsible versus the reckless and the thoughtful with the thoughtless. The plot sees Lucy Emerson, along with her two sons Michael and Sam, moving to live with her father in the coastal town of Santa Carla. Once there, Michael gets involved with a motorcycle gang lead by the mysterious David. We discover that these are in fact vampires and that they are trying to turn Michael into one of their number. It also transpires that Lucy's suitor, who is her boss at the video store, is none other than the King Vampire, Max. The Emerson family, along with the self-styled vampire slayers, the Frog brothers, manage to kill the undead monsters, and save Michael from a fate worse than death. What this story sets up is a tension between the forms of youth available to the adolescent. There are many visions of childhood within the film's story, as Rob Latham observes:

> The film's title can thus be taken to refer not only to David's crew, but also to the Frog Brothers, to Michael and Sam – indeed, to the entire contemporary generation, seduced and abandoned in a garish teenage wasteland presided over by a vampiric image-apparatus that has become a kind of surrogate father.[18]

This somewhat miasmic interpretation befits Latham's Marxist interpretation of the film, where all consumers are made into mindless children in the face of vampiric capitalism. Consequently, Latham sees the film as 'curiously divided in its purposes'[19] but it is a division it fights gamely to cover up, if in a somewhat clumsy binary manor. Michael, as the man-in-waiting of the narrative, must choose between being an adult or remaining a child, which in terms of the film means either doing as his mum says or becoming a vampire.[20] This is not as easy a choice as it may first seem because for the first time the undead are shown to be something desirable in their own right, even if still cursed with challenging eating habits. As Stacey Abbott observes, 'these vampire are no longer interlopers within a modern setting but are born and bred within the urban milieu.'[21] Ken Gelder notes how the teen-vamp films

> introduced a rock'n'roll sound track, developed the connections between special effects, speed and travel, fine-tuned the vampiric puns, and had their vampires getting around in gangs, showing off their leather and their hardware. Young American vampires become highly attractive to others (in terms of their "look", and as a subculture).[22]

This is in stark contrast to the more traditional representations of Count Dracula from around those times, such as *Love at First Bite* directed by Stan Dragoneti, and *Dracula* by John Badham, both from 1979. Even George Romero's *Martin* from 1977, although showing a teenager who may or may not be a vampire, reveals the condition to be as awkward and as ungainly as eternal growing pains, which the eponymous youth never seems to outgrow. In *The Lost Boys*, however, the vampire is amazingly cool and hip. Sporting finely coiffed hair, ripped jeans and chains, they 'cruise' the boardwalk by night. Self-confident and flaunting authority whenever they get the chance, they intimidate passers-by and loiter around shops and the adjoining fairground. They are the 'bad boys' that all boys want to be and all girls want to be with, and parents hate. Julie Plec, in an observation which is equally valid for 1985 as it is now, says: 'The vampire is the new James Dean.'[23] This specifically marks vampires out as being the undesired form of youth because it is uncontainable. As Latham further writes:

> David and his gang represent a delusory fantasy of youthful autonomy ... a seductive vision of rebellious adolescent hipness that is actually merely a cat's-paw of power; on the other hand, they are an unpredictable, even dangerous agency, mercurially resistant to Max's [their creator] authority and perhaps finally uncontrollable.[24]

This is in contrast to Michael whose natural inclination is to the 'good' form of youth where he is responsible for his actions and will become the replacement 'man' of the family, making up for the father that abandoned them.

The 'good' and the 'bad' within the story become inextricably linked, and the centrality of this theme to the film's plot is seen in the similarities between Michael and David: both come from single parent families. Michael's mother is recently divorced and we later discover that David's father is Max (who owns the video store), the unmarried King Vampire. The respective families are made up of all male children but the parents are largely absent from their lives, leaving the eldest male child to ultimately be responsible for himself and the family. This 'mirroring' between Michael and David is further accentuated in that they are not only attracted to the same girl, Star, but in that they are also attracted to each other. This further configures the monstrous nature of David's enactment of childhood for he actively tries to lure Michael over to the other side, not just from life to un-death, but from hetero- to homosexual. As Anne Bilson comments:

> *The Lost Boys* and *Fright Night* have a thinly veiled homoerotic undertone: in each case the token girlfriend seems like a "beard", whose role it is to flag the male characters' heterosexuality, since the central "relationship" in each film is the one between the young hero and the male vampire(s).[25]

This again configures the uncontainable and transgressive nature of the adolescent vampire. As Gelder notes, 'David's question [in the film], 'How far are you willing to go, Michael?' carries this homosexual subtext.'[26] This is emphasised later when David asks Michael to 'be one of us' referring to the lost boys, as I have noted elsewhere:

> Of course, the "us" of the "lost boys" live in a cave that was created by the 'quake' in San Francisco, and where all the boys can "hang out together." It is also the drinking of David's "fluid" that begins to "turn" Michael, and the resolution of the sexual tension between them only comes when Michael has "staked" David, and the vampire expires with a beatific glow to his face.[27]

Homosexuality, whilst being shown as monstrous in its own right, also refers to a wider anxiety over control and containability, and where one's place and role within society is necessarily clearly demarcated. David and his 'gang' disrupt such distinct categories. Elaine Showalter, talking about Stoker's novel, *Dracula*, describes the inherent fluidity of the vampiric body:

> The novel is also about the thrills and terrors of blurred sexual, psychological, and scientific boundaries. Dracula lives in Transylvania, "on the borders of three states," which we might read as the states of living, dead, and undead, or as masculinity, femininity, and bisexuality.[28]

This perfectly captures the liminal state of the 'lost boys.' Geographically, they live on the edge of society, not in a house but a cave. The cave itself was created by the 'shock wave' from San Francisco. Psychologically, they are our worst fears in that they kill indiscriminately and feed off our very life blood, and yet they are alluring and sexually potent. This potency itself knows no bounds, without discrimination between the sexes or differences in biological reproduction.[29] Cynthia Freeland nicely sums up their expression of multi-lateral excess as 'polymorphously perverse.'[30] This, in many ways, constitutes the nature of their eternal youth for in living in the moment they become eternally stuck or caught in the present.

This notion of being 'caught' in time is explained by Ludwig Wittgenstein: 'If by eternity is understood not endless temporal duration but timelessness, then he lives eternally who lives in the present.'[31] This notion is further elucidated by Havi Carel: 'Immortality is possible, Wittgenstein argues, as long as we live in the present. If we have no sense of past and future and do not experience the passing of time as a progression towards death then we become eternal.'[32] Michael's choice, then, becomes one of accepting change or remaining the same forever; of either becoming a 'man' or remaining an eternal 'monstrous' youth who will never grow up. Ultimately, of course, Michael chooses life and responsibility, and he kills David, and any latent urges of dissention within himself, and, consequently, saves both Star, and a missing boy, 'Laddie,' from the vampires. In so doing, he not only 'mends' his own broken family but also creates a symbolic new one, saving both himself and them from the clutches of this monstrous, undead, youth.

Interestingly, within the film, the monstrous youth of David and his gang is shown as being strongly contemporary, not just in the obvious 1980s hair styles and fashions that they wear, but in the notion that, although eternal, they have only recently been made into vampires. Their monstrous enactment of youth is a new one, limiting the possibilities presented to Michael and possibly assisting in his somewhat hasty choice to remain in the land of the living. However, a discarded early version of the script saw this quite differently, and the Lost Boys were shown as being much older than this, and contained photographs from the start of the 20th century, in which they all appeared (not unlike the end of Stanley Kubrick's *The Shining* from 1980). This creates a more curious scenario where the monstrous youth they enact is one that they have performed not just once, but over and over again … and this brings us to *Twilight*.

4. Me, Myself, My Monster

> I stared because their faces, so different, so similar, were all devastatingly, inhumanly beautiful. They were faces you never expected to see except perhaps on the airbrushed pages of a fashion magazine. Or painted by an old master as the face of an angel. It was hard to decide who was the most beautiful – maybe the perfect blond girl, or the bronze-haired boy.[33]

The Twilight Saga, written by Stephanie Meyer, comes almost 20 years after *The Lost Boys* – the first book, *Twilight*, was published in 2005. It now constitutes four books: *Twilight*, *New Moon* (2006), *Eclipse* (2007) and *Breaking Dawn* (2008), which have been made into five very successful films, the last of which, *The Twilight Saga: Breaking Dawn Part 2* directed by Bill Condon, was released in November 2012. Despite the gap in years between them, *Twilight* has at its core a very similar story of what is, and what is not, a monstrous youth.

Not unlike *The Lost Boys*, *Twilight* involves a human and a vampire, a love story between the two, and the choice of whether to conform to what is seen as a normal youth or to choose its monstrous counterpart. The human and vampire are respectively Bella Swan and Edward Cullen, though the almost symbiotic and even violent relationship they have over the course of the narrative is not that different from Michael and David's. However, unlike the earlier film, in *Twilight* the vampires are not obviously monstrous and are, in fact, figures to admire and aspire to be. Here the 'lost boys' are known as The Cullens, the 'All-American' family of two loving parents, Carlisle and Esme, and, five supportive siblings: Edward, Emmet, Rosalie, Jasper and Alice. Where the vampires in Schumacher's film hid in a dark and gloomy lair, here they live in a bright modern house made, almost entirely, of glass. On top of this they are extremely wealthy. In *Breaking Dawn*, Bella, now part of the Cullen family, notes: 'Not even taking into consideration the bloated accounts that existed all over the world with the Cullens' various names on them, there was enough cash all over the house to keep a small country afloat for a decade.'[34]

In contrast, the human part of the love story, Bella Swan, comes from a broken family, not dissimilar to the other human families in the town of Forks where the story is set, and just like the Emerson's from Schumacher's film. Interestingly, adult intervention plays little or no part in the unfolding story, and it is a drama that takes place entirely in the adolescent sphere. There is an argument, however, as intimated in Monica Dufault's chapter on 'Nasty Old Things' in this collection, that the most influential 'adults' are the Volturi who symbolise adult, and subsequently, societal restriction, and as such cast an unseen shadow over all that happens in the narrative. As Kat Burkhart observes, 'The Twilight Saga is full of teenagers acting as adults. The fate of the world sometimes rests on their shoulders, and they confront horrors and trials both alone and together, without the benefit of adults in authority.'[35] However, the nature of the human adolescent sphere and that possessed of the vampire are very different. Whereas in *The Lost Boys* the impression is that these are all newly turned vampires, in *Twilight* the Cullen children have been teenagers for a long, long time.

As one looks more closely one begins to realise that this family has been the 'perfect' family before, in many places and in many times previous to this one, and it is, in fact, a performance. This is seen in the film *Twilight* when we hear Bella ask Edward how old he is, and he replies 'seventeen;' she then asks 'And how long have you been seventeen?' to which he eventually answers 'a while.'[36] Further to this, when Bella visits Edwards house for the first time and sees a curious picture on the wall above the stairs, he explains that it is 'a bit of an in joke' as it is made up of all the different graduation caps that he and his siblings have worn over the years. He then comments to Bella: 'we matriculate a lot.'[37] As such, the vision of perfect youth that Edward seems to enact becomes one that is never natural or spontaneous but one which is both knowing and premeditated. I have commented elsewhere that

> [t]he boyhood that Edward represents, however, is very different to that we saw enacted earlier, not so much in the quality of it but in the quantity, for he has been an adolescent boy for almost one hundred years. This positions him very differently to David and his biker boys as their enactment of boyhood, though disaffected and bored, is only taking place for the first time.[38]

This determination in their performance of humanity and youth, and social acceptance also applies to the Cullens' much publicised refusal to drink human blood. Though labelled as 'vegetarianism' in the film, this actually means hunting for what is termed 'free range' food that lives in the forests around them. One would suspect this is not as clear cut as it first seems, as Abigail Myers points out:

> he [Edward] and the rest of the Cullen family live on the blood of animals, obtained during their "hunting" trips in the forests surrounding Forks. But that doesn't mean that he and his vampire family have totally lost their interest in human blood. Being around humans is a struggle for the whole clan on occasion.[39]

This sentiment we likewise see later in *New Moon*, the second film, when Bella cuts her finger opening a birthday gift and the entire family has to restrain Jasper from pouncing on her to drink her blood. The book describes the scene from Bella's perspective:

> A single drop of blood oozed from the tiny cut. It all happened very quickly then. "No!" Edward roared. He threw himself at me, flinging me back across the table. It fell, as I did, scattering the cake and the presents, the flowers and the plates. I landed in the mess of shattered crystal. Jasper slammed into Edward, and the sound was like the crash of boulders in a rock slide. There was another noise, a grisly snarling that seemed to be coming from deep in Jasper's chest. Jasper tried to shove past Edward, snapping his teeth just inches from Edward's face.[40]

The only one capable of composure is Carlisle who admits it came only through practice. Similarly, Edward admits to Bella that at times he can hardly suppress his true impulses for human blood. As he explains to her in *Twilight*: 'The fragrance coming off your skin … I thought it would make me deranged that first day. In that one hour, I thought of a hundred different ways to lure you from the room with me, to get you alone.'[41] This consequently reveals their abstinence as a thin veneer held in place only through continual re-enactment. This re-enactment has taken place over many periods of American history which is a point made by Kyra Glass von der Osten when she notes that their 'behaviour and sense of morality and norms have not developed according to the norms of a single time and place, but rather through a process that has changed the nature of the family throughout history.'[42]

As such the Cullens' performance of youth, and by extension, Edward's, is one of choice, not compulsion. This contrasts sharply with the other teenagers within the film, and in particular the Quileute Indians that are also based in Forks alongside the vampire family. As Steven Rita-Proctor notes in this volume, their shape-shifting propensity, especially in the figure of Jacob Black, expresses the uncontrollability of adolescence rather than its studied enactment. The Cullens' version of youth becomes monstrous, not because of its voraciousness or impulsiveness, as seen earlier in *The Lost Boys*, but because of its in-human performativity and pre-meditation.

5. Conclusion: Will the Real Monster Please Stand Up?

> With his vampire gaze, Lestat sees subjectivity as possibility, and thus the myriad aspects of subjectivity that mortals take for granted as no more than boats temporarily at anchor in a sea of possibilities.[43]

In conclusion, then, the two version of cinematic and monstrous youth of the teenage vampire in the late 20th century and the early 21st that we have seen are completely different but exactly the same – only their levels of self-awareness change. This in itself reflects society's changing views of agency that can and is accorded to the child and young adult. As Chris Jenks observes,

> More recently, however, a growing number of sociologists and anthropologists have attended to the dissonance which exists between children's own experiences of being a child and the institutional form which childhood takes. This has sharpened a theoretical focus on the plurality of childhoods, a plurality evidenced not only cross-culturally but also within cultures. At the very least, it is suggested, the experience of childhood is fragmented and stratified, by class, age, gender and ethnicity, by urban or rural locations and by particularized identities cast for children through disability or ill health.[44]

The two paradigms of monstrous youth exemplified previously can also be seen to example a 'before and after' in the recognition of this 'dissonance.' In *The Lost Boys* from the 1980s, the vampire youth represented an alternative to that expected, or desired, by a conservative society that wanted responsible adults that conformed to a traditional, hetero-normative ideal of what young adulthood should be. The human or 'good' boy, Michael, is offered only two choices: toe the family line and gain societal acceptance, or be a monster. Monstrous youth here demonstrated an impulsiveness and selfishness that resulted in a wish to never grow up and to never grow old, denying social conformity and promoting individuality above everything. Seemingly in contrast, the early 2000s vampiric teenager, as represented by Edward (and his Cullen siblings,) only wants to conform and be what society wants and expects, to perfection. This very perfection is revealed to be monstrous in its in-human re-enactment of youth and its pre-meditation in every move and gesture of boyhood, and yet its over-determination allows for a further reading. The Cullen children have played both adults and teenagers in their many and varied performances of what is socially expected of them. As Burkhart notes,

> All members of the family were considered adults, or nearly adults, during their human lives; but in twenty – first – century America, Edward, Rosalie, Emmett, Alice, and Jasper now "play" at being modern teenagers without the responsibilities of work or children.[45]

Consequently, their knowing mimicry of youth and what is socially expected of the teenager in fact allows for a strategic staging of cultural expectation as well as a deconstruction and tactical repositioning of its various parameters. Edward is aware of the exterior forces that dictate the form of adolescence that is required from him but his previous enactments also allows him to formulate his own. In this framework, the performance of youth that *The Lost Boys* manifest is ultimately one of exclusion but also containment. Its dark reflection of normative society locks it forever in an eternal repetition of what is not considered good, and so it becomes reactionary rather than reflexive. Almost beyond individual agency they can only be what society is not. The Cullens are monsters of a different order as they are supremely self-aware. However, this is not the aping of the adult, as acted out by a precocious child, but the performance of childhood by an adult that knows what the society of adults within which it lives expects. The Cullens then, unlike the Lost Boys, do not reflect society but rather become a mirror for that same society to see how dark it really is; their monstrosity is actually that of the heteronormative community around them. Edward, then, ultimately shows that it is not the youth of the cinematic vampire that is monstrous but rather the society that restricts what youth can be. What needs to be remembered though is that it is not a dead, or undead, reflection but one which can be changed – the vampire, like the child, exhibits an excess which is not meant to destroy the world that created it but make it more than it is. Their transgressive acts are not meant as answers to society's questions but they interrogate the validity of the question itself, as Jenks astutely observes:

> Their transgressions should not merely complete and affirm our constraints; they might better make us think again about the moral basis of our social bond. This is not a romantic and outmoded plea for us to be led by the "innocent creativity" of children but perhaps a recommendation that we might employ their disruption as a source of critical examination of our dominant means of control. Children explore the very limits of consciousness and highlight, once again, the indefatigable, inherent and infinitely variable human capacity to transgress.[46]

Notes

[1] Adam Rex, *Fat Vampire: A Never Coming of Age Story* (New York: Balzer and Bray, 2010), 85.

[2] The *Brat Pack* is a nickname given to a group of young actors who frequently appeared together in teen-oriented coming-of-age films in the 1980s. The most well-known ones included Emilio Estevez, Rob Lowe, Andrew McCarthy, Demi Moore, Molly Ringwald, and Ally Sheedy.

[3] The Twilight films are the following: *Twilight*, dir. Catherine Hardwicke (Summit, 2008); *The Twilight Saga: New Moon*, dir. Chris Weitz (Summit, 2009); and *The Twilight Saga: Eclipse*, dir. David Slade (Summit, 2010). *The Twilight Saga: Breaking Dawn, Part 1,* dir. Bill Condon (Summit, 2011) and *The Twilight Saga: Breaking Dawn, Part 2*, dir. Bill Condon (Nov. 2012).
[4] Phillipe Aries, *Centuries of Childhood: A Social History of Family* Life, trans. Robert Baldick (New York: Alfred A. Knopf, 1962), 32.
[5] Chris Jenks, *Childhood* (London: Routledge, 1996), 51.
[6] Aries, *Centuries of Childhood*, 412.
[7] Jenks, *Childhood*, 5.
[8] James R. Kincaid, *Child-Loving: The Erotic Child and Victorian Culture* (London: Routledge, 1992), 12.
[9] Paul Hodkinson, *Youth Cultures: Scenes, Subcultures and Tribes* (London: Routledge, 2007), 1.
[10] Timothy Shary, *Generation Multiplex: The Image of Youth in Contemporary American Cinema* (Austin: University of Texas Press, 2002), 4.
[11] Leerom Medovoi, *Rebels: Youth Culture and the Cold War Origins of Identity* (Durham: Duke University Press, 2005), 136.
[12] The closing words of the grandfather in *The Lost Boys*, who has seemingly spent the entire film oblivious to all the vampire-caused chaos around him.
[13] Before this you had had either vampire children such as Claudia in Anne Rice's novel, *Interview with the Vampire*, or the old/young adult and 'real' (?) vampire in George Romero's film, *Martin*, both 1976.
[14] Pat Gill, 'The Monstrous Years: Teens, Slasher Films, and the Family', *Journal of Film and Video* 54, No. 4 (2002): 19.
[15] Sorcha Ní Fhlainn, '"It's Morning in America": The Rhetoric of Religion in the Music of The Lost Boys and the Deserved Death of the 1980s Vampire', in *The Role of the Monster: Myths and Metaphors of Enduring Evil,* ed. Niall Scott (Oxford: Inter-Disciplinary Press, 2009), 149.
[16] Graffiti written on the back town sign which we see as the Emerson family enter Santa Carla.
[17] Laurence A. Rickels, *The Vampire Lectures* (Minneapolis: University of Minnesota Press, 1995), 211.
[18] Rob Latham, *Consuming Youth: Vampires, Cyborgs, and the Culture of Consumption* (Chicago: The University of Chicago Press, 2002), 64.
[19] Ibid., 114.
[20] This is somewhat oxymoronic in terms of what the films sets up, as David and his gang enact the same longing after eternal youth that Lucy and her generation of liberal hippies exhibit. This equivalence between them is shown in the vampire lair

where a huge picture of Jim Morrison of the Doors hangs in pride of place, himself a poster-boy of the 'free-love' generation.
[21] Stacey Abbott, 'Embracing the Metropolis: Urban Vampires in American Cinema of the 1980s and 90s', in *Vampires: Myths and Metaphors of Enduring Evil*, ed. Peter Day (New York: Rodopi, 2006), 126.
[22] Ken Gelder, *Reading the Vampire* (London: Routledge, 1994), 103.
[23] Ruth La Ferla, 'From Film to Fashion, A Trend With Teeth', *The New York Times*, 2 July 2009, Viewed 17 August 2009,
<http://www.nytimes.com/2009/07/02/fashion/02VAMPIRES.html?scp=2&sq=a%20trend%20with%20teeth%20la%20ferla&st=cse>.
[24] Latham, *Consuming Youth*, 65.
[25] Anne Billson, *Let the Right One In: Devil's Advocates* (Leighton Buzzard: Auteur, 2011), 73.
[26] Gelder, *Reading the Vampire*, 106.
[27] Simon Bacon, 'People are Strange: Re-Viewing the Lost Boys', in *Kultur & Geschlect* (June 2011): 10.
http://www.ruhr-uni-bochum.de/genderstudies/kulturundgeschlecht/pdf/Bacon_Re-Viewing.pdf.
[28] Elaine Showalter, *Sexual Anarchy: Gender and Culture at the Fin de Siecle* (London: Virago, 1992), 179.
[29] This last point is arguable depending upon how biological one views vampiric 'turning' or 'siring.'
[30] Cynthia A. Freeland, *The Naked and the Undead: Evil and the Appeal of Horror* (Oxford: Westview Press, 2000), 124.
[31] Ludwig Wittgenstein, *Tractatus Logico-Philosophicus* (London: Routledge & Kegan Paul, 1922), §6.4311.
[32] Havi Carel, *Life and Death in Freud and Heidegger* (New York: Editions Rodopi, 2006), 76.
[33] Stephanie Meyer, *Twilight* (New York: Little, Brown and Company, 2005), 10.
[34] Stephanie Meyer, *Breaking Dawn* (New York: Little, Brown and Company, 2006), 600.
[35] Kat Burkhart, 'Getting Younger Every Decade: Being a Teen Vampire during the Twentieth Century', in *Twilight and History*, ed. Nancy R. Reagin (Hoboken: John Wiley & Sons, 2010), 259.
[36] This is also seen in the novel by John Ajvide Lindqvist *Let the Right One In* (2004) and its subsequent cinematic adaptations *Let the Right One In* (2008) by Tomas Alfredson and *Let Me In* by Matt Reeves, in which the twelve year old boy asks the vampire how old they are and he/she replies twelve but for a long time.
[37] This picture also makes an appearance in the film *Breaking Dawn Part 1* when Bella's father, Charlie, sees it and finds it 'weird.'

[38] Simon Bacon, 'Lost Boys: The Infernal Youth of the Cinematic Vampire', *Thymos: Journal of Boyhood Studies* 5, No. 2 (Fall 2011): 159.
[39] Abigail E. Myers, 'Edward Cullen and Bella Swan: Byronic and Feminist Heroes ... or Not', in *Twilight and Philosophy: Vampires, Vegetarians, and the Pursuit of Immortality*, ed. Rebecca Housel and J. Jeremy Wisnewski (Hoboken: John Wiley & Sons, Inc., 2009), 156.
[40] Meyer, *New Moon*, 28-29.
[41] Meyer, *Twilight*, 152.
[42] Kyra Glass von der Osten, 'Like Other American Families, Only Not: The Cullens and the 'Ideal' Family in American History', in *Twilight and History*, ed. Nancy R. Reagin (Hoboken: John Wiley & Sons, Inc., 2010), 182.
[43] Rosanne Stone Allquere, *The War of Desire and Technology at the Close of the Mechanical Age* (Massachusetts: The MIT Press, 1996), 180.
[44] Jenks, *Childhood*, 122.
[45] Burkhart, *Twilight and History*, 246.
[46] Jenks, *Childhood*, 150.

Bibliography

Abbott, Stacey. 'Embracing the Metropolis: Urban Vampires in American Cinema of the 1980s and 90s'. In *Vampires: Myths and Metaphors of Enduring Evil*, edited by Peter Day, 143-158. New York: Rodopi, 2006.

Aries, Phillipe. *Centuries of Childhood: A Social History of Family Life*. Translated by Robert Baldick. New York: Alfred A. Knopf, 1962.

Bacon, Simon. 'People are Strange: Re-Viewing *The Lost Boys*'. *Kultur & Geschlecht* (June 2011). Viewed 17 February 2012.
http://www.ruhr-uni-bochum.de/genderstudies/kulturundgeschlecht/pdf/Bacon_Re-Viewing.pdf.

———. 'Lost Boys: The Infernal Youth of the Cinematic Vampire'. *Thymos: Journal of Boyhood Studies* 5, No. 2 (Fall 2011): 152–162.

Billson, Anne. *Let the Right One In: Devils Advocates*. Leighton Buzzard: Auteur, 2011.

Burkhart. Kat. 'Getting Younger Every Decade: Being a Teen Vampire during the Twentieth Century' In *Twilight and History*, edited by Nancy R. Reagin, 245-262. Hoboken: John Wiley & Sons, 2010.

Carel, Havi. *Life and Death in Freud and Heidegger*. New York, Editions Rodopi, 2006.

Freeland, Cynthia A. *The Naked and the Undead: Evil and the Appeal of* Horror. Oxford: Westview Press, 2000.

Gelder, Ken. *Reading the Vampire*. London: Routledge, 1994

Gill, Pat. 'The Monstrous Years: Teens, Slasher Films, and the Family'. *Journal of Film and Video* 54, No. 4 (2002): 16-30.

Glass von der Osten, Kyra. 'Like Other American Families, Only Not: The Cullens and the 'Ideal' Family in American History'. In *Twilight and History*, edited by Nancy R. Reagin, 182-201. Hoboken: John Wiley & Sons, Inc., 2010.

Hodkinson, Paul. *Youth Cultures: Scenes, Subcultures and Tribes*. London: Routledge, 2007.

Jenks, Chris. *Childhood*. London: Routledge, 1996.

Kincaid, James R. *Child-loving: The Erotic Child and Victorian Culture*. London: Routledge, 1992.

Latham, Rob. *Consuming Youth: Vampires, Cyborgs, and the Culture of Consumption*. Chicago: The University of Chicago Press, 2002.

La Ferla, Ruth. 'From Film to Fashion, A Trend With Teeth.' *The New York Times*, 2 July 2009. Viewed 17 August 2009.
http://www.nytimes.com/2009/07/02/fashion/02VAMPIRES.html?scp=2&sq=a%20trend%20with%20teeth%20la%20ferla&st=cse.

Medovoi, Leerom. *Rebels: Youth Culture and the Cold War Origins of Identity*. Durham: Duke University Press, 2005.

Meyer, Stephanie. *Twilight*. New York: Little, Brown And Company, 2005.

———. *New Moon*. New York: Little, Brown And Company, 2006.

Myers, Abigail E. 'Edward Cullen and Bella Swan: Byronic and Feminist Heroes ... or Not'. In *Twilight and Philosophy: Vampires, Vegetarians, and the Pursuit of Immortality*, edited by Rebecca Housel, and J. Jeremy Wisnewski, 147-162. Hoboken: John Wiley & Sons, Inc., 2009.

Ní Fhlainn, Sorcha. '"It's Morning in America": The Rhetoric of Religion in the Music of The Lost Boys and the Deserved Death of the 1980s Vampire'. In *The Role of the Monster: Myths and Metaphors of Enduring Evil*, edited by Niall Scott, 147-156. Oxford: Inter-Disciplinary Press, 2009.

Rex, Adam. *Fat Vampire: A Never Coming of Age Story*. New York: Balzer and Bray, 2010.

Rickels, Laurence A. *The Vampire Lectures*. Minneapolis: University of Minnesota Press, 1995.

Shary, Timothy. *Generation Multiplex: The Image of Youth in Contemporary American Cinema*. Austin: University of Texas Press, 2002.

Showalter, Elaine. *Sexual Anarchy: Gender and Culture at the Fin de Siecle*. London: Virago, 1992.

Stone Allquere, Rosanne. *The War of Desire and Technology at the Close of the Mechanical Age*. Massachusetts: The MIT Press, 1996.

Wittgenstein, Ludwig. *Tractatus Logico-Philosophicus*. London: Routledge & Kegan Paul, 1922.

Simon Bacon is an Independent Scholar living in Poznan, Poland. His current research is focused on the eternal child in film and literature.

Mirror, Mirror on the Wall: Youth, Age and the Monstrosity of Beauty in The *Twilight* Saga

Monica Dufault

Abstract
The vampires and werewolves that populate the town of Forks in Stephenie Meyer's *Twilight* series provide a framework through which to read a romantic quest for beauty, youth and eternal love, but also a confirmation of American socio-economic values. Unlike the moral warnings personified by the monsters of traditional fairy tales, the supernatural creatures Bella encounters in the world of *Twilight* embody and celebrate the markers of success and power associated with our twenty-first century youth-centred culture. The members of Edward Cullen's 'family' are stunningly beautiful, superhumanly strong, extremely wealthy, and have all been turned into immortals in their late teens and early twenties: they are forever young. Likewise the shape-shifter wolves of Jacob Black's Quileute tribe, although not wealthy, are physically massive young men caught at their prime. These 'werewolves' are not cursed; rather, their transformative powers are a gift that has been passed down from father to son, so that the men can protect their people. The vampires of Forks are not damned by their condition; these are temperance vampires, who have found their salvation through abstinence from human blood, and in the American family values modelled by the highly moral patriarch Carlisle Cullen. The equation of youth and beauty with all that is desirable informs the entire saga, so that the greatest enemies to Bella and her friends are the foreign and ancient Volturi. These old ones, led by the corrupt trio Aro, Caius and Marcus, maintain a secretive control over the vampire world from their lair beneath a medieval Italian town, confirming that what is very old is very bad. The vampire figure drawn by Meyer is a sublime creature of stone, a perfection of the human form, preserved to stay forever young. For aging, ultimately, is the supreme evil in the *Twilight* world.

Key Words: Vampires, werewolves, *Twilight*, age, youth, cosmetic surgery, beauty, A.S. Byatt.

*****

The cultural phenomenon that is the *Twilight* Saga was conceived by its author, Stephenie Meyer, as a series of romantic fiction for teenage girls. Yet the books and subsequent films have proved incredibly popular with a much wider audience. I propose that this is due, at least in part, to the fascination with youth and beauty that lies at the foundation of these novels. Northrop Frye writes,

> The Romance is the nearest of all literary forms to the wish-fulfilment dream […] In every age the ruling social or intellectual class tends to project its ideals in some form of romance, where the virtuous heroes and beautiful heroines represent the ideals and the villains the threats to their ascendancy.[1]

What *Twilight* and its sequels celebrate is the twenty-first century ideal of being not only young, but, as Katy Perry puts it so eloquently in her song 'Teenage Dream' being 'young forever'.[2] By contrast, all things old in the *Twilight* world symbolize the 'threats' to which Frye refers.

This youth/age binary stretches throughout the saga, informing not only the relationships and drives of the characters, but the socio-political structures of the world in which they live. Likewise, the inter-textuality found in the books supports this ageism, drawing parallels between Bella and other young literary figures. The immortality of the *Twilight* vampires is achieved through a kind of calcification, a turning to stone. In an exploration of the significance of this unique visioning of the vampire figure, I compare the transformation of Bella into one of Meyer's stone vampires to the cosmetic surgery makeovers depicted in reality television, and to the metamorphosis of the main character in A.S. Byatt's short story 'A Stone Woman'.

Despite this romantic celebration of youth within *The Twilight Saga*, Meyer's stories make it clear that the nascent sexuality of her teenage characters is something that must be tempered, controlled. In his chapter from this volume 'Monstrous Sexual Awakenings: Jacob Black and the Monstrosity of the Male Pubescent Experience', Steven Rita-Procter refers to the monstrosity of the teen-age male as symbolized through the lycanthropy of Jacob Black, and this character's struggle to keep his passions in check. Yet the Twilight novels and films also point to the monstrosity of Bella's sexual awakening. Her carnal instincts and desires are repeatedly thwarted by her vampire lover's sense of propriety until finally she agrees to conform to his ideal of marital restraint. Just as Bella concedes to Edward's stricture of marriage before sex, she realizes that her physical youthful appearance is insufficient, that she must alter her human self to attain a more flawless ideal of youth: the stony vampire body. As Simon Bacon notes in this section's 'The Lost Boys!?: The Monstrous Youth of the Cinematic Teenage Vampires', Meyer's Edward Cullen has mastered the performance of 'seventeen'. Similarly, Bella must leave behind the natural fumbling towards adulthood that marks a real girl's life, and instead configure her flesh into the composed perfection of an immortal.

1. Youth and Beauty

The protagonist at the centre of Stephanie Meyer's novels is Bella Swan, the completely average teenaged girl who leaves her mother and her home in Phoenix and travels to the forest of Forks, Washington to live with her father. In the forest, she meets some vampires and some shape-shifter wolves, and is transformed from her lower middle class, ungraceful self into a wealthy, beautiful immortal Bella who will stay young forever. All of these changes occur in only two years.

Throughout the novels, Bella seems caught between the roles of adolescent and adult. At the beginning of *Twilight*, she confesses, 'I didn't relate well to people my age.'[3] She also refers to her relationship with her mother, and how she, Bella, is more the parent than her mom, Renée, of which Bella seems begrudgingly proud. When Bella comes to Forks, she continues that caretaking role as she keeps house for her father, Charlie. Despite her admitted maturity, and disassociation with her peers, Bella is nevertheless obsessed with her age and how old she is perceived to be. With her friend, Jacob, who is in fact a couple of years younger than her, she begins a game in which they calculate their 'real' ages according to skills and life experience. This is played out especially in *New Moon* when Bella finds two motorcycles and brings them to Jacob to be repaired. After Jacob gets the bikes running, Bella exclaims, 'Jacob, you are absolutely, without a doubt, the most talented and wonderful person I know. You get ten years for this one.' Jacob replies, 'Cool, I'm middle-aged now!'[4] In this continuing competition, it is desirable to be considered older than the other, to have the abilities and knowledge associated with adulthood. The physical changes associated with aging are suspect, however, as in Bella's observation of Jacob's accelerated maturation after he begins to shape shift.

> The planes of his face seemed to have hardened subtly, tightened…aged. His neck and his shoulders were different, too, thicker somehow. His hands, where they gripped the window frame, looked enormous, with tendons and veins more prominent under the russet skin.[5]

This sudden change in her friend, from a skinny adolescent to a physically mature man, alarms Bella at first. But soon she admires his new found strength and power, a reality that was emphasized in the film versions in which Jacob frequently appears shirtless, making his newly 'ripped' body that much more noticeable. Fortunately, Jacob and the rest of the Quileute shape shifters seem to reach a plateau of growth that keeps them at a pleasing stasis of twenty-something, at least until the presence of vampires no longer threatens their tribe.

As a way of illuminating the fears and hopes of her protagonist, Meyer has Bella describe many of her dreams. In one, the character's attitude towards growing old is revealed when Bella sees her grandmother:

> Gran hadn't changed much; her face looked just the same as I remembered it. The skin was soft and withered, bent into a

> thousand tiny creases that clung gently to the bone underneath. Like a dried apricot, but with a puff of thick white hair standing out in a cloud around it.[6]

It turns out in this dream that Bella is not seeing her grandmother, but rather her own reflection in a mirror. In perhaps the most graphic nightmare of the many depicted, Bella has become *old.* The description ends: 'There was no Gran. That was *me*. Me in a mirror. Me – ancient, creased and withered.' Edward appears beside her, 'excruciatingly lovely and forever seventeen.'[7] The fear for Bella is not so much that she will be older than Edward; she never will be, as he is already more than one-hundred years older than she is. Rather, her terror is that she will *look* older than him. The ideal, as Bella recognizes, is that she look young. Because Edward will always look seventeen, she feels that she must also, and the method for achieving this has been presented to her: she must become a vampire.

Once Edward has agreed to transform her into a vampire, he and Bella maintain a prolonged negotiation about when this should happen. Bella is adamant that she be turned soon, so that Edward will not seem younger than her for all eternity. 'If you're staying in your teens forever, then so am I', Bella says.[8] He seems less concerned about this comparison, secretly registering her for college, eager that she experience as much as possible while she is still human. But Bella is a young woman, and is a reflection of the North American consumerist society in which she was created, for whom the status of a youthful appearance is paramount.

Bella's willingness to be permanently altered in order to achieve this ideal can be compared to the contemporary drive to undergo cosmetic surgery in order to attain a desired physical appearance. As Victoria Pitts-Taylor writes, the increasing availability of cosmetic surgery techniques, and their popularization through television programs such as *Extreme Makeover,* has led to a shift in attitude towards elective plastic surgeries and their interpretations: 'Cosmetic surgery culture not only creates a surface appearance that is normatively ideal but also produces that appearance's psychic meanings.'[9] For Bella, her conversion to vampirism represents a transcendence of her frail, awkward and weak human body into the powerful stone body of a vampire, but also the implicit celebrity status meaning that physical beauty carries for us in the culture.

Ultimately, Bella's transfiguration is medicalised when she suddenly begins to convulse and is rushed upstairs to Carlisle's study, which has been outfitted like a surgical operating room. Already weakened by her dangerous pregnancy, she endures a gruesome labour that causes fractures and haemorrhages. Her baby is finally delivered through a kind of caesarean section in which Edward bites into the womb. Edward injects his venom directly into Bella's heart via a syringe in order to accelerate the process of vampirization, augmented with doses of morphine. Just as plastic surgery patients must endure pain in order to attain the goal of manufactured youth, so Bella endures great pain as she reaches for her goal of eternal life and beauty as a vampire. The process for Bella is even faster than the cosmetic surgery makeovers profiled on reality television. It takes her just two days rather than the six weeks or more that humans normally require to recover from multiple surgeries.

The way in which Meyer depicts Bella's transformation is not so different from the techniques used in the television portrayals of surgical makeovers. We read in Bella's own voice her experience of the 'procedure', just like the on-camera testimonials of plastic surgery patients.

> The participants' stories, told through interview clips (without an on-camera interviewer, as if they were confessing straight to the audience) as well as the voice-over narrator, emphasize the impact cosmetic surgery has on individuals' psychological health and definitions of self.[10]

Meyer's use of first person narration fulfils a similar function, for this portion of the story giving first Jacob's and then Bella's perspective, allowing both characters to comment on the implications of the procedure. At one point in her experience of the pain of transformation, Bella makes this realization:

> It was sort of the pattern to my life – I'd never been strong enough to deal with the things outside my control, to attack the enemies or outrun them. To avoid the pain. Always human and weak, the only thing I'd ever been able to do was keep going. Endure. Survive.[11]

Finally, Bella's agony comes to an end and she rises from her hospital bed, dressed by Edward's sister Alice in elegant new clothes. Her transformation is complete and her vampire family gathers around to admire the new improved Bella, beautiful, sparkling and eternally eighteen, evoking the 'Big Reveal' of *Extreme Makeover* and other programs like it. The expectation of dramatic alterations through cosmetic procedures that reality television has instilled in the cultural imagination is enacted in the changes that Bella undergoes. At this moment, arguably the climax of the entire *Twilight* Saga, Bella looks in a full-length mirror, for, in a departure from traditional vampire lore, Meyer's undead do cast a reflection. Bella observes her image, and she sees herself to be what she never saw herself to be previously in the novels: beautiful. Here Meyer has Bella describe herself in the third person, accentuating the strangeness, the monstrosity of this inhuman beauty.

> The alien creature in the glass was indisputably beautiful, every bit as beautiful as Alice or Esme. She was fluid even in stillness, and her flawless face was pale as the moon against the frame of

> her dark, heavy hair. Her limbs were smooth and strong, skin glistening subtly, luminous as a pearl.[12]

As with the 'reveals' on television, Bella is amazed at what she sees and cannot believe it to really be her. The Cullens, clustered around her, provide the obligatory appreciative and awestruck audience, witnesses to her extraordinary change.

A few weeks later, in one of the few instances throughout the novels where the character Bella exhibits some agency and independent will, the relationship between power and beauty in the *Twilight* world is made very clear. After her transformation, and with the imminent danger of a grand vampire battle on the horizon, Bella decides to secretly procure illegal passports for her daughter, Renesmee and her friend Jacob, so that they might have an avenue of escape should the Cullens fall. For the first time, Bella experiences the effect of her new physical being on men. On a seedy street corner in Seattle, she encounters a thug who is impressed by her clothes and her beauty. The man describes her to an associate on the phone: 'Well, she looks like a freaking supermodel, that's what she looks like.'[13] This is the first time that an adult male sees her as a sexually mature and powerful adult woman. It is also the first time that Bella sees herself in this way, separate from Edward.

Unlike the other vampires in these stories, who have been transformed against their will, or without their knowledge, Bella chooses to be turned. She knows it will be painful, and she knows that she will no longer be human. She weighs these risks and agrees to the process, like a cosmetic surgery patient who willingly goes under the knife. Bella endures the pain privately, not wanting to make Edward feel bad about inflicting this agony upon her.[14] She believes that this is the cost of beauty, and that only by attaining this beauty and its appearance of youth will she be assured of Edward's undying love. 'That was the deal, the price. I'd agreed to pay it.'[15] Edward's love is the prize that Bella seeks, and it is a potent catalyst, whatever the discomfort she must endure to attain it. As Naomi Wolf points out, 'women see physical suffering as bearable compared with the pain of losing love.'[16] Bella accepts the suffering rather than risk losing love, she conforms to the contemporary ideal of beauty as youth, she endures the most extreme of makeovers, and thereby assures her social and economic future.

2. Supremacy of Youth

The four published novels of the saga, the novella *The Secret Life of Bree Tanner*, as well as the unpublished manuscript, *Midnight Sun* all employ a first person narrative structure. For the most part, it is in the voice of Bella Swan, but there is also narration from other characters. The result is the confessional quality of a journal entry or sometimes a stream-of-consciousness commentary, which emphasizes the perspective and knowledge of the young narrators. Other adult characters are less well drawn, as we never have access to their thoughts or attitudes, and they are always seen from the point of view of the young protagonists. The one exception perhaps is *Midnight Sun*, in which Edward can read the thoughts of characters. The portraits he draws of the adults he encounters are nevertheless unflattering, even comical, such as the school secretary, Mrs. Cope, whom he describes in this way:

> The woman with the unnaturally red hair looked up and her eyes widened. It always caught them off guard, the little markers they didn't understand, no matter how many times they'd seen one of us before.
>
> "Oh," she gasped, a little flustered. She smoothed her shirt. *Silly,* she thought to herself. *He's almost young enough to be my son. Too young to think that way...*
>
> "Hello, Edward. What can I do for you?" Her eyelashes fluttered behind her thick glasses.
> Uncomfortable.[17]

The same character is described by Bella in *Twilight* on her first day at the school:

> There were three desks behind the counter, one of which was manned by a large, red-haired woman wearing glasses. She was wearing a purple t-shirt, which immediately made me feel overdressed.[18]

As Bella is self-described as someone who does not care much about her outward appearance, we have to assume that poor Mrs Cope is pretty pathetic. This marginalization of adult characters in literature aimed at young people is to be expected. It is by drawing a distinction between themselves and the old that the youth establishes its own identity. Meyer appeals to this instinct by drawing parallels to other portraits of young romance. Several examples of intertextuality are inferred, or referred to explicitly, in the *Twilight* Saga. Shakespeare's *Romeo and Juliet* is being read by Edward and Bella for their English class. *Wuthering Heights* is Bella's favourite book, and a dog-eared copy is often lying on the floor of her bedroom. *Pride and Prejudice* is also alluded to through the characterization of Edward as being like the aloof wealthy suitor, Mr Darcy. Each of these inter-texts confirms and even celebrates the perspectives of its young heroes and heroines in opposition to the adults of their respective stories. The passion of Romeo and Juliet is only more profound when seen against the cold matchmaking of Juliet's parents, or the senseless squabbling of their two families. Cathy and Heathcliff's love for each other is thwarted by adults, who are portrayed as drunkards, such as Cathy's brother, and as religious zealots, such as Joseph. Like

Bella, Cathy wants only the 'now' of her youth, and does not care to think ahead to her growing old, proclaiming, 'I have only to do with the present.'[19] The depictions of the older adults in Jane Austen's *Pride and Prejudice*, especially Lady Catherine de Bourgh and Elizabeth's own mother, Mrs Bennet, provide a comic counterpoint to the romantic pursuits of the younger characters. These references by Meyer suggest that the love between Bella and Edward is akin to the timelessness of those in the inter-texts. At the same time, by drawing on models of young passionate lovers, the divide between young and old within the *Twilight* Saga is more clearly drawn.

When we look to the social structures of the saga, the theme of youth versus age appears under several guises. There is Bella's clueless father, Charlie, who is well meaning, but ineffectual in protecting his daughter from the real dangers in this world. He is a small town police chief who has no comprehension of the very real threat of supernatural beings. He is not rich, nor powerful, nor knowledgeable. Charlie's passions seem to revolve around fishing and watching sports on television. His place in this social structure is symbolized by the gift he gives Bella on her arrival in Forks: an ancient rusty truck. He represents the old, the family from which Bella comes, but from which she aspires to ascend.

By contrast, Edward Cullen's family members are stunningly beautiful, superhumanly strong, extremely wealthy, and have all been turned into immortals in their late teens and early twenties: they are forever young. The Cullen vampires are a relatively new coven, according to the norms of Meyer's fictive universe. Unlike others of their kind, they refer to themselves as a 'family'. Their patriarch and leader, Carlisle Cullen, has transformed most of the members of the group himself, and leads them towards a kind of perceived salvation through abstinence from human blood. Yet, even though some of these vampires are in fact hundreds of years old, they seem much younger than all the other adults in the stories. Enlightened by clear-thinking American family values and abstinence morality, the nightmares of our grandparents evolve under Meyer's hand into the conscientious Cullen clan.

These nouveau vampires embody and celebrate the markers of success and power associated with our twenty-first century youth-centred culture. They all wear designer clothes. Their appearance is noticed and commented on favourably by all the teen characters at the high school. They drive expensive cars, and they drive fast. They have a beautiful home on a large piece of property outside of Forks but we are aware that they have travelled all over the world. In *Breaking Dawn* Edward and Bella spend their honeymoon on Isle Esme, a gift to Edward's mother from Carlisle. Back in Forks, Carlisle Cullen is a highly respected physician. The family has wealth and privilege and status. As Sara Buttsworth writes in 'CinderBella', through her marriage into the Cullen family, and subsequent transformation into a vampire, Bella achieves a version of the American dream.[20]

The young/old binary is further depicted by the new-world Cullens versus the old-world Volturi.

> The Cullen coven and Bella illustrate the on-going importance of American culture's vision of itself as different from other nations, not only in their cross-species relationships and puritan diet, but in relation to the European vampire aristocracy, the Volturi.[21]

The Volturi are portrayed as the absolute villains of this world. They are the European rulers of the vampires, and they maintain the laws of secrecy and purity around the globe. Their cabalistic coven lives hidden under a medieval town in Italy. They wear long dark robes and enforce their dictums across the world via emissaries who use torture to ensure compliance, evoking images of the Spanish Inquisition and of secret Catholic sects. The decisions of the Volturi are absolute and unchallenged. That is, until the Cullens come onto their radar.

The American vampires led by Carlisle Cullen refuse to sacrifice human lives so that they may survive, invoking a sense of liberty and equality for all associated with the philosophies of the nation's founding fathers. The Cullens make decisions according to democratic tradition, such as the vote they hold to decide whether or not to turn Bella into a vampire.[22] They have adopted a traditional family structure and maintain a belief in God and in Heaven. Edward insists that he and Bella get married before they have sex, he even asks her father for her hand in marriage. The aristocratic Volturi, led by the corrupt trio Aro, Caius and Marcus, exact their own form of 'justice' unilaterally, unlike the Cullens who discuss crises and make democratic decisions. Most significantly, these three 'ancients' are just that – old. And aging, ultimately, is the greatest evil in the *Twilight* world.

The construct of the decadent amoral foreign power attempting to reign from afar and being challenged by the clean living fiercely moral American vampires certainly begs to be read as a reference to the American War of Independence. The final atrocity comes with the revelation that the Volturi not only feed off the lives of other people, they eat American tourists![23]

But in case the reader has not yet realized how awful the Volturi are, Stephenie Meyer makes it absolutely clear when Bella meets the *ancients* for the first time and observes of Aro:

> I couldn't decide if his face was beautiful or not. I suppose the features were perfect. But he was as different from the vampires beside him as they were from me. His skin was translucently white, like onionskin, and it looked just as delicate – it stood in shocking contrast to the long black hair that framed his face. I felt a strange, horrifying urge to touch his cheek, to see if it was softer than Edward's or Alice's, or if it was powdery like chalk. His eyes were red, the same as the others around him, but the

> color was clouded, milky; I wondered if his vision was affected by the haze.[24]

References to the three decrepit Volturi are numerous in the next few pages: they have 'paper-thin skin'.[25] When Aro raises his eyebrow, Bella wonders 'how his papery skin did not crumple in the effort.'[26] She takes Aro's hand and his skin feels 'brittle – shale not granite.'[27] 'Caius pointed a skeletal finger at me. [...] His voice was papery thin, just like his skin.'[28] These old-world, old-style vampires, the very foreign Volturi are really, really old, and by equal measure really, really bad.

3. Stone Mythology

In a departure from usual vampire lore, Stephenie Meyer depicts her vampires within the *Twilight* Saga as being made of stone. There is some precedence for this idea, as in Anne Rice's novel, *The Queen of the Damned.* Here the ancient Egyptian mother of all vampires, Akasha, as an expression of grief at the loss of her partner, voluntarily takes the form of stone. For Rice, however, this is a kind of stasis, like a statue. Centuries later, Akasha is awakened by the rock music of the superstar Vampire Lestat. Akasha comes back to life and wreaks havoc in the modern world, until a group of vampires attack her, draining her of all her blood, and turning her to dust. In this case, the one who drinks the last drop of Akasha's blood turns to stone. So, unlike the luminous and beautiful stone undead of Meyer's world, Rice perceives a transformation to stone as punishment or atonement, and as a cessation of vampiric life.

Rice's use of this trope is more consistent with the literary tradition of 'turning to stone', as in the Greek myths which recount Medusa turning men who look at her into stone, and of Midas touching his child and turning her to gold. There is also the biblical story of Lot's wife being turned into a stone like pillar of salt. Another literary reference is C.S. Lewis' *The Lion, the Witch and the Wardrobe*, in which characters are placed into a kind of stasis by being turned to stone by the White Witch. However, unlike these other examples, Meyer has conceived of a kind of petrifaction which allows her supernatural beings to still move and speak and function like humans rather than to be statues of stone. Still, the sparkly skin of the *Twilight* vampires comes with a lack of expressive movement, rather like a Botox treatment. Meyer's hybrid construction creates an interesting paradox between the eternal youth, which Bella seeks through becoming a vampire and the ancient, elemental nature of rock and its associations with processes that are slow, nearly imperceptible.

A recent literary exploration of a living person made of stone can be found in the short story 'A Stone Woman,' in which A.S. Byatt explores ideas of age and eternal life and the implications of a human being who turns to stone. Like the first novel of Meyer's series, Byatt's fiction begins with the loss of the main character's mother. While Bella's loss is the result of her leaving her mother and their home in Phoenix, Byatt's main character Ines is grieving the death of her mother. And, although Byatt's is the tale of an old woman, whose hair is grey, and whose body has begun to deteriorate, there are some striking similarities in the way these two stone women develop.

Like Meyer's first novel, A.S. Byatt's story also uses the imagery of twilight to symbolize the in-between time in which the character finds herself.

> At first she did not think of stones. Grief made her insubstantial to herself; she felt herself flitting lightly from room to room, in the twilit apartment, like a moth. The apartment seemed constantly twilit, although it must, she knew, have gone through the usual sequences of sun and shadow over the days and weeks since her mother died.[29]

After her mother's death, Ines has to have an emergency surgery and is left with a large scar on her abdomen, her navel cut away by the surgeon's knife. With the loss of her mother and her umbilical scar, the woman begins to gradually turn to stone: 'Slowly, slowly, day by quick day, her torso was wrapped in a stony corselet.'[30] Ines, at first shocked, soon becomes reconciled to the process, observing that 'her thoughts and feelings had slowed to stone-speed, nerveless and stolid.'[31] This description of the inner effect of becoming stone is similar to Meyer's description of the stillness of her vampires, as in the scene in which Esme and Alice coach Bella on how she must not be too still, in order to seem human when her father Charlie comes to visit her at the Cullen's house not long after Bella has been turned.[32]

Despite her stoicism at these changes to her being, Byatt's Ines recognizes that she is becoming what others would consider a monster.

> She dismissed, with no real hesitation, the idea of consulting the surgeon, or any other doctor. Her slowing mind had become trenchant, and she saw clearly that she would be an object of horror and fascination, to be shut away and experimented on. [...] She assumed it would end with the petrifaction of her vital functions. A moment would come when she wouldn't be able to see, or move, or feed herself...[33]

The process of transformation to vampire stone, as described in the *Twilight* series, leaves less time for this kind of reflection, as the vampire in the making feels the venom spread through her body causing excruciating pain that lasts less than a week and ends in a burning thirst and a sparkling body.[34] By contrast, Ines experiences a metamorphosis that takes months, years, as first the wound from her surgery seems to harden, then turn to rock, and spread across her body, sprouting crystals and gems. Meyer's version of the vampire transformation is complete when the human heart beats for the last time, as in Bella's description of her final human moment.

> My heart stuttered twice, and then thudded quietly again just once more.
>
> There was no sound. No breathing. Not even mine.
>
> For a moment, the absence of pain was all I could comprehend. And then I opened my eyes and gazed about me in wonder.[35]

Having had the opportunity to discuss at length with Edward and the Cullens the process by which she will become immortal, Bella knows what to expect. Ines is less informed and wonders about the moment at which she will stop being 'alive', as her organs slowly evolve into stone. Yet, as Ines continues to ruminate about her own transfiguration, she begins to see the points of confluence between the 'mineral world' and the human, recognizing that many rock formations are in fact comprised of the remains of ancient creatures. 'These were themselves once living stones – living marine organisms that spun and twirled around skeletons made of opal.'[36] One day, Byatt's protagonist cuts herself, and discovers that she no longer has blood moving through her veins.

> She watched the thick red liquid run down the back of her hand, on to the bread, on to the table. It was ruddy-gold, running in long glassy strings, and where it touched the table, it hissed and smoked and bored its hot way through the wood and dripped, a duller red now, on to the plastic floor, which it singed with amber circles and puckering. Her veins were full of molten lava.[37]

It is after this incident that Ines decides to reveal herself to an Icelandic stonemason, Thorsteinn Hallmundursson, whom she has encountered working in a nearby cemetery, saying to him, 'If anyone can bear to look, perhaps you can.'[38] Despite her fears that he will see her as a monster, Thorsteinn's response surprises her: '"Beautiful," he said. "Grown, not crafted."'[39] A different kind of beauty, certainly, than the alabaster perfection that Meyer describes. Nevertheless, this moment is strangely parallel to the scene in *Twilight* in which Edward reveals his sparkling stony skin to Bella in their flower filled meadow.

> He lay perfectly still in the grass, his shirt open over his sculpted, incandescent chest, his scintillating arms bare. His glistening, pale lavender lids were shut, though of course he didn't sleep. A perfect statue, carved in some unknown stone, smooth like marble, glittering like crystal.[40]

While Byatt uses the imagery of stone in its natural formations to detail the transmutation of a woman into rock, Meyer envisions a marble-like being that has been formed into the ideal human shape. Yet both human observers, in these cases Thorsteinn and Bella, see exquisiteness.

While Bella is looking for endless love, Ines is looking for a place where she can rest once this metamorphosis is complete. She imagines that she will eventually become immobile, and hopes to find a suitable location to stand still for the rest of time. Thorsteinn tells Ines of his homeland.

> Iceland is a country where we are matter-of-fact about strange things. We know we live in a world of invisible beings that exists in and around our own. [...] Our tales are full of striding stone women.[41]

Similar to Meyer's references to fairy tales such as Little Red Riding Hood, Cinderella and Sleeping Beauty, Byatt here draws from Icelandic folklore. The folktale that Byatt refers to specifically, Trunt, Trunt and the Trolls in the Fells, tells of the transformation of a man into a troll. Icelandic trolls are known to be able to transform themselves into stones and, as Jacqueline Simpson notes, 'Tales about them are often intended to explain curious rock formations.'[42] Ines accepts Thorsteinn's suggestion, and decides to go with him to Iceland for the summer. In these strange and wild surroundings, she begins to perceive the world in new ways, she sees 'huge dancers, forms that humped themselves out of earth and boulders, stamped and hurtled, beckoned with strong arms and snapping fingers.'[43] Bella's senses are altered, too, after her transformation. In the minutes after her awakening as a vampire, she notices as though for the first time the dust motes, the grains in wood, the filament in a light bulb.[44] For Ines, however, while she begins to see these stone creatures of a previously invisible world around her, she has more and more difficulty bringing her attention to her human friend, Thorsteinn: 'He was becoming insubstantial. His very solid body looked as though it was simply a form of water vapour.'[45] After the years of her metamorphosis, Ines can no longer really see the world as humans do. She has become a part of the living stone. Finally, the stone creatures call to her, and she runs off to dance with them in the hills.[46]

Considered next to the rugged, elemental stone woman that Ines becomes in A.S. Byatt's story, the vampires of Stephenie Meyer's *Twilight* world seem composed, constructed, moulded. It is as though their stone bodies have been sculpted in the same way that Michelangelo's David was carved. Their surfaces are smooth, like polished marble. Despite their strength and capacity for great violence, Meyer's vampires embody the perfect idealized human form. There does not seem to be any molten rock flowing through their veins. The flawlessness of their physical form echoes the inhuman perfection of the surgically altered spectres of aging Hollywood: their perfection is actually their monstrosity. They sparkle and reflect the sunlight of our adoration, rather than burning up in the daytime. As manifestations of our youth-centred cosmetic culture, the *Twilight* vampires are about the surface, the appearance, the skin, as Bella alludes to so often in her descriptions of the Volturi. They contemplate their beauty in the mirror, and find that, indeed, they are the fairest of them all. The transference of these characters from page to screen in the film adaptations provides a further magnification of this idealization. The actors 'become the perfection of the work of art'[47] fulfilling for all of us the desire to change ourselves into something younger and better. The strange irony that Meyer has in store for Bella and for Edward, the immortal lovers, is that if they do live, as Edward promises at the end of the Saga, 'forever and forever and forever'[48] they will eventually become the ancients. And, like the Volturi rulers, Aro and Caius and Marcus, those nasty old things, even Bella and Edward will become papery skinned and will get *old*. Will they have the grace, then, to go dancing with the stone woman in Iceland?

Notes

[1] Northrop Frye, *Anatomy of Criticism: Four Essays* (Princeton: Princeton UP, 1957), 186.
[2] Katy Perry, 'Teenage Dream'. *Teenage Dream.* USA: Capitol Records, 2010.
[3] Stephenie Meyer, *Twilight* (New York: Little, Brown and Company, 2005), 10.
[4] Stephenie Meyer, *New Moon* (New York: Little, Brown and Company, 2006), 168-9.
[5] Ibid., 262.
[6] Ibid., 3.
[7] Ibid., 6.
[8] Ibid., 540.
[9] Victoria Pitts-Taylor, *Surgery Junkies: Wellness and Pathology in Cosmetic Culture* (Piscataway: Rutgers UP, 2007), 34-5.
[10] Ibid., 43.
[11] Meyer, *Breaking Dawn*, 374.
[12] Ibid., 403.
[13] Ibid., 640.
[14] Ibid., 381.
[15] Ibid., 392.
[16] Naomi Wolf, *The Beauty Myth* (London: Chatto & Windus, 1990), 217.
[17] Stephenie Meyer, *Midnight Sun* (Partial Draft.) Viewed March 25, 2011, http://www.stepheniemeyer.com/midnightsun.html, 18.
[18] Meyer, *Twilight*, 13.
[19] Emily Brontë, *Wuthering Heights: The Complete Novels of Charlotte & Emily Brontë* (New York: Avenel Books, 1981), 314.

[20] Sara Buttsworth, 'CinderBella: *Twilight*, Fairy Tales, and the Twenty-First-Century American Dream.' Twilight *and History*, ed. Nancy R. Reagin (Hoboken: John Wiley & Sons, 2010), 52.
[21] Ibid., 52.
[22] Meyer, *New Moon*, 527-529.
[23] Ibid., 482.
[24] Ibid., 467.
[25] Ibid., 469.
[26] Ibid., 470.
[27] Ibid., 473.
[28] Ibid., 478.
[29] A. S. Byatt, 'A Stone Woman,' *Little Black Book of Stories* (London: Chato and Windus, 2003), 129.
[30] Ibid., 139.
[31] Ibid.
[32] Meyer, *Breaking Dawn*, 502.
[33] Byatt, 'A Stone Woman', 140-114.
[34] Meyer, *Twilight*, 414.
[35] Meyer, *Breaking Dawn*, 385-6.
[36] Byatt, 'A Stone Woman', 147.
[37] Ibid., 156.
[38] Ibid., 157.
[39] Ibid., 158.
[40] Meyer, *Twilight*, 260.
[41] Byatt, 'A Stone Woman', 158.
[42] Jacqueline Simpson, *Icelandic Folktales and Legends* (London: Willmer Brothers, 1972), 7.
[43] Byatt, 'A Stone Woman', 177.
[44] Meyer, *Breaking Dawn*, 387.
[45] Byatt, 'A Stone Woman', 176.
[46] Ibid., 182-183.
[47] Sander L. Gilman, *Making the Body Beautiful: A Cultural History of Aesthetic Surgery* (Princeton: Princeton UP, 1999), 328.
[48] Meyer, *Breaking Dawn*, 754.

Bibliography

Austen, Jane. *Pride and Prejudice.* Ware: Wordsworth Editions, 1992.

Brontë, Emily. *Wuthering Heights: The Complete Novels of Charlotte & Emily Brontë.* New York: Avenel Books, 1981.

Byatt, A. S. 'A Stone Woman.' *Little Black Book of Stories.* London: Chato and Windus, 2003.

Click, Melissa A., Jennifer Stevens Aubrey and Elizabeth Behm-Morawitz, eds. *Bitten by* Twilight*: Youth Culture, Media and the Vampire Franchise.* New York: Peter Lang, 2010.

Frye, Northrop. *Anatomy of Criticism: Four Essays.* Princeton: Princeton UP, 1957.

Gilman, Sander L. *Making the Body Beautiful: A Cultural History of Aesthetic Surgery.* Princeton: Princeton UP, 1999.

Meyer, Stephenie, *Breaking Dawn.* New York: Little, Brown and Company, 2008.

———. *Eclipse.* New York: Little, Brown and Company, 2007.

———. *New Moon.* New York: Little, Brown and Company, 2006.

———. *Midnight Sun.* (Partial Draft). An unpublished manuscript. Retrieved at http://www.stepheniemeyer.com/midnightsun.html.

———. *The Short Second Life of Bree Tanner.* New York: Little, Brown and Company, 2010.

———. *Twilight.* New York: Little, Brown and Company, 2005.

Pitts-Taylor, Victoria. *Surgery Junkies: Wellness and Pathology in Cosmetic Culture.* Piscataway: Rutgers UP, 2007.

Reagin, Nancy R., ed. Twilight *and History.* Hobken: John Wiley & Sons, 2010.

Simpson, Jacqueline. *Icelandic Folktales and Legends.* London: Willmer Brothers, 1972.

Wolf, Naomi. *The Beauty Myth.* London: Chatto & Windus, 1990.

Monica Dufault acts, writes and directs for the theatre, and teaches performance at Brock University in St. Catharines, Ontario, Canada.

Part III

Beyond Gender

Print Culture and the Monstrous Hermaphrodite in Early Modern England

Whitney Dirks-Schuster

Abstract
Early modern England was obsessed with hermaphrodites. A first, simple explanation for this phenomenon is that sex sells. There is a variety of evidence to support this assertion, from a pamphlet account of the famous 'Parisian boy-girl', which describes his/her body explicitly and at length, to the short-and-sweet advertisement to see a live hermaphrodite in London for 2s 6d. A second possible reason for the popularity of hermaphrodites is their identification as a kind of monstrous birth. The physical deformity of hermaphrodites, their indeterminate sex, could be read as a sign of God's wrath for the sins of His people. Hermaphrodites could also be problematic in a third, secular sense. Without clear male or female genitals, an hermaphrodite could transgress societal gender boundaries, leading to fears of sodomy and attempts to pin down an hermaphrodite's 'true' sex. This chapter will examine a variety of print sources – from pseudo-scholarly sex manuals to articles dedicated to real-life hermaphrodites in the *Philosophical Transactions of the Royal Society of London* – to investigate why ambiguous sexuality was simultaneously fascinating and monstrous to the people of early modern England.

Key Words: Hermaphrodite, sex, gender, monstrous birth, print culture, England, early modern.

*****

1. Introduction

To begin with modern medical definitions, an hermaphrodite is an individual in whom 'the gonads show both ovarian and testicular components, either in separate organs or as combined ovotestes.'[1] In addition to this 'true' hermaphrodite, modern medicine also identifies the female pseudohermaphrodite, an individual with ovaries and masculinised genitalia, and the male pseudohermaphrodite, a person with testes and feminized genitals. Naturally, short of a post-mortem autopsy, neither seventeenth-century physicians, anatomists, midwives, nor judges could have determined sex based upon such evidence as the existence of ovaries. As a result, the early modern definition of 'hermaphrodite' included this entire range of sexual indeterminacy and was therefore much closer to the modern definition of 'intersexual,' an individual in whom the genitals are not clearly male or female but who may fit into any of the above categories. Rowan Roux likewise discusses the liminal nature of intersexuality in the chapter to follow. It is this blurring of what is typically seen to be a gender binary, Roux suggests, that lends a transgressive quality to the intersexual; difference is inherently monstrous. Also, for a discussion of our fascination with ungendered monstrosity in modern cinema, see Steven Nardi and Munehito Moro's chapter later in this section.

The historian Alice Domurat Dreger claimed that in 1998 roughly 'one to three in every two thousand people [or 0.05 to 0.15%] are born with an anatomical conformation not common to the so-called typical male or female such that their unusual anatomies can result in confusion and disagreement about whether they should be considered female or male or something else.'[2] Anne Fausto-Sterling's estimate from the year 2000, compiled from medical frequency estimates of various categories of intersexuality, was 1.7% of all live births, though she clarifies that this figure should be taken as an order-of-magnitude estimate and not a precise count.[3] By averaging these two statistics (Dreger's 0.05% and Fausto-Sterling's 1.7%), one can come up with the count of 0.875% of all live births or 35,000 intersexed babies born yearly in the United States, giving a total of 2,625,000 individuals in the United States today who can be classified as intersexed. Though this seems an incredibly high number, Dreger is quick to point out that this statistic utilizes a rather broad definition of individuals with non-standard genitals, and many people who could theoretically fit into the intersexual category are never labelled as such.[4] Barring genetic predisposition within a given population, which Dreger cites as the cause of some forms of intersexuality,[5] the incidence of intersexual births today is likely to have been similar to that in the seventeenth century.[6] Given my estimate and that London's population in 1650 was around 400,000 people, approximately 3,500 of London's mid-seventeenth-century inhabitants could have been described as intersexed. One can hardly be surprised, then, that the occasional early modern hermaphrodite came into the public view.

According to the physicians, midwives, and popular authors who posited the existence of hermaphrodites, there were either four or five varieties of hermaphroditic body. The esteemed seventeenth-century French surgeon Ambroise Paré identified four varieties of hermaphrodite:

> The first of which is the male Hermpahrodite, who is a perfect and absolute male, and hath onely a slit in the *Perinœum* not perforated, and from which neither urine nor seed doth flow. The second is the female, which besides her naturall privity, hath a fleshy and skinny similitude of a man's yard [referring to the clitoris], but unapt for erection and ejaculation of seed, and wanteth the cod and stones [scrotum and testicles]; the third difference is of those, which albeit they beare the expresse figures of members belonging to both sexes, commonly set the one against the other, yet are found unapt for generation, the one of them onely serving for making of water: the fourth difference is of those who are able in both sexes, and throughly performe

> the part both of man and woman, because they have the genitals of both sexes compleat and perfect, and also the right breast like a man, and the left like a woman.[7]

According to Paré, hermaphrodites could be male, female, neither, or both. The seventeenth-century midwife Jane Sharp also identified four types of hermaphrodite; however, hers were either male or female:

> There is but one kind of Woman *Hermaphrodites*, when a thing like a Yard [penis] stands in the place of the *Clitoris* above the top of the genital … But three ways a boy may be of doubtful sex. 1. When there is seen a womans member between the Cods and the Fundament [testicles and buttocks]. 2. When it is seen in the cod, but no excrement coming forth by it. 3. When they piss through it.[8]

Agreeing with Sharp's definitions, and opposing Paré, was the anonymous author of *An Historical Miscellany of the Curiosities and Rarities in Nature and Art* (1794-1800) who argued that 'there is no such thing as a perfect androgyne, or real hermaphrodite; that is to say, a living creature which … possesses the genuine powers of both sexes, in such a manner as to be qualified for performing the functions of either with success.'[9]

Those authors who argued for a fifth type of hermaphrodite – such as Nicholas Venette in his *Mysteries of Conjugal Love Revealed* (1703), whose definitions of hermaphrodites were co-opted almost verbatim by Giles Jacob in his *Treatise of Hermaphrodites* (1718) – conflated the above theories. For Venette, there existed three kinds of male hermaphrodite, one kind of female, and one with 'their Privy parts confused, and the Temper of man and Woman so intermixed, that one can hardly say which has the upper hand.'[10] However, 'one of the privy parts of an Hermaphrodite is always useless,'[11] allowing some societal determination of gender to be made. More generally, though, whether split into four or five categories, hermaphrodites were individuals with imperfect sex such that 'hee that vieweth them cannot determine and be resolved of what sex or kinde they may be of.'[12]

2. Sex Sells

Pseudo-scholarly sex manuals – of which the anonymous *Aristotle's Master-Piece* (1690) and its sequels *Aristotle's Compleat Master Piece* (1702), *Aristotle's Last Legacy* (1707), and *Aristotle's Book of Problems* (1710) are excellent examples[13] – presented sex to the reading public through the veil of academic inquiry. In the introduction to the first book, the author pointed to his supposed audience:

> I shall proceed to Unravel the Mystery of Generation, and divers other Mysteries; which I hope will be to the Satisfaction of the Learned and Ingenious of the Age, whose Discretion I need not doubt, will keep them from wresting it to any other end than what it was design'd for … not desiring that this Book should fall into the Hands of any Obscene or Wanton Person, whose Folly or Malice may turn that into Ridicule, that loudly proclaims the Infinite Wisdom of an Omnipotent Creator.[14]

Though the author professed innocent intentions in writing this book, such disclaimers are quite common in texts on the body and reproduction. Whereas Thomas Allen's 'Exact Narrative of an Hermaphrodite Now in London' (1666-7) was originally printed in Latin in the *Philosophical Transactions* 'for the view of the Learned,'[15] *Aristotle's Master-Piece* was written in English and was therefore available to any reader who could afford it. The author again claimed that he was presenting his anatomical information 'for the benefit of Practitioners and Professors of the Art of Midwifry' in the section 'Of the Genital of Women, External and Internal to the Vessels of the Womb,' but the following descriptions read as though aimed at an audience completely unfamiliar with female genitalia: 'the parts that offer themselves to view, without any diduction, at the bottom of the Belly, are the *Fissura Magna*, or the Great Chink, with its *Labia* or Lips, the *Mons Veneris*, and the Hair.'[16] Moreover, though the expensive folio edition of Helkiah Crooke's *Description of the Body of Man* (1615), printed in English with carefully-labelled copper plate anatomy pictures, contains similar anatomical descriptions, *Aristotle's Master-Piece* was printed cheaply in octavo with a few woodcut images of monstrous births tacked on the end. Given this format, the *Master-Piece* was clearly intended to have a popular audience. John Cannon, born in 1684 to a lower-middling-sort family,[17] even admitted in his 'Memoirs' to reading *Aristotle's Master-Piece* and masturbating to Nicholas Culpeper's *A Directory for Midwives* (1651) until his mother caught him and took the book away.[18] Popular sex manuals, and even midwives' handbooks, could certainly be put to such illicit use and indeed 'often drew upon exactly the same material [as erotic works] and presented it in a remarkably similar style.'[19]

As with anatomy in general, hermaphrodites' bodies were likewise available for consumption, both to be viewed in person at private peep shows and to be read about in print. The 'Parisian boy-girl, aged sixteen, named Michael-Anne Drouart,' for example, was 'upon Show in Carnaby-Street, London' in November 1750 and simultaneously described in a 17-page pamphlet.[20] At birth, Drouart was given the two names of 'Michael' and 'Anne,' 'under the Uncertainty of which [sex] it properly belonged to,' though Drouart's parents later determined him/her[21] to be predominantly female. As a child, however, Drouart was widely reported as being an hermaphrodite, which led to 'constant Interruptions and Visits … from all

Quarters.' His/her parents 'had not the least Idea, at that Time of exposing it to View, for any Advantage or Lucre' except to 'some Persons only of the first Distinction [who] were admitted to satisfy their Curiosity.' At the age of sixteen, Drouart became 'an Object so interesting to the public Curiosity' that his/her portrait was engraved and apparently so widely disbursed by 1750 that it 'is at this Time grown pretty rare.' The crowds flocking to Drouart's home eventually became so overwhelming that his/her parents allowed Drouart to stay at the home of 'M. Fage'aise, a Surgeon of great Note and Eminence,' who only allowed in 'Persons of the first Rank and Condition,' at the price of 'thirty *louis-d'ors per diem.*' Early in 1750, Drouart travelled to London, 'where all Curiosities either of Nature or Art find an Encouragement proportionable to their Degrees of Merit,' and where he/she went on display for people such as M. Vacherie, the pamphlet's author, to describe.[22]

After presenting Drouart's background, the following eight pages of the pamphlet are dedicated to a careful description of his/her body and especially genitalia, eventually concluding that Drouart's sex could not be determined and that he/she was therefore 'a complete Hermaphrodite.'[23] In a letter to the Royal Society, however, James Parsons disagreed with Vacherie's conclusions, instead arguing that Drouart, who was 'now shewn at Ludgate as an hermaphrodite' was in fact a female with a 'clitoris, grown to an inordinate size.'[24] This public disagreement between anatomists typifies the prurient nature of many anatomical or pseudo-anatomical accounts of genitalia. As Ruth Gilbert points out, 'such works often straddled an unclear boundary between science and sensation … the authors of vernacular works that discussed hermaphrodites exploited the commercial possibilities attached to the erotic nature of their subject matter.'[25] Indeed, Parsons's letter simultaneously commented on Drouart and advertised Parsons's *Mechanical Critical Inquiry into the Nature of Hermaphrodites*, the same book that he had mentioned in a 1741 letter to the Royal Society. In writing this book, Parsons had apparently capitalized upon 'a Time when the Town was daily entertained with Advertisements of the Angolan [hermaphrodite] that was shewed here publickly.'[26] By the time Drouart appeared, Parsons had already established himself as an expert on hermaphroditism.

Apparently, advertisements to see hermaphrodites were not altogether uncommon. A description of an entirely different Angolan hermaphrodite, for example, survived in a seventeenth-century collection of such promotions:

> An hermaphrodite (Lately brought over from Angola). The Features of whose Face are entirely Fæminine, and something agreeable in Its Countenance when It smiles; there is no appearance of a Beard, nor was there ever any; when It Talks low, the Voice resembles a Woman's, if aloud, a Man's; Its Breast is made wide and Masculine, Its Shoulders and Arms very

> Masculine, the Muscles being strong and large; below the Elbow It has a small neat Arm like a Woman; the Hips are Masculine, the Thighs and Legs Fæminine, the private Parts are equally Masculine and Fæminine, and so perfect in each Sex, that 'tis hard for the Curious Examiner to distinguish which has the Superiority.[27]

The hermaphrodite 'is to be seen at the Golden-Cross, near Charing-Cross, Price 2s. 6d.'[28] A second paragraph of the advertisement, specifically describing the hermaphrodite's genital structure, is in Latin; learned readers, possibly specifically physicians or anatomists, were evidently the targeted audience for these hermaphrodite shows.

3. A Fascination with Monstrosity

Cheap to print and therefore available to a wide audience of readers, popular or ephemeral literature could be bought in a variety of forms in early modern London. Within the genre of broadside ballads alone, one could choose among 'all the Newes in England, of Murders, Flouds, Witches, Fires, Tempests, and what not,'[29] love stories, young women's cross-dressed adventures, murderers' gallows confessions, and tales of monstrous births, in addition to many other entertaining topics.

The *Oxford English Dictionary* cites the English word *monster* as having developed out of the twelfth-century French *mostre* or Latin *monstrum* (a portent, prodigy, or monstrous creature) and the Latin *monere* (to warn), while the naturalist Ulisse Aldrovandi asserted that the word *monstrer* (to show) developed into a monster as being something that could be shown to others.[30] According to the physician Ambrose Paré, monsters were 'what things soever are brought forth contrary to the common decree and order of nature. So wee terme that infant monstrous, which is borne with one arme alone, or with two heads.'[31] The anonymous *Aristotle's Compleat Master Piece* (1702) further clarified that monsters may be 'vicious in Figure, when a Man bears the Character of a Beast … vicious in Magnitude, when the Parts are not equal, … vicious in Situation many Ways; as if the Ears were on the Face … And lastly, … vicious in Number, when a Man hath two Heads, or four Hands.'[32] In *A Directory for Midwives* (1651), the physician Nicholas Culpeper simply defined a monster as 'that which is either wholly or in part like a beast, or that which is ill shaped extraordinary.'[33] Such prayers as 'Give unto this woman thy handmaid neither a monstrous, a maimed, or a dead birth … let thy blessing be upon it'[34] indicate that monstrous births were often on the early modern mind.

Aaron W. Kitch asserts that 'broadside ballads about monstrous births appeared in England during the 1560s and quickly achieved popularity, based on the number of copies that survive relative to other types of ballad from the same period.'

Interestingly, Kitch claims that the authors and printers of the first monstrous birth broadsides were important members of the Stationers' Company and that therefore, 'their choice of subject matter … was dictated as often as possible by the tastes of their consumers, most of whom were probably in London.'[35] Tessa Watt argues for the ubiquity of the broadside ballad at every level of early modern English society; 'ballads were stuck up on the walls in alehouses and private homes' alike. In fact, everyone, whether literate or not, would have had access to this intensely public medium of literature when read or sung aloud.[36] In his *Emblematic Monsters: Unnatural Conceptions and Deformed Births in Early Modern Europe*, A. W. Bates asserts that the sheer availability of printing can explain the apparent upsurge of interest in monstrous births in the sixteenth century: 'for the first time, it was possible to disseminate written accounts quickly enough and in sufficient numbers that readers could hope to go and see a monster for themselves.'[37] Monsters did not become more plentiful in the early modern period, but stories about monstrous births could be more quickly and easily spread in print than in manuscript. For more on monstrous births in early modern cheap print and fairy tales, particularly the tendency to blame the mother for her child's abnormality, see Belinda Calderone's chapter earlier in this volume.

A typical ballad, which happens to describe hermaphroditic conjoined twins, was printed in London in 1566. The title declares this broadside to be 'The true description of two monstrous children' who are then pictured in a woodcut.[38] The image clearly depicts conjoined twins, one female and the other male. Above the woodcut, very specific details of the birth are provided, including the parents' names, where they live, and when the birth occurred: 'laufully begotten betwene George Steuens and Margerie his wyfe, and borne in the parish of Swanburne, in Buckynghamshyre the iiij. of Aprill, Anno Domini 1566.' The infants were baptised John and Joan and lived half-an-hour after the birth.[39] Bates asserts that such specific details were expected by early modern readers, who relied on broadsides for news, and so the burden of truth for the material propagated in the news ballads was on the printers.[40] However, these concrete details only appear in the broadside's introduction; below the woodcut, the remainder of the page – over half – is dedicated to a morality ballad, claiming that such 'vnnaturall shapes and formes, | Thus brought forth in our dayes, | Are tokens true and manifest | How God by dyuers wayes | Doth styrre vs to amendment of | Our vyle and cankred lyfe.' This monstrous birth was a warning from God to 'Bewayle your former lyfe and sinnes, | While you haue time and space.'[41]

Within the broadside literature, monstrous births were quite often presented as God's warning to the people of England, that 'if we will not be instructed by his worde nor warned by his wonderfull workes, then let vs be assured that these straunge monstrous sightes do foreshow vnto vs that his heauy indignation wyl shortly come vpon vs for our monstrous liuyng.'[42] This sentiment was repeated in such chronologically varied accounts as the birth of a pig with 'a dolphines head' in 1562 and of conjoined female twins 'having two Heads, four Arms, and two Legs' from 1664.[43] Less often, ballads presented monsters as emblems whose individual body parts encoded specific meanings, as in *The True Discripcion of a Childe with Ruffes* (1566), which blamed the birth of a girl with 'fleshy skin behinde like vnto a neckerchef growing from the veines of the back vp vnto the neck, as it were with many ruffes set one after another' on women's fashion, 'the ruffes that many do vse to weare about their necks.'[44] This monstrous birth did not merely warn against sin in general but rather expressed God's displeasure over vanity in clothing. Monstrous births could also be interpreted as prodigies. As opposed to the definitions of *monster* mentioned above, a prodigy, said Paré, was one of 'those things which happen contrary to the whole course of nature, that is, altogether differing and dissenting from nature: as, if a woman should be delivered of a Snake or a Dogge.'[45]

The Ravenna prodigy was supposedly born in 1512 'in which yeere, upon Easter day, neere Ravenna was fought that mortall battell, in which the Popes forces were over throwne.' This humanoid monster had a horn on its head, wings, a single foot with raptors' talons, an eye on its knee, and hermaphroditic genitals.[46] Daston and Park trace the origins of the Ravenna monster myth to a 'monster reportedly born in Florence in 1506,' which Bates suggests was linked to the 1512 Ravenna massacre in order to draw attention to contemporary events.[47] This reading of the monster is supported by Pierre Boaistuau's account in *Histoires Prodigieuses* of how each individual defect typified the 'sins that reigned at this time in Italy': 'the horn was the symbol of pride and ambition: the wings, lightness and inconstancy: the lack of arms, the lack of good works: by the raptor's foot, pillage, usury, and avarice: by the eye that was on the knee, the attraction to earthly matters: by the two sexes, Sodomy.'[48] In the Ravenna monster – as it was often called, blurring the line that Paré attempted to draw between anatomical abnormalities and wholly unnatural births – God had projected onto this unfortunate child 'a silhouette of the sins which had infested the body politic.'[49] The Ravenna monster remained a celebrity long after its birth and subsequent death in 1506, appearing in continental and English chronicles for centuries.

The reaction of one early modern reader to stories of monstrous births, and even to hermaphrodites particularly, can be gleaned from the manuscript book 'A Short History of Human Prodigious and Monstrous Births,' compiled by James Paris du Plessis, servant to the diarist Samuel Pepys, between 1680 and 1730. Unlike his master whose ballad collection contains only two monstrous broadsides,[50] du Plessis was obsessed with monsters. Included in his sizeable book are three pages on an hermaphrodite born in Yorkshire in 1680 who visited London in 1702, complete with a painting of him/her wearing a dress. The skirt is painted on a paper flap that can be lifted to bare his/her genitals, the early modern equivalent of a pop-up book! Dudley Wilson suggests that this flap may demonstrate the manner in which hermaphrodites were exhibited to the London public, with very little consideration for the hermaphrodite him/herself.[51] Du Plessis recounts how he met, talked with, and examined the twenty-two-year-old hermaphrodite: 'she seemed to be a Perfect Partaker of boath sexes its viril Verge did Erect by Provocation.' On the following page he continues: 'asked it many Questions but Company Cumming in Interrupted us but I found by Inspections that its viril Member was Perfect as to all outward Aparance. as to the Head Calote Testicules Scrotum &c.'[52] Du Plessis enjoyed unfettered access to this hermaphrodite, as did Vacherie when he examined Michael-Anne Drouart in 1750. In Wilson's words, 'the curiosity of the public was in no way inhibited' when examining bodies on display.[53]

4. Transgressing Gender Boundaries

Uncertainty surrounded hermaphrodites in early modern England. Were they women or men? Who decided? How could one be sure? Thomas Edgar rather unhelpfully posited that hermaphrodites were 'persons' who 'must bée déemed male or female, according to the predominance of the sex most inciting,'[54] and Edward Coke agreed that an hermaphrodite 'aught to be baptized' 'according to that kinde of the sex which doth prevaile.'[55] Anatomists, physicians, and midwives – the early modern medical community – were often called upon, or appointed themselves, to identify the 'true' sex of an hermaphrodite. However, their opinions often varied widely, and physicians appear to have regularly challenged each other's identifications or even denied the existence of hermaphrodites altogether. A very clear medical interest can be seen in these discussions about real, historical hermaphrodites, and while the authors disagree on the details – for example, whether an individual might be better identified as a true hermaphrodite or a woman with excessive genitalia – their writings do demonstrate that the fascination with hermaphrodites reached beyond the purely literary.

In December 1686, Monsieur Veay, a French physician, wrote to the Royal Society about the French hermaphrodite Marguerite/Arnaud Malause. Significantly, the letter was published in the original French, 'it being judged improper to appear in English,'[56] though Gilbert asserts that the case was 'widely discussed in early modern medical, paramedical and pornographic literature,' some of which was printed in English. Malause was baptized 'Marguerite' and lived as a female until becoming ill in 1686; upon being examined by Veay, he declared her[57] an hermaphrodite, with a largely impenetrable vagina[58] and, according to Georges Arnaud de Ronsil, a 'pretty long penis, about eight inches in length, when in a state of erection; it was well formed, but without any preputium.'[59] Urine, semen, and menstrual blood all flowed out of the penis. In consultation with other physicians and the hospital's governors, Veay declared Malause to be 'predominately male and ordered her/him to change her/his name to the masculine Arnaud and adopt the clothes and life-style of a man.'[60] Apparently unhappy with this turn of events – Malause insisted vehemently that 'she believed she heard nature always calling her to the sex she had been forced to abdicate'[61] – Malause returned to female clothing, for which transgression she was arrested in 1691.[62] Gendered clothing was an important signifier of sex in the early modern period, and in choosing to express her internal gender identity through wearing women's clothing, Malause was challenging the socio-medical decision that had rendered her 'male.' In 1693, Malause visited two physicians in Paris who disagreed with Veay's determination of sex and instead concluded that she was predominately female.[63] Throughout her ordeal, Malause was a spectacle for public scrutiny and speculation. According to Barthélemy Saviard, she 'used to appear at public assemblies and allow herself to be examined for a small tip by those who were curious'; more blatantly, the anonymous pornographic work *An Apology for a Latin Verse in Commendation of Mr. Marten's Gonosologium Novum* (1709) suggested that 'she got Mony by shewing herself.'[64] The anonymous *Supplement to the Onania* (1725) even went so far as to blame her 'relaxation of the *Vagina*' on masturbation and claimed that rather than being relieved at legally becoming a female once more, Malause had to be 'forc'd to resume her Female Dress, to her great regret.'[65] Public accounts of hermaphrodites did not necessarily get all the details right.

Anna Wilde's story is told in a letter to the Royal Society by Thomas Allen, a physician and member of the Society; it was originally written in Latin in 1667 when Wilde was to be seen in London and reprinted in English in 1745. Wilde was born on 2 February 1647 at Ringwood in Hampshire. At the age of six, 'there appeared two Tumours like Hernia's or Ruptures; in reducing which, all the Care of Surgeons was ineffectual; for they proved to be Testicles,' each contained within skin flaps which were either labia or a bifurcated scrotum. However, Wilde's sex was not called into question until she[66] was thirteen years old: 'once happening to be kneading Dough, all of a sudden a Penis, which till then lay concealed, broke forth, to the great Surprize of the Patient.' At the age of sixteen, Wilde menstruated for two years, whereupon her courses stopped, her voice dropped, and she grew a beard. Allen included two accounts of Wilde's sexual preference, first saying that 'at the Sight of a Woman her Penis was erected, and at the Sight of a Man it became flaccid' and going on to relate how 'one Night she was making merry with her Companions, she cast her Eyes upon a handsome Man, and became so much in Love with him, that the Excess of her Passion made her hysterick.'[67] Though Allen likely intended the observation and story to demonstrate Wilde's double nature – as a man, she was aroused by women, while as a woman, she was capable of succumbing to hysterical passion for a man – a modern reader is instead led to question whether Wilde may in fact have been bisexual or at least attracted to members of both sexes.

An anonymous response to Allen's letter sharply contradicted Allen's conclusions and even called his professional credentials into question. The author of this review, entitled 'A True and Accurate Account of an Hermaphrodite,' began his own account of Wilde's case by questioning not Allen's identification of Wilde as an hermaphrodite but rather whether hermaphrodites even exist. He asserted that 'we are not to wonder that People, unacquainted with the Structure of a human Body, and the Laws of Nature in its Formation, should credit Impossibilities concerning it' and later claimed that all the so-called hermaphrodites he had seen in London since Allen's letter was published were actually 'Women whose Clitoris was longer than ordinary, and nothing more.' Moreover, he identified Wilde as one of these women, who through 'Frequent Titillation' had made her 'Clitoris grow longer than it would naturally have done.' The author continued on to berate Allen for his lack of scientific method as, he claimed, Allen received all his information about Wilde's genitalia from her handler, 'the Man who shewed her to People for Money: A Man … whose Business it was to tell as strange a Story as he could.' The author even questioned how Wilde could have grown a beard and become physically more masculine around age eighteen, as Allen had claimed, if she was seen in Holland by the anatomist Ysbrand van Diemerbroeck 'some years after this, but she was then as much a Woman as ever.' According to the author, Diemerbroeck even reported that Wilde menstruated when he examined her and called Allen's 'penis' an enlarged clitoris. 'However false Conclusions Dr. Allen may have drawn from the Facts he lays down in this Paper,' the author asserted at the end of his review, 'the Facts themselves serve our Turn to prove the contrary to what he intended to make out by them. They perfectly convince us that what he means to describe as an Hermaphrodite, was not an Hermaphrodite, but a mere Woman.'[68]

Anna Wilde's story leads us to a highly-debated question in early modern Europe: Are spontaneous sex changes possible? Among the works concurring with this theory were Ambroise Paré's *The Works of that Famous Chirurgion* (English trans. 1634), *The Compleat Midwifes Practice* (1656), Jane Sharp's *The Midwives Book* (1671), *Aristotle's Master-Piece* (1690), and John Dunton's periodical *The Athenian Oracle* (compiled 1704). Sex changes, these sources argued, 'however held for a Fable, hath chanced many times in nature.'[69] Paré presented his arguments in a bit more detail:

> It is not impossible that the virile members, which hitherto sluggish by defect of heat, lay hid, may be put forth, especially if to that strength of the growing heat some vehement concussion or jactation [agitation] of the body be joined … it is not fabulous that some women have beene changed into men: but you shall find in no history men that have degenerated into women; for nature always intends and goes from the imperfect to the more perfect, but not basely from the more perfect to the imperfect.[70]

These authors contended that female-to-male sex change was possible, but not *vice versa*.

On the other side of the sex-change debate were the anatomists: Kaspar Bartholin, John Bulwer, Helkiah Crooke, Ysbrand van Diemerbroeck, Jacques Duval, and Alexander Ross. These men said that the 'stories which tell us of maids turned into boyes, are false and ridiculous'[71] and could only be believed by 'them who were ignorant in Anatomy.'[72] 'The vessels of generation in the male and female are not the same, as some have thought, supposing they differ onely in scituation, the one being inward, the other outward.'[73] The arguments used against spontaneous sex change are that male and female genitals are not identical in substance, and so sex change is not possible. Interestingly, however, both Ross and Giles Jacob, author of the popular *Treatise of Hermaphrodites* (1718), asserted that *perceived* sex change was possible in the case 'of Hermaphrodites, or of such boyes, in whom the vessels of generation have not at first appeared outwardly for want of heat and strength, which afterwards have Thrust them out.'[74] Such individuals were mistaken for girls at birth, but when their bodily heat rose at puberty, their genitals were thrust out from where they had been hidden within the body, revealing that they had actually been male all along. The sole difference between Ross's and Jacob's assertions and those of Paré and Sharp above is in the terminology: the individuals labelled 'female' by the sex change proponents are called 'hermaphrodite' by their opponents.

5. Conclusion

There can be no question that hermaphrodites appealed to a wide audience in early modern England. Cheap print was available to anyone; a labourer could easily afford a ballad or two a week, the occasional pamphlet, and sporadically even inexpensive books. Live hermaphrodite shows, anatomy books, and accounts published in the *Philosophical Transactions*, on the other hand, would have been aimed at a learned audience of anatomists, physicians, and moneyed gentlemen with an interest in natural philosophy. Though these more highly educated individuals likely also read popular literature – Samuel Pepys, for example, was a notorious collector of broadside ballads – these scientific works were not generally available to a popular audience. In each of these guises, the hermaphrodite was available for public consumption, and the public eagerly indeed consumed such accounts of erotica, monstrosity, and transgression.

Notes

[1] David J. B. Ashley, *Human Intersex* (Edinburgh: Williams and Wilkins, 1962), 148.

[2] Alice Domurat Dreger, *Hermaphrodites and the Medical Invention of Sex* (Cambridge, Massachusetts and London: Harvard University Press, 1998), 42.

[3] Anne Fausto-Sterling, *Sexing the Body: Gender Politics and the Construction of Sexuality* (New York: Basic Books, 2000), 51.
[4] By means of comparison, Dreger provides data for the prevalence of cystic fibrosis (one in two thousand, or 0.05%) and Down syndrome (one in eight hundred, or 0.125%). Dreger, *Hermaphrodites*, 43.
[5] Ibid., 40.
[6] Unlike Down's syndrome which can be detected through amniocentesis and therefore allows for selective abortion of affected fetuses, intersexuality cannot be determined before birth.
[7] Ambroise Paré, *The Works of that Famous Chirurgion Ambrose Parey*, trans. Thomas Johnson (London, np, 1634), 973.
[8] Jane Sharp, *The Midwives Book* (London, np, 1671), 115.
[9] Anonymous, 'Of Androgynes, or Hermaphrodites', *An Historical Miscellany of the Curiosities and Rarities in Nature and Art* (5 vols., London, np, 1794-1800), II, 257.
[10] Nicolas Venette, *The Mysteries of Conjugal Love Reveal'd* (London, np, 1707), 455.
[11] Ibid., 465.
[12] Jacob Rueff, *The Expert Midwife ... Six Bookes Compiled in Latine by the Industry of James Rueff ... and Now Translated into English* (London, np, 1637), 155.
[13] *Aristotle's Master-Piece* was published at least sixteen times between 1690 and 1798, pointing to its clear public appeal.
[14] Anonymous, *Aristotle's Master-Piece: or, The Secrets of Generation Displayed in all the Parts Thereof* (London, np, 1690), A4v.
[15] Thomas Allen, 'An Exact Narrative of an Hermaphrodite Now in London', in *Philosophical Transactions (1665-78)* (12 vols., London, np, 1666-7), II, 624.
[16] Anonymous, *Aristotle's Master-Piece*, 98.
[17] Tim Hitchcock, *English Sexualities, 1700-1800* (New York: Palgrave Macmillan, 1997), 28.
[18] Ibid., 29.
[19] Ruth Gilbert, 'Seeing and Knowing: Science, Pornography and Early Modern Hermaphrodites', in *At the Borders of the Human: Beasts, Bodies and Natural Philosophy in the Early Modern Period*, eds. Erica Fudge, Ruth Gilbert and Susan Wiseman (Basingstoke and New York: Palgrave Macmillan, 1999), 154.
[20] M. Vacherie, *An Account of the Famous Hermaphrodite, or, Parisian Boy-Girl, Aged Sixteen, Named Michael-Anne Drouart, at This Time* (November, np, 1750).
[21] Vacherie refers to Michael-Anne Drouart throughout the pamphlet with the gender-neutral pronoun 'it'. In this narrative and in a conscious attempt to

acknowledge the 'double' nature of Drouart's genitals, I will instead refer to Drouart with the pronouns 'he/she', 'him/her', etc.

[22] Vacherie, 'Account of the Famous Hermaphrodite', 4-6.

[23] Ibid., 14.

[24] James Parsons, 'A Letter to the President Concerning the Hermaphrodite Shewn in London', in *Philosophical Transactions (1683-1775)* (91 vols., London, np, 1751-52), XLVII, 142.

[25] Ruth Gilbert, *Early Modern Hermaphrodites: Sex and Other Stories* (Aldershot: Palgrave Macmillan, 2002), 142.

[26] James Parsons, 'A Letter from James Parsons, M.D. F.R.S. to the Royal Society, Giving a Short Account of his Book Intituled', *A Mechanical Critical Inquiry into the Nature of Hermaphrodites (1683-1775)* (91 vols., London, np, 1739-41), XLI, 651.

[27] Anon., '*Fœmina, Mas, Maurus, Mundi Mirabile Monstrum.* An Hermaphrodite (Lately Brought Over from Angola', in compiler unknown, 'A Collection of 77 Advertisements Relating to Dwarfs, Giants, and Other Monsters and Curiosities Exhibited for Public Inspection' (London, 1680-1700), n. p.

[28] Ibid.

[29] Quoted in Tessa Watt, *Cheap Print and Popular Piety, 1550-1640* (Cambridge and New York: Cambridge University Press, 1991), 11.

[30] 'monster', Oxford English Dictionary, last modified March 2003, Viewed 12 December 2011, http://dictionary.oed.com/cgi/entry/00315137?query_type= word&queryword=monster&first=1&max_to_show=10&sort_type=alpha&result_ place=1&search_id=0h5w-Rein3E-17988&hilite=00315137; Ulisse Aldrovandi, *Monstrorum Historia* (Bononi, 1642), quoted in A. W. Bates, *Emblematic Monsters: Unnatural Conceptions and Deformed Births in Early Modern Europe* (Amsterdam and New York: Rodopi, 2005), 12.

[31] Paré, *Works*, 961.

[32] Anonymous, *Aristotle's Compleat Master Piece. In Three Parts; Displaying the Secrets of Nature in the Generation of Man* (23rd ed., London, np, 1749), 88-9.

[33] Nicholas Culpeper, *A Directory for Midwives, or, a Guide for Women, in Their Conception, Bearing and Suckling Their Children* (London, np, 1651-62), 152.

[34] David Cressy, *Travesties and Transgressions in Tudor and Stuart England: Tales of Discord and Dissension* (Oxford: Oxford University Press, 2000), 30.

[35] Aaron W. Kitch, 'Printing Bastards: Monstrous Birth Broadsides in Early Modern England', in *Printing and Parenting in Early Modern England*, ed. Douglas A. Brooks (Aldershot: Ashgate, 2005), 221, 231.

[36] Watt, *Cheap Print*, 12-13.

[37] Bates, *Emblematic Monsters*, 15.

[38] Kitch, 'Printing Bastards', 223.

[39] Anonymous, 'The True Description of Two Monsterous Children …' (London, 1565).
[40] Bates, *Emblematic Monsters*, 55.
[41] Anonymous, 'The True Description of Two Monsterous Children'.
[42] Anonymous, 'The Description of a Monstrous Pig, the which was Farrowed at Hamsted Besyde London, the XVI Day of October, this Present Yeare of our Lord God, M. D. LXII [Reprint. Originally Published: London, 1562]', in *Ancient Ballads & Broadsides Published in England in the Sixteenth Century: Chiefly in the Earlier Years of the Reign of Queen Elizabeth, Reprinted from the Unique Original Copies, in the Library of Henry Huth, Esq.*, ed. unknown (London, 1867), 164.
[43] W[illiam] F[ulwood], 'The Shape of II Monsters, M D LXII' (London, np, 1562). Anonymous, 'Nature's Wonder? Or, a True Account How the Wife of One John Waterman an Ostler in the Parish of Fisherton-Anger, Near Salisbury, was Delivered of a Strange Monster upon the 26th of October 1664 …' (London, 1664).
[44] Anonymous, 'The True Discription of a Childe with Ruffes, Borne in the Parish of Micheham, in the Countie of Surrey, in the Yeere of our Lord MDLXVI [London, 1566]', in *Ancient Ballads & Broadsides Published in England in the Sixteenth Century: Chiefly in the Earlier Years of the Reign of Queen Elizabeth, Reprinted from the Unique Original Copies, in the Library of Henry Huth, Esq.* (London, 1867), 360-1.
[45] Paré, *Works*, 961.
[46] Ibid., 962. Paré's account is repeated practically word-for-word in Anonymous, *Aristotle's Master-Piece*, 181.
[47] Lorraine Daston and Katharine Park, *Wonders and the Order of Nature, 1150-1750* (New York: Zone Books, 1998), 178; Bates, *Emblematic Monsters*, 27.
[48] Quoted in Kathleen P. Long, *Hermaphrodites in Renaissance Europe* (Aldershot: Ashgate, 2006), 34.
[49] Alexandra Walsham, *Providence in Early Modern England* (Oxford and New York: Oxford University Press, 1999), 195.
[50] Anon, 'The Lamenting Lady [London, n.d.],' in *A Pepysian Garland: Black-Letter Broadside Ballads of the Years 1595-1639, Chiefly from the Collection of Samuel Pepys*, ed. Hyder Edward Rollins (Cambridge: Cambridge University Press, 1922), 124-31. Significantly, both ballads describe fictional accounts of monstrosity: respectively, a woman who gives birth to 365 children at once and a pig-faced woman living in Holland.
[51] D. B. Wilson, *Signs and Portents: Monstrous Births from the Middle Ages to the Enlightenment* (London and New York: Routledge, 1993), 92.
[52] James Paris du Plessis, 'A Short History of Human Prodigious and Monstrous Births' (unprinted manuscript, British Library, 1680-1730), f. 34r.

[53] Wilson, *Signs and Portents*, 92.
[54] Thomas Edgar, *The Lawes Resolutions of Woemens Rights: or, The Lawes Provision for Woemen* (London, 1632), 5.
[55] Gilbert, *Early Modern Hermaphrodites*, 42.
[56] Quoted in Gilbert, 'Seeing and Knowing', 161.
[57] Marguerite/Arnaud Malause self-identified as a woman throughout her ordeal; I will therefore utilize feminine pronouns while describing her case.
[58] Gilbert, 'Seeing and Knowing', 162.
[59] Georges Arnaud de Ronsil, *A Dissertation on Hermaphrodites* (London, 1750), 54.
[60] Gilbert, 'Seeing and Knowing', 162.
[61] Quoted in Lorraine Daston and Katharine Park, 'The Hermaphrodite and the Orders of Nature: Sexual Ambiguity in Early Modern France', *GLQ: The Journal of Lesbian and Gay Studies* 1 (1995): 427.
[62] Gilbert, 'Seeing and Knowing', 162.
[63] Ibid.
[64] Quoted in Ibid., 163.
[65] Anonymous, *A Supplement to the Onania* (London, 1725?), 164-5.
[66] Anna Wilde was never identified as male and was invariably referred to by feminine pronouns, a practice I will follow here.
[67] Thomas Allen, 'An Hermaphrodite,' in *Medical Essays and Observations Relating to the Practice of Physic and Surgery: Abridg'd from the Philosophical Transactions, from their First Publication*, ed. S. Mihles (London, 1745), 25, 26.
[68] Anonymous, 'A True and Accurate Account of an Hermaphrodite [Reprint. Originally Published: London, n. d.]' in *A Review of the Works of the Royal Society of London; Containing Animadversions on Such of the Papers as Deserve Particular Observation*, ed. Sir John Hill (London, 1751), 97-102.
[69] Anonymous, *The Compleat Midwifes Practice, in the Most Weighty and High Concernments of the Birth of Man* (London, 1656), 288.
[70] Paré, *Works*, 975.
[71] Alexander Ross, *Arcana Microcosmi; or, the Hid Secrets of Mans Body Disclosed: First, in an Anatomatical Duel between Aristotle & Galen, about the Parts Thereof. Secondly, by a Discovery of the ... Diseases, Symptomes, and Accidents of Mans Body* (London, 1651), 84.
[72] John Bulwer, *Anthropometamorphosis: Man Transform'd ...* (London, 1650), 226-7.
[73] Ross, *Arcana Microcosmi*, 84.
[74] Ibid., 125.

Bibliography

Allen, Thomas. 'An Exact Narrative of an Hermaphrodite Now in London'. In *Philosophical Transactions (1665-1678)*. 12 vols., London, 1666-1667, vol. II.

———. 'An Hermaphrodite'. In *Medical Essays and Observations Relating to the Practice of Physic and Surgery: Abridg'd from the Philosophical Transactions, from their First Publication*, edited by Samuel Mihles, 24-26. London, 1745.

Anonymous. *Aristotle's Compleat Master Piece, In Three Parts: Displaying the Secrets of Nature in the Generation of Man.* 23rd ed., London, 1749.

Anonymous. *Aristotle's Master-Piece: or, The Secrets of Generation Display'd in All the Parts Thereof.* London, 1690.

Anonymous. *The Compleat Midwifes Practice, in the Most Weighty and High Concernments of the Birth of Man.* London, 1656.

Anonymous. 'The Description of a Monstrous Pig, the Which was Farrowed at Hamsted Besyde London, the XVI Day of October, this Present Yeare of our Lord God, M. D. LXII [Reprint. Originally Published: London, 1562]'. In *Ancient Ballads & Broadsides Published in England in the Sixteenth Century: Chiefly in the Earlier Years of the Reign of Queen Elizabeth, Reprinted from the Unique Original Copies, in the Library of Henry Huth, Esq.*, London, 1867.

Anonymous. '*Fœmina, Mas, Maurus, Mundi Mirabile Monstrum*: An Hermaphrodite (Lately Brought Over from Angola)'. In *A Collection of 77 Advertisements Relating to Dwarfs, Giants, and Other Monsters and Curiosities Exhibited for Public Inspection*, compiler unknown. London, 1680-1700. British Library N Tab 2026/25.

Anonymous. 'The Lamenting Lady [Reprint. Originally Published: London, n.d.]'. In *A Pepysian Garland: Black-Letter Broadside Ballads of the Years 1595-1639, Chiefly from the Collection of Samuel Pepys*, edited by Hyder Edward Rollins, 124-131. Cambridge: Cambridge University Press, 1922.

Anonymous. 'Nature's Wonder? Or, a True Account How the Wife of One John Waterman an Ostler in the Parish of Fisherton-Anger, Near Salisbury, was Delivered of a Strange Monster upon the 26th. of October 1664 …' (London, 1664).

Anonymous. 'Of Androgynes, or Hermaphrodites'. In *An Historical Miscellany of the Curiosities and Rarities in Nature and Art*, 5 vols., London, 1794-1800, vol. II.

Anonymous. *A Supplement to the Onania.* London, 1725.

Anonymous. 'A True and Accurate Account of an Hermaphrodite [Reprint. Originally Published: London, n. d.]'. In *A Review of the Works of the Royal Society of London; Containing Animadversions on Such of the Papers as Deserve Particular Observation*, edited by Sir John Hill, 97-102. London, 1751.

Anonymous. 'The True Discription of a Childe with Ruffes, Borne in the Parish of Micheham, in the Countie of Surrey, in the Yeere of Our Lord MDLXVI [Reprint. Originally Published: London, 1566]'. In *Ancient Ballads & Broadsides Published in England in the Sixteenth Century: Chiefly in the Earlier Years of the Reign of Queen Elizabeth, Reprinted from the Unique Original Copies, in the Library of Henry Huth, Esq.*, London, 1867.

Anonymous. 'The True Description of Two Monsterous Children …' London, 1565.

Arnaud de Ronsil, Georges. *A Dissertation on Hermaphrodites.* London, 1750.

Ashley, David J. B. *Human Intersex.* Edinburgh: Williams and Wilkins, 1962.

Bates, A. W. *Emblematic Monsters: Unnatural Conceptions and Deformed Births in Early Modern Europe*. The Wellcome Series in the History of Medicine, Amsterdam and New York: Rodopi, 2005.

Bulwer, John. *Anthropometamorphosis: Man Transform'd.* London, 1650.

Cressy, David. *Travesties and Transgressions in Tudor and Stuart England: Tales of Discord and Dissension.* Oxford: Oxford University Press, 2000.

Culpeper, Nicholas. *A Directory for Midwives, or, A Guide for Women, in Their Conception, Bearing and Suckling Their Children.* London, 1651-62.

Daston, Lorraine and Katharine Park. 'The Hermaphrodite and the Orders of Nature: Sexual Ambiguity in Early Modern France'. *GLQ: The Journal of Lesbian and Gay Studies* 1 (1995): 419-38.

———. *Wonders and the Order of Nature, 1150-1750.* New York: Zone Books, 1998.

Dreger, Alice Domurat. *Hermaphrodites and the Medical Invention of Sex.* Cambridge, Massachusetts and London: Harvard University Press, 1998.

Du Plessis, James Paris. 'A Short History of Human Prodigious and Monstrous Births'. Unprinted Manuscript, c. 1680-1730. British Library Add. MSS 5246

Edgar, Thomas. *The Lawes Resolutions of Woemens Rights: or, The Lawes Provision for Woemen.* London, 1632.

Fausto-Sterling, Anne. *Sexing the Body: Gender Politics and the Construction of Sexuality.* New York: Basic Books, 2000.

F[ulwood], W[illiam]. 'The Shape of II Monsters, M D LXII'. London, 1562.

Gilbert, Ruth. *Early Modern Hermaphrodites: Sex and Other Stories.* Aldershot: Palgrave Macmillan, 2002.

Gilbert, Ruth. 'Seeing and Knowing: Science, Pornography and Early Modern Hermaphrodites'. In *At the Borders of the Human: Beasts, Bodies and Natural Philosophy in the Early Modern Period*, edited by Erica Fudge, Ruth Gilbert, and Susan Wiseman, 150-70. Basingstoke and New York: Palgrave Macmillan, 1999.

Hitchcock, Tim. *English Sexualities, 1700-1800.* New York: Palgrave Macmillan, 1997.

Kitch, Aaron W. 'Printing Bastards: Monstrous Birth Broadsides in Early Modern England.' In *Printing and Parenting in Early Modern England*, edited by Douglas A. Brooks, 221-236. Aldershot and Burlington, VT: Ashgate, 2005.

Long, Kathleen P. *Hermaphrodites in Renaissance Europe.* Aldershot: Ashgate, 2006.

LP. 'A Monstrous Shape. Or a Shapelesse Monster'. London, 1639.

Oxford English Dictionary. 'monster'. Last modified March 2003. http://dictionary.oed.com/cgi/entry/00315137?query_type=word&queryword=monster&first=1&max_to_show=10&sort_type=alpha&result_place=1&search_id=0h5w-Rein3E-17988&hilite=00315137.

Paré, Ambroise. *The Works of That Famous Chirurgion Ambrose Parey: Translated Out of Latine and Compared with the French by Th: Johnson.* Translated by Th. Johnson. London, 1634.

Parsons, James. 'A Letter from James Parsons, M.D. F.R.S. to the Royal Society, Giving a Short Account of his Book Intituled, *A Mechanical Critical Inquiry into the Nature of Hermaphrodites*. London, 1741. in 8vo.'. In *Philosophical Transactions (1683-1775)*, 650-652. 91 vols., London, 1739-41.

———. 'A Letter to the President Concerning the Hermaphrodite Shewn in London'. In *Philosophical Transactions (1683-1775)*, 142-145. 91 vols., London, 1751-52.

Ross, Alexander. *Arcana Microcosmi; or, The Hid Secrets of Mans Body Disclosed: First, in an Anatomatical Duel Between Aristotle & Galen, About the Parts Thereof. Secondly, by a Discovery of the ... Diseases, Symptomes, and Sccidents of Man's Body.* London, 1651.

Rueff, Jacob. *The Expert Midwife ... Six Bookes Compiled in Latine by the Industry of James Rueff ... and Now Translated into English.* London, 1637.

Sharp, Jane. *The Midwives Book.* London, 1671.

Venette, Nicolas. *The Mysteries of Conjugal Love Reveal'd.* Unknown translator. London, 1707.

Walsham, Alexandra. *Providence in Early Modern England.* Oxford and New York: Oxford University Press, 1999.

Watt, Tessa. *Cheap Print and Popular Piety, 1550-1640.* Cambridge and New York: Cambridge University Press, 1991.

Wilson, D. B. *Signs and Portents: Monstrous Births from the Middle Ages to the Enlightenment.* London and New York: Routledge, 1993.

Whitney Dirks-Schuster is a PhD Candidate at The Ohio State University. Her dissertation is titled 'Monstrous Births and the Spread of Knowledge in Early Modern Britain.

Monstrous Hermaphrodites: Jeffrey Eugenides's *Middlesex*, the Intersexed Individual and the *Bildungsroman*

Rowan Roux

Abstract

A child born with ambiguous genitalia will discover early in life that being born different leads to association with the monstrous. This chapter examines Jeffrey Eugenides's exploration of the intersexed individual in his novel, *Middlesex*. The protagonist, Calliope Stephanides, is born with 5-alpha-reductase-deficiency syndrome, which means that although the infant presents as female at birth, the child is, biologically speaking, more male than female. Having been designated as female, Callie struggles to identify with the gender role which is expected of her, and consequently Eugenides begins an examination of the complex constitution of gender as Callie is caught in a struggle between societal expectation and biological fact. As Anne Fausto-Sterling has argued, the idea that there are only two sexes is erroneous, but those who cannot be easily categorised have long been seen as a deviation from what is understood to be human. When Callie discovers the 'truth' about her biological make-up, s/he learns that hir very condition of existence is defined as a gruesome deviation from the norm. In Webster's Dictionary, Callie finds 'hermaphrodite' defined as: 'Anything comprised of a combination of diverse or contradictory elements. See synonyms at MONSTER'.[1] At first Callie is convinced that the synonym is 'official, authoritative'; 'the verdict that culture gave on a person like her'.[2] But, as this chapter will explore, through embracing the category of 'monster' and mapping its contradictory elements into existence on the body, Callie is able to achieve a stable, legitimate subject position in society and discover that intersexuality is a condition shared in some degree by all human beings.

Key Words: *Bildungsroman*, intersexuality, Jeffrey Eugenides, *Middlesex*, gender performativity, gendered identity, monsters.

*****

1. Introduction

'[M]y genitals have been the most significant thing that have ever happened to me',[3] reflects the intersexed protagonist of Jeffrey Eugenides's *Middlesex*. While '[s]ome people inherit houses,' Calliope Stephanides reveals a personal inheritance of 'a recessive gene on [the] fifth chromosome and some very rare family jewels indeed'.[4] Medically speaking, Calliope is born with 5-alpha-reductase-deficiency syndrome, which means that although the infant presents as female at birth, the child is, biologically-speaking, more male than female. Having been designated as female, Callie is a perfect example of how, according to Morgan Holmes, 'people, for the most part, have an expectation that genitals correspond to gender',[5] and Calliope's genitals, thus, serve as what would appear to be a 'logical and accurate predictor of an entire sexual and social future'.[6] In her seminal essay, 'The Five Sexes', Anne Fausto-Sterling argues that the common belief that human beings have only two sexes is erroneous, and that those who cannot be easily categorised as either male or female have long been seen as a deviation from what is understood to be human.[7] This is why, as human beings, 'a morphological defect is, to our living eyes, a monster'.[8] For Calliope, then, the apparent ambiguity in biology suggests an ambiguity in her status as human.

As Whitney Dirks-Schuster argues in the preceding chapter, 'Print Culture and the Monstrous Hermaphrodite in Early Modern England', despite these bodies being viewed as defective anomalies their occurrence is, in fact, more common than many may realise. Dirks-Schuster gives a rough estimate of 2,625,000 individuals alive today in the United States who would fall along the spectrum of 'intersexed', often meaning that their genitals are only slightly different, but sometimes completely beyond the limiting binary of male/female. This figure, she says would account for 35, 000 intersexed babies being born annually in the United States alone. In 2007, Milton Diamond speculated that one in every two to four thousand infants born presents with ambiguous genitalia.[9] Despite the frequency of such births, these infants still suffer a cruel fate: they do not neatly fit the precise categorisation of male or female, and therefore, in order for society to accept them as either, or really, to be able to view them as something beyond monstrous, surgery is the usual port of call. Diamond comments that just a decade prior:

> Doctors had been taught in medical school to make their decisions based on the length of the penis. The child is called a boy if it is longer than an inch. If shorter, the doctor typically recommended that that the genitals be operated on to appear as a girl's. After designating the child a girl, regardless of its actual sex, doctors would tell the moms to raise the child as such.[10]

As such, before a child is even a few weeks old, a huge life decision is already made for them. Cheryl Chase, founder of the Intersex Society of North America (ISNA), comments that 'Intersexuality is a psychiatric emergency on the part of the doctors and parents,' who believe the only option, is to 'treat it by cutting in to the body of the infant, even though the adults … are the real patients'.[11] This process is sometimes referred to as intersex genital mutilation (IGM), and what doctors seek to do in cases like these is 'cure' or 'restore' a child to their 'true' sex, because as Riki Wilchins argues, it does not register that 'these infants are whatever sex they are because that non-binary outcome appears to the medical community (and indeed to most of society) as a logical impossibility'.[12] It is for this reason then, that the child appears to be monstrous, something which has no place in the world.

There is no place for these children then, because their bodies are literally expunged of that which makes them appear different, making their existence a continued impossibility. With each surgery performed, the categorisation of monster becomes more rigid in opposition to the fixed binary of male/female.

This chapter expands on the historical positioning of the hermaphrodite, examining the ways in which the intersexed body of Calliope Stephanides transgresses and destabilises the boundaries of both biological sex and gender, as well as questioning what it is that makes difference so inherently monstrous.

2. The *Bildungsroman*

My reading of the novel is heavily centred on the developing sense of gendered identity in the narrator. For this reason, it becomes useful to read *Middlesex* against the typically masculine tradition of the *Bildungsroman*. Usually, this type of novel follows a character's journey into adulthood; a journey which requires assimilation into one of only two possible gender roles. For the intersexed child, however, the binary supposedly inherent in gender roles complicates this process. Aside from the occasional moment of intuition that something may be different, it is only when two testicles are discovered 'squatting illegally'[13] that Calliope undergoes a full identity reassessment. The *Bildungsroman* is defined by M.H. Abrams as 'a "novel of formation" or "novel of education".'[14] Typically, the 'subject of these novels is the development of the protagonist's mind and character, in the passage from childhood ... into maturity, which usually involves recognition of one's identity and role in the world'.[15] Similarly, Pratt adds that this genre of novel is centred on the 'quest of the youthful self for identity, an adventure often formalised into a ritual which the individual undergoes in order to be initiated into the mysteries of adulthood'.[16] Furthermore, a *Bildungsroman* should end with either the protagonist's 'assimilation or non-assimilation into society'.[17]

Fraiman, however, notes that 'heterosexual adventures are favoured in the world's curriculum',[18] meaning that the journey of a character from any marginalised group is always going to be fraught with additional factors of alienation. Thus, we can conclude that if the purpose of a *Bildungsroman* is to chart the development of a character's sense of identity, and if Morgan Holmes is correct in assuming that 'one must be recognised as either a boy or a girl, as either a man or a woman, in order to live securely, unthreatened at a basic level of access to a 'legitimate' subject position',[19] then it is clear that Calliope, as an intersexed individual, will 'experience, at a particularly obvious corporeal level, the logical impossibility of a nature that has to be constructed through cultural measures'.[20] Using an understanding of the theories on gender performativity, as pioneered by Judith Butler, this chapter focuses on the idea that '[i]dentity is not something planted in us to be discovered, but something that is performatively produced by acts',[21] and follows Calliope's transformation from a girlhood as Callie into the adult male, Cal.

Already, from the moment of birth, an infant's genitals determine the particular 'appropriate' path of development which the child should follow. The notion of gender itself then is already defined by and ostensibly determined at birth: a child is either male or female and nothing in-between. This assertion is, of course, a problematic one for a child who is born with 'ambiguous' genitals. Morgan Holmes argues that 'the trouble with the 'ambiguous' body of the intersexed infant is that it suggests an ambiguous future'.[22]

3. The Ambiguity of Bodily Representation

The ambiguous body of the intersex infant also presents the text, and any critical discussion thereof, with another challenge: the problem of how to refer to an intersexed individual. Early in the novel, Eugenides's narrator comments on being 'first one thing and then the other',[23] but still fails to discern an adequate middle ground of terminology with regards to establishing a consensus on non-gendered pronouns. Although various attempts have been made to develop non-gendered pronouns for use in the English language, there is seldom a consensus as to the most 'correct' way to refer to an individual who is neither male nor female. In her afore-mentioned chapter, Whitney Dirks-Schuster demonstrates that these questions of gendered identity, acceptance, and pronoun use have existed within Western culture for centuries. Dirks-Schuster herself opts for using the functional 'he/she', rather than subscribe to her primary text's use of 'it'. Although the latter may be gender-neutral, it is in calling Godzilla 'it', argue Steven Nardi and Munehito Moro in their chapter 'Who Mourns for Godzilla? *Gojira* and De-Asianization of Postwar Japan' that the creature is left faceless and, although something beyond gender, Godzilla is still left profoundly othered. Nardi and Moro also argue that this lack of gender is what places Godzilla in stark contrast to King Kong. Kong, they state, exudes a typically masculine presence and his rampage is shown to be emotionally motivated. This, in turn, allows him to evoke a sympathy that is only available to those with a 'legitimate' subject position, while Godzilla, and anyone relegated to the pronoun 'it' simply moves further away from the category of human. When it comes to other texts, even the progressive use of hir and many similar variants still prove dissatisfactory and appear inherently political, calling more attention to the author than to the individual being described.

In *Middlesex*, when referring to his patient, Dr Luce, at least at first, does not 'use any pronouns at all',[24] demonstrating the awkward extreme: avoidance. Eventually, the narrator makes it clear that because of her 'sex of rearing',[25] Callie Stephanides is to be considered, for all intents and purposes, female. Only as 'the easily rechristened Cal Stephanides',[26] does the narrator begin to use masculine pronouns to refer to himself. For the sake of clarity, and out of respect for Cal's personal decision to reassign his own gender, this chapter uses feminine pronouns when referring to the adolescent Callie's actions, and male pronouns for the retrospective insights provided by Cal, who prefers to 'operate in society as a man'.[27]

The novel opens with Cal, now a 'forty-one-year-old man with longish, wavy hair, a thin moustache, and a goatee',[28] revealing that at birth his 'sex was revealed in the usual manner: by spreading the legs apart and looking'.[29] The reason for no one realising that Calliope was born with genitalia more complicated than it appears, is because '5-alpha-reductase deficiency syndrome is a skilful counterfeiter'.[30] The reader is told that, until Callie reached puberty 'the ways in which [she] differed from other little girls were hard to detect',[31] and could not be superficially discernible. At birth, when spreading her legs apart Callie describes what the doctor saw:

> The clean, saltwater mussel of the female genitalia. The area inflamed, swollen with hormones. That touch of the baboon all babies have. Dr Philobosian would have had to pull the folds apart to see any better, but he didn't.[32]

As the second child born to Milton and Tessie Stephanides, Calliope, is the realisation of her mother's dreams, and this is why, having been 'starved for a daughter, Tessie [goes] a little overboard dressing [Callie in] Pink shirts, lace ruffles [and] Yuletide bows'.[33] Tessie's use of decidedly feminine clothing is explained by Judith Butler's suggestion that 'clothing is part of the performative nature of power and gender,' revealing that 'that which many consider essential gender identity is in fact created by signs that are inscribed on the surface of the body over the course of time by repeated actions dictated by social norms'.[34] Through the imposition of 'feminine' clothing, Tessie actually inscribes her daughter's body as that of a little girl. This type of action is, effectually, what places Callie into the category of female. It is important at this point to distinguish 'between 'sex' as the anatomical difference between male and female bodies and 'gender' as the meanings attached to those bodily differences in various cultures'.[35] Butler, of course, argues that because of what can be termed 'genital determinism',[36] even biological sex projects certain behavioural imperatives which an individual is meant to follow. Because Tessie is told that her child is female, she enforces certain actions and behaviours which are to be expected of a female child. Cal notes that, in his medical investigations, Dr Luce concludes his study with the assertion that:

> gender identity is established very early on in life, about the age of two. Gender [is] like a native tongue; it [doesn't] exist before birth but [is] imprinted in the brain during childhood, never disappearing. Children learn to speak Male or Female the way they learn to speak English or French.[37]

Holmes notes that, with 'infants we assign a sex first and then build a gender upon it',[38] and this is why Cal, even after making the decision to function as a male, cannot help but 'remain in essential ways Tessie's daughter ... the one who remembers to call her every Sunday'.[39] Gender is not something which can ever be 'erased', but it is also not something entirely inherent; at some point in a child's development, the parental figure serves to reinforce certain 'gender appropriate' behaviours while dissuading characteristics 'inherent' in the opposite sex. This lends to Cal's disclosure of the age-old wisdom: 'We're all the children of our parents'.[40] More importantly though, '[t]he way we style our bodies is neither a matter of sex (nature) nor simply an adjunct of the prevailing order (culture), rather it is one of the techniques through which we perform, enact and 'do' gender'.[41]

As suggested by the definition of the *Bildungsroman,* as well as the idea that gender is something which is enacted, it is necessary for Callie to undergo a certain rite-of-passage, serving to induct her into the world of being female. The most visible welcoming to womanhood is at Sophie Sassoon's beauty parlour, The Golden Fleece. Here, 'gendered identity is socially produced through repetitions of ordinary daily activities',[42] such as waxing in order to win the 'battle of unsightly hair'.[43] The idea of gender separation is suggested early on in the novel when Cal mentions that Desdemona and Lefty's house was 'sex-segregated ... men in the *sala*, women in the kitchen. Two separate spheres with separate concerns [and] duties'.[44] This is why, as puberty approaches, Callie starts shaving her legs and using makeup; these are performative activities which effectively create a feminine identity. As Wilchins elucidates, ''[b]eing' a gender is always a *doing*, a continuous approximation of normative ideals that live outside of us and were always there before we arrived'.[45] Over and above styling her body, and 'hidden in the back of the cabinet, was the box of Kotex pads', which Tessie gives to Callie with the words 'We better keep these on hand,' and 'no further explanation'.[46] Realising the importance of this activity, and in response to her mother's worries that Callie has not yet started to menstruate, Callie begins faking her period. The best indication that this activity is a performance aimed at 'attaining' the feminine gender is when Cal reflects 'I did cramps the way Meryl Streep did accents'.[47]

4. Gender and Sexuality

Long suggests that we can 'connect gender ambiguity to moral and epistemological confusion',[48] and this relates to Callie's growing feeling of disassociation with her own body, which ultimately leads her to belief that she is something indecent; something monstrous. The first instance of this is when, as a child, she experiences her first kiss with a female neighbour, Clementine Stark, who asks if Callie 'want[s] to *practice* kissing'.[49] Cal remembers that 'Clementine swivelled her head back and forth the way the actresses did in the movies'.[50] But when Callie attempts to do the same, Clementine tells her 'You're the man',[51] implying, firstly, that a man has a certain role to play; secondly, that such an activity is only performed between a female and a male, and finally, that Callie is not supposed to be performing the role of a woman. Thus, from observing adults, and especially from watching films, Clementine has already been 'imprinted' with the type of behaviour which is deemed 'acceptable', and, in performing it for herself, she serves to construct the heterosexual, female identity expected of her. Callie, however, is, for the first time, relegated to the role of the deviant. Already, Callie is performing the masculine role in this encounter; something which may serve as the basis for Cal later identifying as male.

The description of this encounter, as well as Callie's later encounters with the girl known only as the Obscure Object, is very problematic for Morgan Holmes, who argues that 'Eugenides makes the very same assumption that nineteenth-century physicians and courts did: that desire reveals something innate, and inherently true, about one's sex'.[52] Holmes argues that:

> what is deeply problematic about *Middlesex* is the issue of the erasure of the visibility and vitality of lesbian desire, lesbian sex(uality), and lesbian experience. Calliope cannot be allowed to love the Obscure freely, but Cal can love Julie openly. Eugenides' characterisation of Cal/liope falls right along the matched values of prescientific and biologistic explanations for sexual dimorphism as the appropriate mode of being.[53]

Eugenides does ask whether 'Callie feel[s] any inkling of her true biological nature',[54] suggesting that this has already been pre-determined, while Warhol argues that 'Cal's decision to identify as male is motivated partly by sexual desire ... partly by physical cues'.[55] Cal, on the other hand, asserts 'I've got a male brain. But I was raised a girl'.[56] In utero, Calliope Stephanides followed a primarily female line of development, as all foetuses do, but 5-alpha-reductase deficiency syndrome 'allows for normal biosynthesis and peripheral action of testosterone, in utero, neonatally, and at puberty' and, furthermore, Cal does 'possess all the secondary characteristics of a normal man'.[57] The implication is clear: Callie is, biologically speaking, more male than female, and, as the novel is being written retrospectively, has already 'become' male before beginning to tell this story, a fact bound to influence the manner in which the narrator constructs and recalls his memories of childhood. Holmes's argument, thus, is also problematic. It is impossible to argue that lesbian desire is being erased if the character in question does not, in fact, identify as a lesbian. Thus, I argue, it is unfair to hold such allegations against Eugenides, and from an analytical point of view, it is much more interesting to pay attention to how the *character* relates to these feelings of desire. Not only does Callie struggle to identify with her assigned gender, but she also possesses a problematic body, one which defies conventional categories of sexual orientation. But, as Cal asks the reader, 'Why should [Callie] have thought

[she] was anything other than a girl? Because [she] was *attracted* to a girl? That happened all the time'.[58] This means that both Eugenides and his central character acknowledge the power of female to female attraction without ascribing it any monstrous dimensions. Cal just does not identify as either female or a lesbian. Callie's feelings of desire are only increased by the appearance of a girl referred to only as 'the Obscure Object'. Cal reflects that 'Any girl suspected of being attracted to girls was gossiped about, victimised, and shunned. I was aware of all this. It scared me'.[59] Because of this, Callie is uncertain of whether her feelings for 'the Obscure Object are normal or not'.[60] Finally, the two girls are required to share a bed for their summer vacation. Their night time dalliances are soft, under-the-blanket, with the beginnings of sexual exploration, but these evenings are more characterised by innocence and desire than by overtones of transgression.

After several sexual interactions, the Object's brother, Jerome, catches Callie pleasuring the Object in the pool, and, from his reaction, Callie judges that she is doing something 'wrong'. 'Carpet munchers',[61] Jerome calls them as he makes obscene gestures. By embarrassing the two girls, Jerome is enforcing the idea that they are engaging in something which is wrong when it occurs between two women, as well as asserting his own masculinity by denouncing this activity. Butler suggests that 'nothing is natural, not even sexual identity',[62] as this is regulated by societal intervention, such as Jerome's response. Being told that their behaviour is deviant is what makes the girls feel ashamed; not the behaviour itself. What is revealed during the summer of 1974 is Callie's realisation that she not only desires to be with the Object, but that she desires to be fulfilling the masculine role during such an act. Cal's later reflection reveals that he does not believe that it is desire alone which results in him identifying as male; rather he says that it is 'desire *and* the facticity of my body'.[63]

5. The 'Monstrous' Body

At this point in the novel, the intuition Callie seems to have about her body and her 'unnatural' desires, is revealed to be true, when an accident leads to her being admitted to hospital, where the truth is finally uncovered. From the terms Dr Luce uses during his diagnostic process, Callie is able to search in the dictionary for the details that the doctors seem unwilling to have her hear. She eventually arrives at 'hermaphrodite', defined in Webster's as: 'Anything comprised of a combination of diverse or contradictory elements. See synonyms at MONSTER'.[64] To Callie, this term 'explain[s] so much', and she is convinced that the 'synonym was official, authoritative; it was the verdict that the culture gave on a person like her'.[65] Dr Luce claims he can 'cure' Callie by offering the following 'treatment':

> First, hormone injections. Second, cosmetic surgery. The hormone treatments will initiate breast development and enhance her female secondary characteristics. The surgery will make

> Callie look exactly like the girl she feels herself to be. In fact, she will be that girl. Her outside and inside will conform. She will look like a normal girl. Nobody will be able to tell a thing. And then Callie can go on and enjoy her life.[66]

Holmes argues that the reason why 'treatment' is considered to be necessary is because 'the hermaphrodite can only become recognisable as human once all the queer desire, embodiment, and sex have been erased'.[67] Callie's body is deemed monstrous or abnormal as it threatens how gender is understood; the very existence of an intersexed body proves that 'the gendered body is a highly dubious zone upon which to anchor difference and a treacherously slippery surface on which to sustain gender meaning'.[68] This, in turn, suggests that how we structure our identity is severely flawed, and thus the existence of the intersexed individual serves to 'crack' the 'agreed-upon fiction … that there are but two clearly marked, distinct sexes that require no work to exist as distinct types'.[69]

This is what makes the intersexed body appear so threatening: not only does it transgress gender, but it appears to 'fracture' the very notion of the male/female binary. Riki Wilchins explains:

> It appears that gendered identifications are only meaningful within a binary framework in which one term's separation from the other gives it meaning. Which points to a second problem: Each gendered identity must maintain a strict coherence among sex, gender identity, gender expression, and desire. Female is to woman as woman is to feminine as feminine is attracted to Male. Breaking any link causes a gender to fall right off the grid of cultural intelligibility.[70]

In effect, the unaltered intersexed body is able to terrify many by the very suggestion that the way we have constructed our bodies may be flawed. Marginalising Callie's body, attempting to make it 'female', is an attempt to keep the binary rigid. Truly, attempts at labelling the intersexed body as 'incorrect' rather than 'variant' are attempts to keep the societal structure. As Wilchins suggests, the intersexed body is the corporeal evidence that could collapse the very notion of biological sex even existing. For a discussion on the Lacanian Real and the Symbolic, and how difference can force societal reorganisation, see Nardi and Moro's chapter on Godzilla.

In an attempt to prove herself as female, however, and thus by extension prove that she is neither hermaphrodite nor monster, Callie provides Dr Luce with false data. This leads Dr Luce to his conclusion that Callie 'manifests a feminine gender identity and role, despite a contrary chromosomal status',[71] and this informs his suggested treatment. Olivia Banner notes that Dr Luce is a satirised version of Dr

John Money, 'a professor at Johns Hopkins University who was cofounder of its Gender Identity Clinic and who established himself as the nation's expert on intersex in the 1960s'.[72] Money, however, was soon an advocate of genital reconstruction surgery, and, despite being progressive in his beliefs that nurture was as important in deciding gender as nature, still attempted to determine the 'true' gender of the intersexed children brought to his clinic. Of course, his oversight was that, for the intersexed child, 'assigning sex reinscribe[s] the traditional understanding of sex as a fixed, dichotomous system'.[73] Money, in effect, 'further entrenched the power of biomedicine over intersexed lives,' and therefore, as Banner argues:

> became an extension of the nineteenth century's consolidation of medical authority into the hands of men, especially as that authority was used to define masculinity and femininity and claimed its justification through such work.[74]

When her difference is revealed to Callie, however, she realises Dr Luce's plan is to 'make' her 'fully-female'. Unsure of her identity, she decides to run away, saying 'I don't think anyone knows for sure what is best'.[75] More importantly, she also asserts: 'I am *not* a girl. I'm a *boy*'.[76] Milton Stephanides, however, cannot 'fathom why [his child] wouldn't want to be fixed, cured'.[77] Banner explains his response by commenting that 'the main problem for intersexed babies comes from parents' responses of anxiety and shame to their children's perceived difference'.[78] Parents fear that without a 'true gender', the child will be unable to establish a stable sense of identity. Wilchins, however, argues that:

> Gendered identification is not an integral part, independent feature of experience, but two accepted sets of meanings through which we are called to understand ourselves and to be understood by others.[79]

Cal soon realises this, and comments that '[g]ender identity is very complex [and] not a matter of sheer genetics'.[80] For him, it is more than just about desire; rather it is about feeling comfortable with his own body and gender role, as well as how he wishes to function in society. As he becomes more comfortable as a male, Cal reflects: 'Not long ago I'd fretted over my failure to develop. That worry was gone now… I felt a vast relief'.[81] As already discussed, the *Bildungsroman* is usually characterised as being 'defined in terms of works by, about, and appealing to men'.[82] There is also little place for a heroine in such stories as she is usually seen as a rebel. This means that the place for an intersexual *Bildungsroman* is even more limited, and, certainly, previously unheard of. Perhaps, this is why 'choosing'

6. Conclusion

Retrospectively, Cal comments: 'I've lived more than half my life as a male, and by now everything comes naturally'.[83] But, despite this, Cal still admits that he needs 'the cigars, the double-breasted suits,' as they 'make [him] feel better'.[84] 'Identity is the effect of performance and not vice versa',[85] and this is why Cal still performs masculinity in his everyday life. As for the Stephanides family, we are told that, '[c]onfronted with the impossible, there was no option but to treat it as normal',[86] and Cal, thus, returns home, the prodigal son/daughter, having established an identity in 'a borderland or 'third space' where mixed races and intersex identities can co-exist'.[87] While 'texts interested in women do indeed rework the old *Bildungsroman* pattern',[88] it is hard to say exactly what *Middlesex* achieves for the intersexed individual on a grander scale than just tracing how Cal establishes his sense of belonging. Although, simply helping the intersexual movement progress from the 'margins of cultural awareness to the mainstream of popular culture',[89] *Middlesex* is certainly one of the first novels which proves beneficial to the intersexed individual's positioning in society, and, thus, as a *Bildungsroman*, depicts a successful journey of an individual's development from adolescence to adulthood. More importantly, the novel has, as Olivia Banner points out, 'helped ease the medical profession's transition from a policy of immediate surgical intervention to the acceptance of ambiguous genitalia'.[90] Considering that at the time of publication, in the United States alone, the number of infants having their genitals surgically altered for purely cosmetic reason stood at about 1,000 surgeries per year,[91] the novel could be considered to have had some real-world influence.

Many, like Morgan Holmes may accuse Eugenides of prescribing to 'retrenchant heterosexist politics',[92] as Cal decides to choose a gender which makes him feel comfortable instead of living as a non-gendered individual, while others believe that Eugenides opens a 'third space'. *Middlesex* is, indeed structured 'to provide readers with a prescient view of the end result that finds Calliope transformed from the impostor/female child, Callie, to the true male adult, Cal',[93] but it is more likely that Callie is an 'impostor' only to Cal, who describes the moments when she does resurface as similar to 'being possessed',[94] and not to Eugenides himself. The decision to assimilate into a gender role which makes Cal feel comfortable with himself appears to be the character's personal choice, and not a critique of any intersexed individuals who may choose to remain neither male nor female. After all, even the Intersex Society of North America (ISNA) does not advocate raising a child without a sex, 'which is a social impossibility anyway, at least right now'.[95]

'Belonging is an achievement at several levels',[96] and *Middlesex*, in the end, serves both as the tale of how Cal Stephanides forms his own, mostly stable, identity, and also as an affirmation of the aim which Cal says the intersex movement promotes: 'to convince the world – and pediatric endocrinologists in particular – that hermaphroditic genitals are not diseased'.[97] More importantly, the body of the intersexed child is not something to be considered 'monstrous'.

Notes

[1] Jeffrey Eugenides, *Middlesex* (London: Bloomsbury Publishing, 2003), 430.
[2] Ibid., 431.
[3] Ibid., 401.
[4] Ibid.
[5] Morgan Holmes, *Intersex: A Perilous Difference* (Selinsgrove: Susquehanna University Press, 2008), 70.
[6] Ibid.
[7] Anne Fausto-Sterling, 'The Five Sexes: Why Male and Female Are Not Enough' *The Sciences*, March/April 1993, viewed 28 April 2011, http://frank.mtsu.edu/~phollowa/5sexes.html.
[8] Georges Canguilhem, 'Monstrosity and the Monstrous', in *The Body: A Reader*, eds. Mariam Fraser and Monica Greco (London: Routledge, 2004), 187.
[9] Milton Diamond, '"Is it a boy or a girl?" Intersex Children Reshape Medical Practice', *Science & Spirit* (Sept/Oct 2007): 36.
[10] Ibid.
[11] Riki Wilchins, *Queer Theory, Gender Theory* (Los Angeles: Alyson Publications, 2004), 73.
[12] Ibid., 75.
[13] Eugenides, *Middlesex*, 294.
[14] M. H. Abrams, *A Glossary of Literary Terms* (Boston: Wadsworth Cengage Learning, 2009), 200.
[15] Ibid., 200-201.
[16] Annis Pratt, 'Women and Nature in Modern Fiction', *Contemporary Literature* 13.4 (1972): 476.
[17] Marianne Hirsh Gottfried, 'Defining Bildungsroman as a Genre', *PMLA* 91.1 (1976): 122.
[18] Susan Fraiman, *Unbecoming Women: British Women Writers and the Novel of Development* (New York: Columbia University Press, 1993), 7.
[19] Holmes, *Intersex*, 66.
[20] Ibid., 19.
[21] Vincent Leith, et al., *The Norton Anthology of Theory and Criticism* (New York: W.W. Norton & Co., 2001), 2487.
[22] Holmes, *Intersex*, 66.
[23] Eugenides, *Middlesex*, 3.
[24] Ibid., 414.
[25] Ibid., 437.

[26] Ibid., 441.
[27] Ibid., 41.
[28] Ibid., 42.
[29] Ibid., 125.
[30] Ibid., 226.
[31] Ibid.
[32] Ibid., 216
[33] Ibid., 224.
[34] Kathleen Perry Long, 'Hermaphrodites Newly Discovered: The Cultural Monsters of Sixteenth-Century France', in *Monster Theory*, ed. Jeffrey Jerome Cohen (Minneapolis: Minnesota UP, 1996), 191.
[35] Leith, et al., *Theory and Criticism*, 2485.
[36] Holmes, *Intersex*, 69.
[37] Eugenides, *Middlesex*, 411.
[38] Holmes, *Intersex*, 17.
[39] Eugenides, *Middlesex*, 520.
[40] Ibid., 240.
[41] Anoop Nayak and Mary Jane Kehily, 'Gender Undone: Subversion, Regulation and Embodiment in the Work of Judith Butler', *British Journal of Sociology of Education* 27.4 (2006): 467.
[42] Leith, et al., *Theory and Criticism*, 2485.
[43] Eugenides, *Middlesex*, 308.
[44] Ibid., 92.
[45] Wilchins, *Queer Theory*, 131.
[46] Eugenides, *Middlesex*, 312.
[47] Ibid.
[48] Long, 'Hermaphrodites Newly Discovered', 192.
[49] Eugenides, *Middlesex*, 264.
[50] Ibid., 265.
[51] Ibid.
[52] Holmes, *Intersex*, 91.
[53] Ibid., 93.
[54] Eugenides, *Middlesex*, 327.
[55] Robyn R. Warhol, 'Physiology, Gender, and Feeling: On Cheering Up', *Narrative* 12.2 (2004): 227.
[56] Eugenides, *Middlesex*, 19.
[57] Ibid., 41.
[58] Ibid., 388.
[59] Ibid., 327.
[60] Ibid.

[61] Ibid., 391.
[62] Leith, et al., *Theory and Criticism*, 2485.
[63] Eugenides, *Middlesex*, 479.
[64] Ibid., 430.
[65] Ibid., 431.
[66] Ibid., 428.
[67] Holmes, *Intersex*, 94.
[68] Nayak and Kehily, 'Gender Undone', 463.
[69] Holmes, *Intersex*, 66.
[70] Wilchins, *Queer Theory*, 130.
[71] Eugenides, *Middlesex*, 437.
[72] Olivia Banner, '"Sing Now, O Muse, of the Recessive Mutation": Interrogating the Genetic Discourse of Sex Variation with Jeffrey Eugenides' *Middlesex*', *Signs* 35.4 (2010): 847.
[73] Ibid.
[74] Ibid.
[75] Eugenides, *Middlesex*, 438.
[76] Ibid., 439.
[77] Ibid., 466.
[78] Banner, 'Sing Now', 862.
[79] Wilchins, *Queer Theory*, 131.
[80] Eugenides, *Middlesex*, 464.
[81] Ibid., 452.
[82] Fraiman, *Unbecoming Women*, 3.
[83] Eugenides, *Middlesex*, 41.
[84] Ibid.
[85] Vicki Bell, *Performativity & Belonging* (London: Nottingham Trent University, 1999), 3.
[86] Eugenides, *Middlesex,* 516.
[87] Francisco Collado-Rodríguez, 'Of Self and Country: U.S. Politics, Cultural Hybridity, and Ambivalent Identity in Jeffrey Eugenides's *Middlesex*', *The International Fiction Review* 33 (2006): 71-83.
[88] Fraiman, *Unbecoming Women*, 12.
[89] Holmes, *Intersex*, 22.
[90] Banner, *Sing Now*, 844.
[91] Wilchins, *Queer Theory*, 74.
[92] Holmes, *Intersex*, 94.
[93] Ibid., 92.
[94] Eugenides, *Middlesex*, 41.
[95] Wilchins, *Queer Theory*, 74.

[96] Bell, *Performativity & Belonging*, 3.
[97] Eugenides, *Middlesex*, 106.

Bibliography

Abrams, M. H. *A Glossary of Literary Terms*. Boston: Wadsworth Cengage Learning, 2009.

Banner, Olivia. '"Sing Now, O Muse, of the Recessive Mutation': Interrogating the Genetic Discourse of Sex Variation with Jeffrey Eugenides' *Middlesex*'. *Signs* 35.4 (2010): 843-867.

Bell, Vicki. *Performativity & Belonging*. London: Nottingham Trent University, 1999.

Canguilhem, Georges. 'Monstrosity and the Monstrous'. In *The Body: A Reader*, edited by Mariam Fraser and Monica Greco, 187-293. London: Routledge, 2004.

Cohen, Jeffrey Jerome. 'Monster Culture (Seven Theses)'. In *Monster Theory*, edited by Jeffrey Jerome Cohen, 3-25. Minneapolis: University of Minnesota Press, 1996.

Collado-Rodríguez, Francisco. 'Of Self and Country: U.S. Politics, Cultural Hybridity, and Ambivalent Identity in Jeffrey Eugenides's *Middlesex*'. *The International Fiction Review* 33 (2006): 71-83.

Diamond, Milton. '"Is it a boy or a girl?" Intersex Children Reshape Medical Practice'. *Science & Spirit* (Sept/Oct 2007): 36-38.

Eugenides, Jeffrey. *Middlesex*. London: Bloomsbury Publishing, 2003.

Fausto-Sterling, Anne. 'The Five Sexes: Why Male and Female Are Not Enough'. *The Sciences*, March/April 1993. Accessed 28 April 2011.
http://frank.mtsu.edu/~phollowa/5sexes.html.

Fausto-Sterling, Anne. 'The Five Sexes Revisited'. *The Sciences*, Jul/Aug 2000. Accessed 28 April 2011.
http://www.neiu.edu/~lsfuller/5sexesrevisited.html.

Fraiman, Susan. *Unbecoming Women: British Women Writers and the Novel of Development.* New York: Columbia University Press, 1993.

Gottfried, Marianne Hirsh. 'Defining Bildungsroman as a Genre'. *PMLA* 91.1 (1976): 122-123.

Holmes, Morgan. *Intersex: A Perilous Difference*. Selinsgrove: Susquehanna University Press, 2008.

Leith, Vincent et al., eds. *The Norton Anthology of Theory and Criticism*. New York: W.W. Norton & Co., 2001.

Long, Kathleen Perry. 'Hermaphrodites Newly Discovered: The Cultural Monsters of Sixteenth-Century France'. In *Monster Theory*, edited by Jeffrey Jerome Cohen, 183-201. Minneapolis: University of Minnesota Press, 1996.

Nayak, Anoop and Mary Jane Kehily. 'Gender Undone: Subversion, Regulation and Embodiment in the Work of Judith Butler'. *British Journal of Sociology of Education* 27.4 (2006): 459-472.

Pratt, Annis. 'Women and Nature in Modern Fiction'. *Contemporary Literature* 13.4 (1972): 476-490.

Warhol, Robyn R. 'Physiology, Gender, and Feeling: On Cheering Up'. *Narrative* 12.2 (2004): 226-229.

Wilchins, Riki. *Queer Theory, Gender Theory.* Los Angeles: Alyson Publications, 2004.

Rowan Roux is an M.A. candidate at Rhodes University, South Africa. His dissertation focuses on trauma and memory in contemporary South African fiction.

Who Mourns for Godzilla? *Gojira* and De-Asianization of Post-War Japan

Steven A. Nardi and Munehito Moro

Abstract
In its 1954 Japanese release the original *Gojira* terrified audiences. Far from being seen as a camp farce, it was recognized as tapping into the terror of not only the atomic bombings (then less than ten years in the past), but also a national anxiety over the Japan's post-war vulnerability. The film reflects the modern, high-tech society emerging in post-war Japan, but it is also symptomatic of the historical and ideological contradictions that the country faced. These dislocations are particularly evident in the way gender and memory are treated in the film. Godzilla is portrayed as an inhuman thing, and so comes to stand for elements that have been foreclosed from the gender matrix and from the historical memory. As the film concludes, the old systems and agents of imperialism are purged, and the future of the nation emerges through the production of a young couple. The film finally offers a fantasy in which it resolves the ideological contradictions of Japanese society – purging the memory of its wartime crimes and adopting an identity as a nation dedicated to peace. The extended sequence of mourning that ends the film is particularly resonant here. The mourned object is ostensibly Serizawa, the hero scientist who finds a means to kill the monster, but monster and hero are tightly interwoven. Rather than presenting the triumphant overcoming of an invading force, the film at last portrays a psychic substitution in which its faceless wartime victims (represented by Godzilla) are finally mourned for through the figure of Serizawa.

Key Words: Japan, media, gender, Asia-Pacific War, imperialism, Godzilla, mourning, melancholia, Japanese history.

*****

1. Introduction

When Terry Morse's *Godzilla: King of the Monsters* was released in the United States in 1956 it was a hit, but as a camp icon; but in its Japanese release the original *Gojira*[1] terrified audiences. Our focus here is on this 1954 original. Far from a farce, it was recognized as tapping into the terror of not only the atomic bombings (then less than ten years in the past), but also a national anxiety over the Japan's post-war vulnerability. Occupied by a foreign army for the first time in its history, Japan faced crises the way the nation understood its identity, and in the way that the massive social dislocations flowing from the war were remaking the national social fabric. This is particularly evident in the way gender was organized. In its Japanese release the film plays on those anxieties, but also constructs a narrative of post-war Japan as risen entirely new. The film is to be taken as a symptom of the historical and ideological contradictions that the country faced, and it offers a fantasy resolution in which those contradictions could be resolved. Godzilla is a native of Japan, and even more, a native of the moment it emerged.

Ten years prior to *Gojira*'s release, Japan had been an imperial power. Since the late nineteenth century, the nation had been expansionist – absorbing first Okinawa, then Taiwan, Korea, and in the thirties and forties parts of China and South East Asia as colonies. In the 1954 film Godzilla's emergence is a symptom of this loss, and the ideological reorganization that the nation went through as it confronted the sudden rejection of the ideological underpinnings that had created the modern expansionist state in Japan, and the social ferment that emerged as those ideological supports collapsed. Godzilla's presence destabilizes both the gender matrix and the ideological notions of political citizenship that structure Japan. As such, the monster enables a realignment of the meaning of gender, as well as a political shift. In the film's fantasy romance, the post-war nation had to undergo destruction by the monster to emerge as a new whole. In a way, the monster is a cry for Japan's taking account of its expansionist deeds.

2. Border Violations

In one of the first reviews of *Gojira*, a reviewer in the Japanese newspaper compared the film with the 1933 US movie King Kong, unfavourably. The criticism revolved around the kind of monster Godzilla is. 'The film's obvious flaw,' the critic writes, 'is that Godzilla does not show any personality at all.' In contrast, 'King Kong [...] presented the tragic character of the monster [....] However, Godzilla is frigid and far from being charming. No sense of tragedy can be seen there that it was driven out of the peaceful nest because of the H-bomb experiment.'[2] In hindsight, the contrast to King Kong seems not a flaw but the very point of the film. While Kong is indelibly human, Godzilla is impersonal. Kong is sympathetic because his rampage is motivated by emotions we can empathize with – revenge, love, fear. The giant ape is an embodiment of unrestrained masculine eroticism, complete with a blond starlet as a love interest. Godzilla, on the other hand, without explanation or reason thunders directly into the heart of Tokyo and destroys it ruthlessly. There are no recognizable human emotions to motivate its actions; unlike Kong, Godzilla is inhuman, faceless, elemental.

One manifestation of this is that Godzilla's refusal of the basic attributes of gender. Unlike the obviously sexualized Kong, Godzilla can be addressed by neither 'he' nor 'she.' In the film the monster is referred to almost only by name, and never grammatically gendered (this is partly because of the Japanese linguistic custom, by which creatures are seldom called with gendering pronouns). The monster can be, and should be, called only as 'it,' in the strict psychoanalytical parlance of Es or Id. In other words, the monster does not yield to the heterosexual matrix of assertive male and passive female.

In Rowan Roux's essay on Jeffery Eugenides's novel *Middlesex* (included in this volume), Roux analyses the socially ambiguous status of 'hermaphrodites,' that is, intersexed individuals. According to Roux, hermaphrodites have the bodily conditions elusive to the dichotomous framework of sexuality, such as the absence of noticeable, intelligible genitalia. Similarly, Godzilla does not at all show any sign of gender. In a sense, Godzilla's unique body could be seen as that of the intersexual. However, it is too hasty a move to identify the condition of monstrosity with the corporal unintelligibility. Intersexed individuals, as Roux elucidates, keep negotiating with the gender matrix in the developmental process of their life; intersexed individuals are not monstrous because of the very struggle against and performative interaction with the gender norm that (dialectically) make them human.

What gives Godzilla the precise status of the monstrous is, therefore, not only its sexually unintelligible body but also its utter lack of interaction with the gender norm. In other words, Godzilla undergoes no developmental process in which it interacts with the norm (the monster knows no dialectics that makes one a human; it affects the norm, but remains immune to the counter-effect). In fact, the film repudiates any anthropomorphous attempt to read the monster as a gendered being. Near the beginning of the film, an old man on a remote island explains to a reporter that the island people used to sacrifice virgins to the monster to placate it, the practice which has ceased to exist for a long time. The old man believes that the cessation of the (feminine) sacrifice has angered the (male) monster. As argued below, the film gives no credence to this old-fashioned, gendering discourse. The film does not take seriously the necessity of sacrifice precisely because the discourse misses the ungenderable nature of Godzilla, which makes it all the more monstrous. By mercilessly excluding the gendered view on the monster, the view that the monster can be gendered, the film allows Godzilla to have no performative interaction with the norm. This is the line by which Godzilla is demarcated even from intersexed individuals, the line between humanity and monstrosity.

It is not so much that Godzilla exists outside borders, but that the monster creates them. The monster is understandable best through Derridean terms, as what he calls a supplement. The meaning of the word 'supplement' is paradoxical, he points out. A 'supplement' is something that, once added to another part, creates a whole. 'It culminates and accumulates presence,' Derrida writes.[3] Yet the same term is used for something that is extra, something added to a whole. In that sense, Derrida writes, the supplement 'adds only to replace. [...] As substitute, it is not simply added to the positivity of a presence, it produces no relief, its place is assigned in the structure by a mark of emptiness.'[4] In this formulation, Godzilla is a supplement. It is nothing but the margin encroaching upon the national body of Japan, demanding the re-organization of the latter in terms of the sexual arrangement in the social context. Precisely because of its being outside the grid of sexuality, it provides a drive for the society to change into something new.

In March 1954, the exposure of a fishing boat Lucky Dragon Five to a lethal dose of radiation from an American nuclear test on Bikini Island caused a scandal across Japan, followed by a surge in the anti-nuclear movement.[5] Because the film is widely known to have been inspired by the incident, *Gojira* has been associated with anti-nuclear sentiments, anti-American feeling, or with a generalized anti-war feeling. Nancy Anisfield summarizes this tradition of critique as 'Humans made the bombs. The bombs created the monsters. The monsters punish the humans.'[6] In general, these arguments assume that the film is anti-American, and so the monster represents an invader, coming from outside of Japan.

The film, however, conspicuously avoids taking an obvious shot at the United States; it is never revealed which country conducted the experiment that enraged the monster. Critics, particularly American ones, have often been puzzled by this aspect of the film. And there are many comments in the film to demonstrate that the monster has a much more complicated relationship to the nation. Professor Yamane, the palaeontologist who identifies Godzilla as a dinosaur driven out of its nest by the H-bomb experiments, argues that Godzilla is a distinctly Japanese creature: it is 'a precious life form manifested only in Japan.'

It is not clear, in other words, from where the monster originates. Even the etymology of the name 'Godzilla' has twin origins; one from inside Japan, and one from without. It is a combination of a Japanese word, 'kujira' (whale) and a foreign word, 'gorilla.' One origin, from outside Japan, is of course the nuclear test. But there is a second origin story in which the Godzilla emerges from Japan's mythological roots. On Ohto-jima, the fictional island where the monster first appears, we hear that Godzilla has been haunting the island through the centuries. We are told by an old fisherman that the monster has returned because the old rituals of sacrificing virgins to it have been abandoned.

Despite the old man's story, the island is not easily read as a mythical pre-history. While an island like the one that Kong inhabits represents geographical otherness as the outside of civilization, Godzilla's island sits in an in-between state – neither inside nor outside Japan. The island is filled with allusions to the past; people dwelling there are mostly old peasants and fishermen in ragged clothes and speaking in a regional dialect. But the voice of that past – in this case the old man – is marginalized; while some islanders are summoned to the Diet's committee in which Yamane first makes his appearance, the old man who has long known of the monster is absent and his mythological explanation never mentioned again.

The geography of the island is similarly unclear; it is vaguely located in the south of Tokyo across the sea. The monster, therefore, emerges from a gap in knowledge, where the past fades into oblivion and the peripheral region is out-shined by the glamour of the metropolis. The island forms a rupture at the periphery of the nation through which the faceless other pays a visit.

On the face of it, the old man's story would seem to ally Godzilla with a deeply conservative, mythologized ideal of Japan's tradition (the monster is wreaking vengeance on those who would abandon the past). Similarly, critic Kato Norihiro sees the monster through a nostalgic and nationalistic lens. Godzilla, Kato argues, embodies the return of Japanese soldiers killed in the Asia-Pacific War: the angry dead return. He compares the war dead to the Freudian uncanny, and the return of a once-familiar object. For Kato, the monster embodies a remnant of Japanese empire buried with the war heroes in Yasukuni shrine, the national institution that enshrines the war dead, and so a history that retains a death-grip on the present. Kato writes:

> Godzilla first appeared out of the blue on the screen as the fearful, spine-chilling 'uncanny' in 1954. Even its producers could not have understood what they had been making. Why does this film mesmerize us so strongly? I believe it is because of the defence mechanism among Japanese that averts our eyes from the 'uncanny,' the mechanism whose working is echoing in such common explanations as 'because it is an anti-nuclear movie' or 'because it is about anti-war movements and the pursuit of peace.'[7]

The uncanny, for Kato, explains why Godzilla focuses his attacks only on Japan. It haunts the national ego. The changing character of the monster, from the terror of *Gojira* to the domesticated friendly Godzilla later, Kato argues, represents Japan collectively working through its historical trauma. The monster had to be 'tamed' and 'sterilized'[8] so that the people could come to accept he past that it represents. Godzilla, in other words, suggests the lingering grip of the imperial era.

Kato's argument is convincing to the degree that the monster seems to represent something unresolved in the national psyche. Whether because humans have disturbed the natural order, or because Japan has left its war dead un-mourned, Godzilla's destruction feels like a rough kind of justice.[9] But the unresolved force that Godzilla represents does not simply seem to be a naive, nostalgic longing for the imperial past. It is not for nothing that the revelation of Godzilla's origin in Japan's ancient mythology is shunted aside – put in the mouth of an old man whom the crowds tease for being backwards. 'Oh again you babble about that so-called Godzilla, old man,' says one of the island girls upon hearing his account. The Japan Kato recalls nostalgically is a leftover dream that only occupies the old.

Against Kato's suggestion, it could be better said that the monster represents the return of the emperor's faceless victims in other Asian nations, rather than his dead soldiers. Historian John Dower, in *Embracing Defeat*, notes that the victims of the Japan's soldiers represented an extremely difficult loss for the nation to come to terms with. Dower writes, 'The millions of deaths inflicted by the Emperor's soldiers and sailors [...] remained difficult to imagine as humans rather than just abstract numbers. The non-Japanese dead remained faceless. There were no familiar figures among them.'[10] Godzilla embodies that faceless presence, a presence that remains excluded also from the post-war politico-ideological framework.

In this light the geography of the monster's island makes more sense. The island, physically remote and culturally backward, suggests a residual trace in the present of imperial Japan and its colonies. It is the outside sneaking into the post-war universe of Japan: a colony within the country, a disruption at the national margin. It floats in an unspecified ocean, and as such fixes the memory of imperial Japan within a kind of cloudy half-remembered story. The nation's links to Asia, only ten years ago defended to the last, are pushed out beyond the field of intelligibility projected by the newly technological post-war Japan.

3. The New Japan

In another key aspect, the film diverges from Kato's argument. The Japan of *Gojira* is free of nostalgic attachments. To the contrary, *Gojira* celebrates the cutting-edge modernity of a new society saturated by media technology. The Japan of the film, though seemingly set in the present, is in an alternate present, a new Japan. This Japan is fully rearmed, fielding modern tanks and airplanes and so apparently unhampered by Article nine of the constitution, the US-imposed disarmament clause. In this Japan, there is no foreign military left behind, nearly no foreign presence at all. The super-connected, ethno-techno-logical society the film portrays appears to be complete within itself.[11]

That field of technological heightening is most evident in a rarely observed habit of the film: the images of electronic media that serve as a recurrent trope in the film. Images of spinning printing presses, close ups of radio towers and speaker grills, and radio operators punching at buttons serve as transitions between many scenes. The media perspective is the point of view of the film itself. Throughout the film, reporters appear as characters, advancing the story and filling in plot holes, while the camera often supplies the point of view. Godzilla's arrival in Tokyo is pulsed through radio transmission; people witness the burning destruction via television monitors; evacuation orders are announced through radio.

The electric media system, in particular, plays an outsized role in mediating the viewer's knowledge of the monster.[12] The media serve as the movie's eyes and ears. When Godzilla is first seen, the monster is shot from the neck up as it emerges over a ridge – a perspective equated with the camera-wielding journalists in the crowd of witnesses. There are many scenes of characters listening to reports of his movements. In Professor Yamane's house, a TV set occupies the centre of the living room from which he (sadly) learns the military action is commenced against the monster. There is also a slippage between media sources and the characters' points of view. While hundreds of female students sing a hymn for the dead, the scene is simultaneously transformed into the electric waves and reaches the underground laboratory where Dr. Serizawa agonizes over the use of his powerful weapon, offering a deciding factor to his decision. Although Serizawa never sees the sites of destruction by his own eyes, his TV set is able to influence what course of action he eventually has to take.

Godzilla's abrupt entry is portrayed as a disruption of the smooth superimposed surface created by the media net. In the initial scenes, the loss of radio contact is the only indication that something has gone very wrong. The crowd seems panicked by the failure of the otherwise seemingly gapless net of electronic visibility. In fact, throughout the film Godzilla is able to appear and disappear, dropping off and on the screens of the electronic system tracking him at will. The monster remains something outside of the new technological system of knowing.

The film is quite self-conscious about its play with the media's gaze. This is most strikingly true of the scenes where Godzilla attacks Tokyo. The skyline view of the city burning at first seems to be merely a camera angle, but it is later revealed to be footage shot from atop a television tower. We realize that the footage is a live broadcast being watched by the characters in the film. As Godzilla advances towards the tower, a TV reporter within, reporting live, screams: 'Dear audiences; this is neither a theatrical performance nor movie!' This self-referential joke would have been particularly striking in 1954; because of the care with which Tokyo was recreated in the film, the first audiences were often sitting in the same Tokyo movie theatres that were being destroyed on the screen. *Gojira* invites audience to confuse the camera's eye with a direct record of history, transforming the latter into an imaginary fiction. Providing a vicarious reality of life, the film weaves the nation into a different world: the world where the monster attacks, and as we argue below, the world where political responsibility is dealt with.

Perhaps the most striking characteristic of this New Japan is that although it is internally tightly connected, internationally it is cut off. Not only are the US and Soviet Union barely acknowledged, but the countries neighbouring Japan remain unmentioned as well. When the map of the country appears on the screen, it shows only Japan's archipelago – as if the rest of Asia did not exist.

This consistent exclusion is even stranger considering the historical context. Only a decade before the making of the film, the map of Imperial Japan included vast territories throughout Asia: Korea, Manchuria, part of China, Taiwan and countries in South-East Asia. The severance of Japan from its former colonies was not only a political move, but also the reinvention the psychological links that bound Japan to the region that the Empire used to dominate. What followed the war's end was, Lori Watt argues, 'the recasting of Japan from its position at the nexus of a multi-ethnic empire in East Asia into a new position as a mono-ethnic nation.'[13] According to historian James J. Orr, in the decade after the end of the war a gradual shift happened in the way war responsibility was understood in Japan. By 1954, the year *Gojira* is released, the country was reinventing itself as yet another victim of the war, shedding the militarist past and burden.[14]

According to Orr, one of the key moments in the shift to victim consciousness was the Lucky Dragon Five incident that also inspired the script of *Gojira*.[15] In the aftermath of that incident, the anti-nuclear movement in Japan gained force. Japan's post-war identity shifts from being formed by its aggressive actions, and becomes formed by its atomic victimhood. Orr writes, 'it was in the realm of antinuclear pacifism that Japanese war victimhood was most easily detached from Japanese wartime aggression.'[16]

In the mid-fifties, Japan discovered that it could assert a special status and moral authority in the world community as the only people ever to suffer an atomic bombing. This was evident in the goals of the anti-nuclear movement, which relied in its early years on a sense of Japan as having been given a unique dedication to peace from the aftermath of Hiroshima and Nagasaki.[17] This thread of thinking is apparent in *Gojira*, for example in the characters' frequent ruminations about the special role that Japan gains from the monster's attacks. In the film's final minutes, Professor Yamane draws a moral from the attack and Godzilla's death; mankind must change or anticipate Godzilla's rebirth.

4. Gender Reorganization

In *Gojira*, then, part of the drama is that the monster's destructive drive is also evidence of a creative will. As Godzilla tears apart the physical fabric of Japan, it exposes elements that were waiting for this act of clearing away to be born. This is particularly true of the monster's relationship to gender roles. Against the monster's un-genderable body, the norms of sexuality and family come apart. If the monster at first impedes the emergence of the new couple represented by Ogata and Emiko, in the end Godzilla facilitates this emergence. In this, Godzilla is a discursive disruption of the gender matrix, an un-genderable noise in the symbolic universe of Japan. Its presence leads to a new model for heterosexual practice (represented by Emiko and Ogata), while questioning the established ones (Yamane, Serizawa, and other marginalized figures).

We have already noted that the monster itself stands in a supplemental relationship to gender, to borrow Derrida's terminology. But surrounding the monster, within the New Japan, there are analogous figures of gender indeterminacy. Some aspects of this have been frequently noted, for example the scene in which the widow with small children, about to be crushed by the monster, longs to be reunited with her husband (who we assume was killed in the war). But there are other, less frequently noticed, such figures. The old man on the island, we have mentioned, is an example of a masculine authority uprooted and marginalized. As the Diet deliberates how to respond to Godzilla, a group of female politicians rail against their male counterparts. In two vignettes, first on a commuter train, and then on a cruise with her boyfriend, a young, fashionably dressed woman laments the current disaster. Her new social mobility seems to have drawn her directly into the path of the attacking monster. In these scenes we see the rapidity and variety of the changes in gender roles in Japan after the war. The film, then, presents a variety of gender roles, both male and female, for scrutiny. Which is appropriate in the new emerging social order?

Even the leading figures cannot escape such scrutiny. Professor Yamane himself is plagued by a series of incidents that reveal his paternal as well as social impotence in dealing with the monster. Despite the respect he receives, Yamane is portrayed as a weak, fading man.[18] In a subplot that shows how hollow Yamane's authority has become, Emiko, Yamane's daughter, and Ogata, his young friend, have fallen in love. Although Emiko has already been arranged to marry Dr. Serizawa (another friend of Yamane and a brilliant scientist who eventually provides a way to destroy the monster), Yamane is unable to prevent his daughter's scandalous attachment. Indeed, Yamane is entirely, and rather comically, unaware of the affair budding right under his nose. As the film concludes, he watches from the margins as the love triangle between Ogata, Emiko, and Serizawa unfolds.

In contrast to his inability to notice his daughter's wanderings, Yamane develops an attachment to Godzilla so obsessive it seems libidinal. Prior to Godzilla's second attack on Tokyo, Yamane insists on the need for studying Godzilla so furiously that he expels Ogata from his house for arguing that the monster should be killed. Yamane's sense of mission as a scientist comes at increasing odds with others, including his own daughter, whose conviction is shared with Ogata. As Yamane becomes more and more attached to the monster, his credibility as a scientist gets endangered further.

In a way, the monster serves as a replacement for Yamane's missing wife. While the film boasts unlimited supply of feminine figures ranging from hoarse island women to antagonistic feminist politicians, the mother figure that is supposed to occupy the centre of the feminine domain remains completely missing. However, the two phenomena – proliferation of femininity and the absence of the mother figure – should not be taken by any way coincidental. On the contrary, it is the very absence of Yamane's wife (the ultimate figure of maternity and reproduction) that allows the examination of alternative feminine models, while simultaneously discrediting Yamane's paternal authority. The unfolding process of the narrative is, therefore, nothing but a screening process, in which various types of gender are contested, combined, discarded to find eligible candidates for the future generation.

Ironically, it is the monster's attack that resolves these disorganized gender roles into a new coherence. Japan emerges from disaster as young and fertile. In fact, the very modernized couple of Ogata and Emiko emerges from what has seemed throughout the film as an impossible entanglement. The two lovers spend much of the film looking for and failing to find opportunities to announce their relationship to Emiko's oblivious father and taciturn betrothed. The love triangle subplot, in fact, has a rather comic undertone. In several scenes, Emiko and Ogata's bumbling attempts to reveal the truth are interrupted by Godzilla's attacks.

The monster therefore functions as a psychological and sexual block; their romance is infected by impotence.

Despite the comedy, the subplot also raises what was, in the 1950s, a serious social conflict. Although arranged marriages were still widely practiced among middle-class workers, dating was beginning to be popular among young people; Andrew Gordon notes that in the fifties slowly 'the ideal of the 'love marriage' won the day.'[19] Emiko's choice aligns her with this more modern lifestyle that was rapidly gaining force. In the context of this social change, as Kato points out, Serizawa represents the past, whereas Ogata the future.[20] Emiko's choice is an embrace of the love marriage, and implicitly an abandonment of tradition in which Yamane and Serizawa have lived.

Emiko's rejection of the past is most evident in the figure of Serizawa himself. In the love triangle's key scene, Emiko and Ogata confront Serizawa with his unwillingness to use the Oxygen Destroyer, a fearsome weapon that Serizawa has created, to save Japan. The question underlying the scene is exactly whose future using the weapon would create. Although Emiko had made a promise to Serizawa not to tell about the weapon to anyone, she has told the secret to her lover. Considering the fear Serizawa feels about his technology, it is so apparent that the use of it is equal to a death sentence to him; since he cannot allow his knowledge to be shared, the weapon can be used only once, with his death entailed.

When Serizawa finally relents, it is a dual acceptance. He acknowledges that the weapon must be used, and that he is surrendering Emiko to Ogata. In fact, Serizawa's resignation to his fate removes the need for Emiko and Ogata to even bother announcing their engagement. By the end of the film, having said nothing, they have been accepted as a couple not only by Yamane, but also by the media system watching as the weapon is employed. In effect, by removing himself, Serizawa solves the puzzle. In confronting his own status as impediment, Serizawa recognizes that his role is to reduce himself into vanishing supplement; he both brings the new whole into being, and renders himself superfluous. The future of the new nation and its new couple is one from which Serizawa is going to be expunged.

5. Resolution by Mourning

In the post-war world, Serizawa is uneasy and ambivalent. He is much more than simply a depressed or alienated personality. Serizawa has become something that, like Godzilla, cannot be integrated into the present. Like the monster, he is a brooding holdover from the past who has no place in the present. If Yamane's desire to keep Godzilla alive comes out of his libidinal substitution, Serizawa's refusal to use his invention is more grounded and pragmatic. More than Godzilla, it seems, Serizawa fears countries of the world, including Japan, wielding a new form of mass destruction. 'A-bombs against A-bombs, H-bombs against H-bombs; as a scientist, no, as a human being, adding the Oxygen Destroyer to humanity's arsenal is something I can't allow,' exclaims Serizawa. He is more afraid of exacerbating military ambitions, including Japan's imperialist expansionism, than he is of the monster.

Little wonder, then, that Serizawa's secret knowledge opens the only narrative discontinuity in the film. When he first reveals the Oxygen Destroyer to Emiko in his underground laboratory, the camera focuses on the horror in her face and then cuts away. We next see Emiko staggered but promising not to reveal what she has seen. At this stage, audiences are given no clue as to what kind of weapon was shown. Like Godzilla, Serizawa's point of view extends outside the rest of the film; the shift away from the invisible Oxygen Destroyer – the limits of the film's point of view – parallels Godzilla's ability to disappear. This is the only point where the film intervenes with a stagy trick: this opacity is a void of knowledge that echoes the monster's unknowable presence. In other words, the twisted narrative of the flashback structure shows that both Serizawa and the monster share an element of mysterious terror. And the only way to dispel that terror is to reveal the film's secrets.

Serizawa reluctance to make his weapon public has a historical correlate: the Emperor Showa's cowardice in ending the war and taking war responsibility for the atrocities committed by his army. Hirohito's delay in surrendering, even after Germany's defeat, when it became clear that Japan would eventually lose, is partly responsible for the catastrophic air raids on Japan's cities and the atomic bombings in Hiroshima and Nagasaki.[21] After the war, it was only collusion with the US occupation army that enabled him to survive in power and emerge as the symbol of the new peaceful nation.

To pursue the psychoanalytic analogy, Hirohito behaved like an analyst who never withdraws, and so seeks only to prolong the session. He does not dissolve the transference to allow his subjects/patients to have a healthy life; instead, the emperor successfully maneuverer to remain at the centre of nationwide authority, at least symbolically, for forty years after the defeat. Even when he renounced his divinity in the 1946 Declaration of Humanity, the renunciation was hedged and nuanced to preserve aspects of the claim.[22] His refusal to assume responsibility had a domino effect in Japan. Orr writes, 'The belief that the emperor had been abused by the militarists, suffered, yet nevertheless emerged from the dark war years with his nobility intact encouraged a similar sentimentality among his newly liberated subjects who might identify with him in their postwar construction of themselves as innocent pacifists.'[23] For some Japanese, the end of the American occupation of the mainland marked the last chance for Hirohito to resign gracefully and accept the ultimate responsibility for the disaster of the war.[24]

In contrast to the emperor Serizawa cannot evade his role in the war; the memory is engraved on his body (he has lost the eye during the war; Ogata reflects, 'If it had not been the war he had not had to suffer such a bad wound.'). This wound, together with his dangerous research, never let him forget Japan's imperial past. In this sense, while Godzilla embodies the faceless dead of Japan's wartime victims, Serizawa functions as a stand-in for the inhuman side of the emperor that needed to be forgotten – the divinity supposedly discarded by the Declaration of Humanity. Serizawa's self-sacrifice, therefore, along with Godzilla's death, completes the task of expunging the imperial system out of the new universe. He enacts the self-sacrifice that Hirohito should have done, even as the traces of Japan's victims are subsumed with the monster.

In this light, it seems natural that the film concludes with an extended mourning.[25] As the ensemble watches the oxygen destroyer's work from the ship, the mood turns sombre. This tone of loss, we have noted, seems out of place considering the damage that Godzilla inflicted. Although Serizawa's death is the surface justification, that is simply not enough of a reason. The characters barely speak of him specifically, instead focusing on more general angst, in particular, voicing the fear that humanity has opened a dangerous door which killing Godzilla does not entirely shut.

But the overlap of Serizawa and Godzilla makes this sense of loss more explicable. Working as the stand-in for the emperor, Serizawa offers himself to pacify the Asian victims, not the dead Japanese soldiers. When the monster is terminated, the process of mourning as a step toward healing can finally kick in. The object being mourned, in other words, is not incorporated into the newly formed social whole as a transitional object, but actually foreclosed from it. The post-war society builds itself upon the loss of the loss; it no longer recognizes what it is mourning for. Asian people's anger was, due to Serizawa's sacrifice, finally ceased to destroy the nation. The faceless, impersonal, aspect of both Godzilla and Serizawa is exactly what enables this act of mourning to be productive. Their physical death does not suffice; in addition to obliterating material bodies, the history of their existence must be consigned to the darkness of the national unconscious.

The ultimate object of mourning in *Gojira* is, therefore, Japan's ability to imagine itself connected to the region it used to dominate. The loss is that of memories of having been a part of Asia. Although the country was apparently striding forward, from out of the Asia from which Japan is pulling itself, a monster arrives. It is only the monstrous rupture, the disjunction of history, which reveals that something has been eclipsed. The nation finally gets untied from its colonies, drifting away from them as a newly fashioned society lying within the archipelago. And the nation would keep mourning for the region of the faceless, wishing its return even in a form of the monstrous.

Notes

[1] For the sake of clarity throughout the essay we refer to the 1954 film as *Gojira* (the title in Japanese) and to the monster as 'Godzilla.'

[2] Yomiuri Shinbun, 'Mimono wa tokushu satsuei dake: Kaiju eiga Gojira' (The Beauty is only in its Special Effects: King of the Monsters Godzilla), Nov. 3 1954.

[3] Jacques Derrida, *Of Grammatology*, trans. Gayatri Chikravorty Spivak. (Baltimore: John Hopkins UP, 1974), 144.

[4] Ibid., 145.

[5] Andrew Gordon, *A Modern History of Japan: From Tokugawa Times to the Present*, 2nd Edition (Oxford: Oxford UP, 2009), 272.

[6] Nancy Anisfield, 'Godzilla/Gojira: Evolution of the Nuclear Metaphor,' *The Journal of Popular Culture* 29.3 (1995): 53-62.

[7] Norihiro Kato, *Sayonara, Gojira Tachi* (Tokyo: Iwanami Shoten, 2010), 167-168.

[8] Ibid., 168.

[9] This kind of rough justice is especially invited by Godzilla's destruction of the Diet Building, as Jonathan M. Reynolds points out, a symbol of Japan's state legitimacy. See Jonathan M. Reynolds, 'Japan's Imperial Diet Building: Debate Over Construction of a National Identity,' *Art Journal* 55.3 (1996): 38-47. Reynolds is unsure, however, if this imagery is truly an attack on a symbol the Japanese nation itself; he writes, 'The Diet Building may serve as a symbol of nationhood, but it is a flawed and uninspired one' (38). Instead, the destruction can be understood as a sweeping away of the remnants of the non-functional past power structure.

[10] John W. Dower, *Embracing Defeat: Japan in the Wake of World War II* (New York: WW Norton & Company, 1999), 486-487.

[11] The common conception of the ego tends to show visual and technological implications. As Daniel C. Dennett argues in his 'Consciousness Explained,' the ego taken as a holistic, transparent entity is commonly but implicitly conceived as a theatrical model which he names 'Cartesian Theater.' In that model, the secluded ego is placed in front of a screen on which the outside world is shown. The national subjectivity newly emerging out of the media system undoubtedly has this quality; a viewer participates in the world through watching news on the electric monitor.

[12] Barak Kushner discusses the film itself as a media event in 'Gojira As Japan's First Postwar Media Event,' in *In Godzilla's Footsteps: Japanese Pop Culture Icons on the Global Stage*, eds. William M. Tsutsui and Michiko Ito (New York: Palgrave Macmillan, 2006), 21-40. Kushner notes that the release of the film was an international hit, and a return of Japan to the international stage (21). This is a different argument from noting that the film portrays a media event.

[13] Lori Watt, *When Empire Comes Home: Repatriation and Reintegration in Postwar Japan* (Cambridge, MA and London: Harvard University Asia Center, 2009), 5.
[14] See, in particular, chapter three in James J. Orr's *The Victim as Hero: Ideologies of Peace and National Identity in Postwar Japan* (Honolulu: University of Hawai'i Press, 2001).
[15] Ibid., 37.
[16] Ibid., 36.
[17] Orr summarizes this argument several contemporary sources that make this argument. For one example, discussing a 1951 article by Kuno Osamu, Orr summarizes, 'His argument also took advantage of the high moral ground of the victim who, by definition it seemed, could not be a victimizer. Victims, being disempowered, cannot be held accountable for the misuse of power; but they can empower themselves by bearing witness to their victimhood' (44).
[18] Yamane is played by the actor Shimura Takashi, a proverbial father-figure of wisdom in postwar Japan's film industry. Takashi, for example, played the samurai leader Kanbei in Akira Kurosawa's *Seven Samurai*, also released also in 1954. The strength of this typecasting gives Yamane's weakness a special resonance, but also renders it nearly invisible. Contemporary, even current, audiences would be apt to take the character at face value.
[19] Gordon, *A Modern History of Japan*, 255.
[20] Kato, *Sayonara, Gojira Tachi*, 151.
[21] The most aggressive account of Hirohito's direct responsibility for the war time actions done in his name is in Herbert P. Bix, *Hirohito and the Making of Modern Japan* (New York: Harper Collins, 2000).
[22] Dower, *Embracing Defeat*, 308.
[23] Orr, *The Victim as Hero*, 31.
[24] For an account of the persistent rumor that Hirohito would abdicate as the occupation ended, see Orr, pages 27-29. It was thought that, once the Americans withdrew, the emperor could assume responsibility for wartime actions without the fear of prosecution as a war criminal.
[25] There are many attempts to explain this mournful sequence in the English language critical literature. Most resort to historical arguments or broad statements about the difference between Japan and the West, for example, see Chon Noriega, 'Godzilla and the Japanese Nightmare: When "Them!" Is U.S.' *Cinema Journal* (1987): 67-68.

Bibliography

Anisfield, Nancy. 'Godzilla/Gojiro: Evolution of the Nuclear Metaphor.' *The Journal of Popular Culture* 29.3 (1995): 53-62.

Anderson, Mark. 'Mobilizing Gojira: Mourning Modernity as Monstrosity.' *In Godzilla's Footsteps: Japanese Pop Culture Icons on the Global Stage*, edited by William M. Tsutsui and Michiko Ito, 21-40. New York: Palgrave Macmillan, 2006.

Bix, Herbert P. *Hirohito and the Making of Modern Japan*. New York: Harper Collins, 2000.

Butler, Judith. *Bodies that Matter: On the Discursive Limits of 'Sex.'* New York & London: Routledge, 1993.

Dennett, Daniel C. *Consciousness Explained*. New York: Little, Brown and Company, 1991.

Derrida, Jacques. *Of Grammatology*. Translated by Gayatri Chikravorty Spivak. Baltimore: John Hopkins UP, 1974.

Dower, John W. *Embracing Defeat: Japan in the Wake of World War II*. New York: WW Norton & Company, 1999.

Gojira [Motion Picture]. Tanaka, Tomoyuki (Producer). Honda, Ishiro (Director). (2009). Japan: Toho Visual Entertainment.

Gordon, Andrew. *A Modern History of Japan: From Tokugawa Times to the Present*, 2nd Edition. Oxford: Oxford UP, 2009.

Kato, Norihiro. *Sayonara, Gojira Tachi*. Tokyo: Iwanami Shoten, 2010.

Kushner, Barak. 'Gojira as Japan's First Postwar Media Event.' In *Godzilla's Footsteps: Japanese Pop Culture Icons on the Global Stage*, edited by William M. Tsutsui and Michiko Ito. New York: Palgrave Macmillan, 2006. 21-40.

Noriega, Chon. 'Godzilla and the Japanese Nightmare: When "Them!" Is U.S.' *Cinema Journal* (1987): 63-77.

Orr, James J. *The Victim as Hero: Ideologies of Peace and National Identity in Postwar Japan*. Honolulu: University of Hawai'i Press, 2001.

Reynolds, J. M. 'Japan's Imperial Diet Building: Debate over Construction of a National Identity.' *Art Journal* 55.3 (1996): 38-47.

Watt, Lori. *When Empire Comes Home: Repatriation and Reintegration in Postwar Japan*. Cambridge, MA and London: Harvard University Asia Center, 2009.

Stephen Nardi, Medgar Evers College, CUNY.

Munehito Moro, International Christian University, Tokyo, Japan.

Part IV

Monstrosity, Racism (and Imperialism)

Spectres of Capitalism: Ghostly Labour and the Topography of Ruin in Post-Industrial Japan

Norihiko Tsuneishi

Abstract

The rocky outcropping of Hashima, off the coast of Nagasaki in Japan, has been a ghost island since its coalmines stopped operations in 1974. Abandoned ferroconcrete structures dot the islet, colloquially known as Gunkanjima (Battleship Island) in reference to its jagged skyline, which, seen from the distance, resembles a military vessel. The desertedness and dilapidation of the place has attracted many tourists in recent years, furnishing a prime example of what some Japanese commentators describe as a 'ruins boom.' However, the phantom nature of Hashima is a matter of more than just visual aesthetics. This chapter uses grotesque monstrous imageries, put forth by Mikhail Bakhtin, to analyse various kinds of 'labour' that, across Japan's modern history, have shaped Hashima into a deeply scarred physical space as well as a rich site of post-industrial phantasmagoria. This chapter looks at a contemporary movement by a group of former island residents to transform Hashima into a World Heritage Site. In monumentalizing Hashima's industrial debris, the memorial movement renders the island's grotesque past(s) into a symbolically flattened history. Memorialists seldom touch upon Hashima's significant role in building an imperial nation-state despite Hashima's ownership and day-to-day administration by the industrial conglomerate Mitsubishi, a de facto government agency until after WWII. Disquietingly, the movement submerges various labours, including that of wartime colonial subjects who worked like slaves in Hashima's coalmines. Instead, the memorialists' narrative glorifies the post-war era when the island reached an economic zenith as a sort of always-already vanished ideal home. At the same time, the memorial movement commodifies Hashima even further as a tourist attraction, extracting 'spectral labour' out of the island's historically more palatable forms of ghostliness. Capturing the kaleidoscope of historical as well as contemporary labours 'still existing' on the island, the chapter analyses modernity as a phantasm that haunts and continually re-enchants Japan's capitalist landscape.

Key Words: Urban ruins, history, colonialism, tourism, grotesque monstrosity, spectral labour.

*****

This is the story of an abandoned battleship, tossed out off the coast from Nagasaki in Japan. This dead military vessel had never sailed to any war fronts when it was still 'alive,' nor had it moved since it was born at the dawn of the twentieth century. From the outset, even before its birth, the ship remained in the same spot. Anchored in the midst of ocean, the very extremity of Nagasaki Peninsula, the dead battleship has patiently been fighting against the brutal waves and strong winds emanating from the East China Sea. The ship never sailed elsewhere because it was originally a natural rocky outcrop, and in fact, it still is a small island called Hashima (Periphery Island). The islet, during the course of its history, was forcibly turned into a grotesque monster – a mixed breed of island/battleship, or nature/machine – floating like a flickering mirage on the sea. This is the story of that phantasmagoric metamorphosis.

1. Introduction

The Angel of History, the protagonist of Walter Benjamin's historical materialism, sees the past as the colossal debris of a single catastrophe, which keeps 'piling wreckage upon wreckage.' [1] Despite the angel's attempt to awaken the dead from the dilapidated landscape of history, the storm emanating from paradise, which Benjamin calls progress, keeps blowing him away from it, submerging the dead further into the heap of rubble. This imagery – history as the catastrophic ruin of the dead – provides a fantastical gateway to unravel the body of Hashima.

Hashima is colloquially known as Gunkanjima (Battleship Island) in reference to its jagged skyline delineated by abandoned ferroconcrete structures, which, seen from a distance, resembles a military vessel – in particular, the pre-war Japanese ship *Tosa*. The locale has been a ghost island ever since its coal mines, under the day-to-day administration of Mitsubishi, stopped operations in 1974. In contrast to the growing as well as inapproachable ruins of Benjamin's angel, Hashima is always there waiting to be seen, yet constantly crumbling under ceaseless exposure to the salty waves and breezes from the ocean. Yet, while drifting toward its own disappearance, this 'already-dead-battleship' is simultaneously growing into a very gay thing, as the desertedness and dilapidation of this locale has attracted many tourists in recent years, furnishing a prime example of what some Japanese commentators describe as a 'ruins boom (*haikyo buumu*)' which began in the 1990s. Photographs of Hashima's ruins have appeared in various magazines, fanzines, photo-book and personal Internet-based travelogues, portrayed as 'Floating Abandoned Metropolis (*kaijo-haito*),'Hidden Monster Island' or 'Ruins of Forbidden Island.'

Just as, par Munehiro Moro and Steven Nardi's investigation in their essay, Godzilla embodied 'faceless victims' of Japan's wartime colonialism through the electronic eyes, the phantom nature of Hashima consists of more than its appearance on the media. The appearance of the island, like Benjamin's Angel of History, internalizes its own catastrophe and buries various dead beneath the ruined topography. What we can hear now is the moaning of the invisible dead taking their ghost walks. In order to give contours to the spectral nature of this locale, this chapter uses the grotesque monstrosity postulated by Mikhail Bakhtin as a theoretical optic to analyse various kinds of labour that have shaped Hashima into a deeply scarred physical space as well as a phantasmagoric site.

Focusing on a contemporary movement by former island residents to monumentalize Hashima into a World Heritage Site, the chapter argues that their labours transmogrify the grotesque history of this locale to a symbolically flattened historical narrative through the institutional framework of UNESCO. In contrast, this analysis conceives Hashima as a grotesque landscape, unfolding its polymorphic as well as its transformative characteristics. The essay then applies this landscape image to render the isle's equally grotesque past in order to debase the sanitized gaze of the memorialists, creating gaping holes within their two-dimensional history. The essay does so by deploying the downward movement – Bakhtin's method of grotesque realism – of human excrements, which shift our historical gaze toward the bodily lower stratum of the polymorphic island. Thus the investigation reaches the ghost of colonial subjects, mainly Koreans, who were taken to Hashima virtually as slaves during WWII and have been wriggling beneath the deserted topography ever since. Following this 'excavation,' the essay looks at the way in which that very abyss, the colonial history of the island, is represented in the tragic novel written by Han Soosan, which unlocks multivalent colonial monstrosities that were orchestrated by Japan's wartime imperial capitalism.

The last section examines the memorialists' portrayal of post-war Hashima, when it reached an economic zenith, as their always–already vanished ideal home. While superscripting over the grotesque history and submerging the dead colonial workers, memorialists superimpose this phantom image of their desired 'home' – not only to save but also to re-modernize this locale as a tourist attraction by extracting ghostly labour from the island's historically more palatable forms of ghostliness. Activated by Benjamin's 'the storm from paradise' – historical progress – Hashima becomes an undead-battleship setting off for its spectral voyage to the mythical sea of post-industrial capitalism, reincarnated as a tourist commodity. Capturing these various forms of monstrosity, the chapter analyses modernity as a phantasm that continually re-enchants Japan's capitalist landscape.

2. Hashima: The Grotesque Body

In *Rabelais and His World*, Mikhail Bakhtin identifies transformative and polymorphic as characteristics of the grotesque body. In contrast to the static and individuated body of the new canon that emerged in sixteenth-century France with the advent of more censored languages – 'an entirely finished, completed, strictly limited body'[2] – the grotesque body, which had existed until the fifteenth century, is constantly in the state of becoming and at the threshold between species. The grotesque body is dynamic, ambiguous, and thus always incomplete, without an end, operating against the more institutionalized body of the new canon. The following sections will apply the image of these two opposing bodies to examine Hashima's history.

Given this image, Gunkanjima's topography is quintessentially the embodiment of a becoming body. The original shape of this reef in plan is described by Goto Keinosuke of the memorialist group as the 'fossil foot of a dinosaur,'[3] with a size of approximately 125m (east-west) x 300m (south-west). The island had been a natural uninhabited reef until coal was found on the site in 1810 by local fishermen. Since then, its footprint was gradually transmogrified in parallel with Japan's industrialization, which accelerated from the second half of the nineteenth century onward, turning the site into a manmade 'battleship.' To borrow Karl Marx's words, 'The mechanical monster . . . bursts forth in the fast and feverish whirl of its countless working organs.'[4]

Utilizing slag (*zuri*) produced from the assortment of coal, Mitsubishi launched a series of land reclamations to produce a flat plain attached to the original jagged landscape, which allowed for construction of various facility buildings required for the operation of the coal industry. This added area – a deck, so to speak – was guarded by colossal retaining walls, a hull protecting the circumference of the body of the battleship from raging waters that attack the site especially during the typhoon season. As a result, the size of the island grew to 160m (east-west) by 480m, three times larger than the original reef. Furthermore, reinforced concrete high-rise apartments, among the earliest of their kind in Japan, were constructed on the island as early as 1916. As those apartments and other structures started to look like superstructures or smokestacks of a ship, Hashima gradually became an in-between species – the mechanized island/naturalized machine. As such, by the 1920s, this precipitous artificial landscape gave Hashima an appearance resembling the Japanese military vessel *Tosa*. Their visual alignment was, as Brian Burke-Gaffney describes, 'so uncanny that a local newspaper reporter dubbed it *Gunkanjima* (Battleship Island), a nickname that soon replaced the official name in common parlance.'[5] The Battleship was finally born. New buildings continued to be built until the 1960s, further transforming the skyline of the island.

However, set adrift under the hegemony of Mitsubishi in 1974, Hashima lost its functional and thus its economic value, becoming nothing more than a ghost ship. Its abandoned concrete landscape was relentlessly exposed to sea wind and tossed in heavy swells. Seasonal typhoons often annihilated portions of its body. Without having any access to maintenance work, the structures on the island deteriorated, and in fact are growing more dilapidated at this very moment. As Kasahara Michiko puts it, the abandoned site is currently in 'a process of dying.'[6] Hashima thereby has been and always will be in a state of becoming.

Beyond the trait of transformability, Bakhtin's conceptualization of polymorphic landscape offers a crucial schema. As a grotesque body is open, rough and penetrable, it forms a flexible, if not ambiguous boundary, which 'leads beyond the body's limited space or into the body's depths.' Furthermore, Bakhtin continues, it presents 'mountains and abysses, such is the relief of the grotesque body; or speaking in architectural terms, towers and subterranean passages.'[7]

Hashima's physical topography indeed expresses this polymorphic landscape of high and low. The mining tunnels of the island go as deep as 1000m underground, creating an abyss, and yet the mine is colloquially referred to as *yama*, the mountain.[8] Furthermore, despite soaring concrete structures on the site, Hashima as a whole can be conceived as an underworld. The architectural historian Akui Yoshitaka expressed the difficulty in identifying the level on which he was standing when working on his land survey on the island. The spatial disorientation was caused due to the way in which each building was erected, jostling each other on the steeply rugged terrain and creating a gloomy labyrinth-like space. Consequently, for the purpose of the survey, Akui set up the virtual ground level of the island at the roof level of the buildings, which, as he describes, 'made it easier to understand the spatial composition as well as floor levels.'[9] This strategy conceptually reconfigured all the levels below the roof as underground space.

Hashima thus internalizes this elevation dialectic: an abyss that is mountain, and towers that are subterranean passages at once, or vice versa. Conceiving the *transformation* and *polymorph* as essential constructs of Hashima, the following sections use these theoretical categories in unfolding the historical topology of the artificial reef inside out. In doing so, the next section looks at the way in which the memorialists, a group of former residents, moulds the history of the island based upon the institutional criteria set forth by UNESCO in their attempt to turn this locale into a World Heritage Site, wherein Hashima's catastrophe – colonial history in particular – is conveniently buried underneath the heap of rubble. For this analysis, the chapter mainly interrogates their publications. As the storm from paradise ruthlessly keeps distancing Benjamin's angel from the historical ruin, making it harder to reach the dead, the memorialist puts the colonial pandemonium of this locale to sleep.

3. 'Universal': Memorialists' History

In 2003 a group of former residents of Hashima formed the NPO organization, Gunkanjima for World Heritage Site (*gunkanjima wo sekaiisan ni surukai*).[10] The inception of the project occurred at their reunion meeting in 1999, the first assembly since they left the island in 1974. It was also motivated by the visit made in 2002 by British industrial heritage expert, Stuart Smith, to the island along with other industrial sites that are interspersed throughout Nagasaki City.[11] In 2007, the site was recognized by the Ministry of Economy, Trade and Industry (METI) under the rubric Heritage of Industrial Modernization for the purpose of 'regional revitalization.'[12] Following this designation, the abandoned island has been valorised into a cultural site of the state, nominated by the Ministry of Culture in 2008 to the States Party's Tentative List for inscription on the World Heritage Site List, under the guidelines of UNESCO.

As part of their efforts, the group Gunkanjima for World Heritage Site made several publications on Hashima. The book *The Legacy of Gunkanjima* (Gunkanjima no Isan), published in 2005, was co-authored by Goto Keinosuke, professor at the University of Nagasaki, and Sakamoto Dotoku, a former resident of Hashima. Goto and Sakamoto are, respectively, the vice president and the president of Gunkanjima for World Heritage. The group also produced the catalogue, *Gunkanjima: The Memory of Living* (Gunkanjima: Sumikata no Kioku) in 2008.

The Legacy of Gunkanjima starts with a brief sketch of the formation of Japan's coal industry, and reveals an overview of Hashima's history. In the following chapter, they introduce Sakamoto's actual lived experience at Hashima during the 1960s, growing up there as a child. The book then highlights the distinctive urban as well as social characteristics of the island when the coal industry was still in operation, a period which has been attracting various scholarly works, ranging from architecture, urban engineering, and sociology to the history of industry. As a whole, these studies have become, as Goto claims, *gunkanjima-gaku* (Gunkanjima Studies). Lastly, the book concludes with the authors' argument for why Hashima is worth being considered a world heritage site, based on claims made in the body of the work.

While they make a valid claim considering the history of the island, their narrative can be also seen as the by-product of the criteria set forth by UNESCO. The memorialist version of the history is in a sense their construct of 'the impenetrable surface' of the island's history, utilizing the framework of the international organization.

The UNESCO World Heritage Centre states that 'to be included on the World Heritage List, sites must be of outstanding universal value and meet at least one out of ten selection criteria.' The list consists of six cultural and four natural criteria. Out of the former, Goto claims that Hashima will meet criteria 1, 4 and 5, which are defined by UNESCO as follows.

> I. to represent a masterpiece of human creative genius;
> IV. to be an outstanding example of a type of building, architectural or technological ensemble or landscape with illustrates (a) significant stage(s) in human history;
> V. to be an outstanding example of a traditional human settlement, land-use, or sea-use which is representative of a culture (or cultures), or human interaction with the environment especially when it has become vulnerable under the impact of irreversible change.[13]

Goto believes that Hashima, being 'a artificial island, rising in the middle of ocean as if a battleship,' satisfies criterion I. Japan's earliest ferroconcrete apartment buildings on the island, which 'shines brilliantly in the course of the history of Japanese architecture,' will qualify the island for criterion IV. Furthermore, he continues, Hashima, as a highly concentrated 'coal mining metropolis on the ocean,' signifies 'an outstanding example of a land use' that is 'representative of the culture of coal mining.' Goto summarizes:

> Gunkanjima, as a whole, embodies the outstanding example of the masterpiece of human creative genius. At the same time, as exemplified by the cluster of reinforced concrete high-rise apartments that entails significant historical and scholarly values, the island can be seen as 'cultural heritage,' which had demonstrated the efficient use of land in response to its restricted premise.[14]

Now, let's return to the earlier part of the book in depth. The authors introduce the history of Hashima in Chapter 2; and in the section 'Birth of Hashima' they stress the artificiality of the island, immediately discussing the land reclamations and the construction of retaining walls which protected the island from heavy waves during seasonal typhoons. They claim that the 'history of Hashima cannot be told without its battle (*tatakai*) against typhoons,'[15] foregrounding the battleship characteristic of the islet from its inception. What follows is their description of 'Japan's first reinforced concrete high rise apartments'; and the section ends with explaining how the island became colloquially referred to as Battleship Island due to its skyline. Thus, the birth of Gunkanjima in their discourse is constructed through the emphasis largely on the physical characteristics, noting the artificiality as well as 'Japan's first' concrete apartments on the island, elements that are part and parcel of UNESCO's criteria.

Briefly touching upon the structures of underground mining tunnels and the period during WWII, the rest of the chapter is dedicated to introducing the revitalized post-war era in the section entitled 'Life on Hashima' (*Hashima no seikatsu*). This section highlights how life on the island was improved through a series of spatial practices. For instance, in addition to retrofitting old buildings and erecting new ones, service water was secured by constructing undersea water pipelines connecting the island with the nearby land. A new pier was installed – as the big waves during typhoons destroyed previous piers – allowing for safer boarding and alighting to a packet boat, the only transportation that linked the islet to neighbouring areas. A town hall, retirement home, schools and various shops were built, creating a self-contained micro-metropolis; as the authors claim, 'the island had everything (*shima niwa nandemoari*).'[16] Despite its circumscribed place, inhabitants were still able to organize diverse recreational events. Here, the book emphasizes the distinctive 'land-use' aspect, which is expressed in UNESCO's criterion V.

After the illustration of Sakamoto's personal experience in Chapter 3, which will be discussed later in this chapter, Chapter 4 stresses the aforementioned Gunkanjima Studies to highlight the historical, scholarly and thus 'universal value' of this locus. This discussion is followed by the chapter that argues for making Hashima into a World Heritage Site. Thus, the book's portrayal of Hashima as a whole represents a strategic build-up to mould its history into UNESCO's heritage site framework, forming that 'closed, smooth' narrative which underplays, if not ignores, the intrinsically transformative and polymorphic character embedded in the history of Hashima. Instead, the abyss must be dug out to awaken the dead sleeping in the darkness.

In order to foreground this historical abyss, the disciplinary boundary of Gunkanjima Studies that the memorialists have set up provides at least a convenient entry point. Emphasizing the scholarly value of this locale, the authors list urban engineering, architecture, sociology and the history of industry as disciplines that emerged as part of Gunkanjima Studies. The book, however, does not seek other potential 'studies' that Hashima could entail. For example, discussing the concrete apartment structures as 'a type of building that illustrates significant stages of human history,' the memorialists situate the significant stage only within architectural history, but not within the much larger 'human history' to elicit the greater symbolic nature of these towering edifices. Or, while addressing the representation of culture, they merely focus on the culture of coal mining, but not on other potential cultures that one can extract from the history of these post-industrial ruins. This narrow focus can lead to a critique of their rather light touch on the history of the island during the war period, as Hashima could provide an ideal site for study of Colonial History, or of the Fascist Culture of Wartime Japan.

Kawamura Minato claims that Gunkanjima transformed into a locale that 'symbolized the Japanese militarism' and was 'at the core of *fukoku kyouhei* (enrich the country, strengthen the military) policy' that was promoted by the Meiji Government since the end of the nineteenth century.[17] The critical turn came in 1890 when the industrial conglomerate Mitsubishi Corporation took over the operation of the coal mining industry from the local clan, and Hashima, equipped with a modern mechanized coal mining technique, began producing the largest amount of coal among the neighbouring coal mining islands. Japan's industrialization heavily relied on coal energy from the last half of the nineteenth to the mid-twentieth century; and Gunkanjima, the 'fossil foot of a dinosaur,' became a 'battleship' for imperial Japan by the 1930s, steered by the de facto government agency Mitsubishi.[18]

Although *the Legacy of Gunkanjima* briefly touches upon the wartime period and how the island's mine produced a large amount of coal under the state policy 'Five Year Plan for Increase in Coal Production, Supply and Demand,' the book merely provides the numerical figures showing the production rate during the war period.[19] It does not fully uncover how Hashima insidiously became a state organ by pumping up the blood – coal – for the colonial economy, supported by its deadly labour from the underground depths, supplied in large part by colonial coal miners.

When the war intensified, the Japanese government promulgated the 'National Mobilization Law' in 1938 to cover a wartime shortage of labour, which 'established the structure that enabled the state power to mobilize a means of production and labour force.'[20] Furthermore, The National Service Draft Ordinance was proclaimed in 1939, by which mobilization of the population was fully enforced. As the law was also applied to all Koreans, who by then were already colonial subjects of the Japanese empire, consequently thousands of them, including teenagers, were 'recruited' to various munitions works to support Japan's wartime economy. Many of them were in fact abducted by Japanese or pro-Japanese Koreans and were sent to work sites where they laboured virtually as slaves. In other words, those recruited to the work force represented essentially 'forced labour.' As Oka Masaharu asserts, 'Japanese imperialists, without exception, sent Korean workers to the most difficult and brutal work sites, such as mines, engineering works, and constructions for military facilities, and sucked their sweat and blood by forcing them to work for twelve or even fifteen hours a day virtually as a beast of burden (*gyūba no youni kokitsukai*) .'[21] The chapter will revisit this image of Korean labourers as beasts, or dehumanized creatures, in a later section.

Between 1939 and 1945, over one million Koreans were mobilized as forced labourers. Many lost their lives due to various forms of colonial violence; some were killed by Japanese, some died due to harsh working conditions, and some committed suicide. About six thousand Koreans were 'killed' in mining work for Japan's empire during wartime. Hashima was no exception. By 1943, there were approximately 500 Korean and 240 Chinese slaves on the island, including women who worked as 'comfort women' at brothels administered by Mitsubishi – a fact conveniently dismissed from the memorialist 'human history.'[22]

The Legacy of Gunkanjima indicates that there were foreign labourers on Hashima during that time, stating that '[in 1939] Patriotic Labour Force, consisting of foreign labourers, such as Korean, were implemented.'[23] They also give the numbers of those foreign populations, describing them as 'coal miners.' However, the authors never used terms such as 'forced labour (*kyōsei rōdō*),' nor do they reveal the fact that the death rate of those colonial slaves exceeded, mysteriously, that of Japanese workers during the war-intensive years between 1944 and 1945. Hence, the 'lived' experience of those who worked in the island's underground tunnels as 'beasts' has been further buried beneath the memorialist 'universal' history.

Reintroducing Bakhtin as a theoretical optic, the following section investigates a particular gaze that the memorialists deployed to 'sanitize' the grotesque body of Hashima wherein its debased terrain – the subterranean space where the abovementioned catastrophe of wartime history took place – is cropped out. Simultaneously, the section traces the spatial passage that navigates us to the very basement, just as Bakhtin found 'the greatest treasures and the most wonderful things' in the underworld of Rabelais's literary space. Bakhtin claims that, through 'downward movement,' Rabelais directs the reader's gaze toward the underground, and this movement for Bakhtin is an essential gesture for grotesque imagery, turning upside down and inside out, or vice versa, any given established hierarchies (e.g., the God-centred universe during the medieval age). Being part and parcel of the downward movement, 'debasement,' he continues, 'is the fundamental artistic principle of grotesque realism; all the sacred and exalted is rethought on the level of the material bodily stratum or else combined and mixed with its image.'[24] Likewise, chasing the particular 'material bodily lower stratum' that vertically runs across Hashima, the following section defaces the 'sacred and exalted' image of the islet, constructed by the memorialist gaze. What follows is the portrait of Hashima in the grotesque realist manner.

4. Downstream: Dung and Urine

Hashima's topography indeed resembles the future world depicted in the science fiction novel *The Time Machine* by H.G. Wells. In this novel, the story takes place in the imagined world of the year 802701 A.D., comprised of underworld and upperworld connected through a series of interconnected wells. 'Ant-like' creatures called Morlocks inhabit the former and beautiful creatures called Eloi reside in the latter. This Wellsian topography of 'high and low' can also be found in Hashima's 'mountains and abysses' or 'towers and subterranean passages,' introduced earlier in this essay. Those two realms on the islet were, on the one hand, symbolically identical as the mine (abyss) was colloquially called *yama* (mountain). On the other hand, they were physically linked together through various passages, much like the connected wells in *The Time Machine*. For example, the elevator-like shaft, the so-called 'cage' that was located at the southeast part of the island, took the miners to the underground tunnels on a daily basis. The stairs within the ferroconcrete apartments connected the Island's subterranean-labyrinth-like lower realm to the upper floors of those towering edifices. Furthermore, each realm possesses temporal dimensions, as various inhabitants lived in these realms at different historical moments. Bridged by multiple 'connecting wells,' thereby, the two-sidedness of Hashima's elevation is tangled up with heterogeneous axes of time, conjuring up an intricate maze and, at the same time, offering multiple sightlines, so to speak. Despite this nature of the locale, however, the memorialist gaze is drawn largely toward the upperworld and projected from the post-war era, as if the spatio-temporal labyrinth of the underworld were to dissipate into a vanishing point of their perceptual memoryscape.

For example, in the introduction to the catalogue *Gunkanjima: The Memory of Living* (Gunkanjima: Sumikata no Kioku), the memorialists claim that 'although there will only be a mere memory with one person, once the former residents of Hashima gather around, they will awaken the collective memory of the island at its height of prosperity.'[25] 'The former residents' referred to here are those who lived on the island during the post-war era. In other words, their collective memory only resides in the era of Hashima's euphoric zenith, not in its grotesque abyss. Likewise, in *the Legacy of Gunkanjima*, it should be noted that the word 'life (*seikatsu*)' never appears before the section 'Life of Hashima' which illustrates the postwar era. The omission suggests there was no life existing on the island prior to WWII. In addition, the catalogue and Chapter 3 of the book start chronicling the life of Hashima by introducing the memory reposited in the island's towers – apartment Hall 65 (Patriotic Hall) and Hashima Elementary School – both of which were constructed at the eve of or after the end of WW II. Although these publications touch upon some buildings that were constructed in the pre-war period, including Hall 30 (1916), they foreground only the post-war memory that owns these spaces. Also, delineated through a peculiar perspective, their personified memoryscape seems to further flatten and sanitize the grotesque form of this locale, by only looking at the idealized surface. This is also exemplified in the 'eye-level' of Sakamoto.

Sakamoto and his family came to Hashima in the mid-1960s and lived for the most part on the top floors of towering concrete apartments. While nostalgically remembering the morning view of the ocean from the ninth floor of Hall 16, Sakamoto confesses, 'We have lived on the fourth floor of Hall 17 for a while, but, unlike the ninth floor, the room was damp and clammy, so I do not have much memory there.'[26] This gaze from above seems to weave together the group's post-war memoryscape. Sakamoto emphasizes air corridors as the distinctive architectural space on the island, as these 'allowed people to move from one building to the other without them descending to the ground level.'[27] Furthermore, he asserts that roof gardens were the key component for Hashima's community formation, functioning as the viewing platform, evening date route for young couples, and micro-agricultural site for school children.[28] Hence, although those are indeed quite remarkable spatial characteristics of this locale, the memorialist gaze is largely drawn to the top surface of this ruined topography, not the space underneath it.

However, there is one moment, among a few, where their flattened history plunges into the island's 'damp and clammy' space via the 'downward movement' of a Bakhtinian grotesque element – human excrements – hinting at the link between zenith and abyss. As Sakamoto explains the toilet system of the high-rise apartments, he points out that there were no flush toilets in his apartments. Instead, there were plopping toilets (*otoshi benjo*) on each floor connected through sewage pipes. Of this system without flushing water, Sakamoto writes:

> The people on the upper floor did not care much. However, as the lower the level is, the more human excrements (*mono*) were dropped along the sewage pipe, thus going to bathroom was always amidst the din. The lower it reached, the worse the smell and noise were.[29]

The dung and urine are considered by Bakhtin as 'the material bodily lower stratum,' connecting the body and the earth (or sea) and simultaneously embodying cosmic catastrophe, i.e., 'the destruction of the world by flood and fire.' Human excrements become for him the instrumental materials for the image of grotesque. Through laughter, writes Bakhtin, 'cosmic catastrophe represented in the material bodily lower stratum is degraded, humanized, and transformed into grotesque monsters. Terror is conquered by laughter.'[30]

Similarly, in the memorialists' narrative above, the dung and urine link the upper realm and the ground through its downward movement within the sewage pipes, which function just like the wells linking the upper and lower realms in Wells's future world. While still remaining in the post-war era and residing in the upper floors, the memorialists' sanitized gaze was at least subverted by the human excrement, shifting attention toward the island's lower stratum. In other words, their 'sacred and exalted' perspective of Hashima was debased by the downstream, summoning in effect the elevation dialectic of the island. Their memory thereby shows a glimpse of polymorphism – tower and abyss – from within. The downstream of dung and urine takes our gaze to the very bottom of Hashima, where 'cosmic catastrophe' – the dehumanization of coal miners by colonial violence – took place and left various traces on the bodies of its inhabitants, transmogrifying them into, like Wells's underworld Morlocks, grotesque subterranean beasts. While the topographies of Hashima and Wells's future worlds are isomorphic, however, the power structures embedded are diametrically opposed to each other. In Wells's novel the Morlocks, the offspring of the nineteenth-century proletariat, prey upon the once-capitalist Eloi as 'fatted cattle.'[31] Thus, the labour-capital relationship of power is reversed. In contrast, in the early1940s, while Hashima's upperworld people stayed in power, subterranean creatures remain as marginalized and dehumanized labour. The former mostly comprised Mitsubishi's personnel, while the latter included Korean slaves.

These slaves were often forced to labour at the harshest work site in Hashima's mining tunnels. These tunnels were too small for any mechanical equipment to fit in, so the miners instead needed to lie down with a pickaxe in their hand, manually digging out the coal. Trapped in the island cavity, many workers were killed by gas explosions or by roof cave-ins. In addition, they had to endure working at least 12 hours a day, and hundreds of them were packed into small, 'damp and clammy,' basement-like living quarters with scarce foods. Although under such conditions their bodily and psychological health soon deteriorated, most of them were forcibly dragged to the underground work site by Mitsubishi personnel, who allegedly put them to torture on many occasions.

This catastrophe was not revealed until 1986, almost a decade after the closing of Hashima's mine, when a set of documents was discovered in the former town hall of the isle, illuminating Hashima's colonial history for the first time. The documents, consisting of over a thousand sheets of paper, are known collectively as the Hashima Document (*Hashima Shiryō*), and consist of Application for a Cremation Permit and Death Certificate for each of the people who died on the island from 1925 to 1945. Included were Japanese from all age groups, from infants to seniors. In addition, the document recorded deaths of Korean and Chinese who worked at the mining tunnels during that time. Those deaths, having been already turned into inscriptions on a piece of paper, were sleeping under the heap of rubble, just like the dead that Benjamin's angel helplessly wants to awaken from the ruin of history, patiently waiting to be discovered ever since the island became a ruin. From this 'archaeological' discovery of the Hashima Document, the grassroots organization the Society for the Human Rights of Koreans (*zainichi chōsenjinjin no jinken wo mamorukai*), led by Oka Masaharu, was able to unearth the voices of dead through its 'downward' gaze.

The Hashima Document showed that the total number of deaths between 1925 and 1924 was over a thousand people, among whom were 1162 Japanese, 123 Koreans and 25 Chinese (male).[32] Carefully studying the document, the Society for the Human Rights of Koreans (SHRK) discovered not only that the death rate of Korean workers exceeded that of Japanese workers toward the end of WWII but also that many of their deaths during that time resulted from strange causes. Some died by cave-ins within mining tunnels, the number exceeding that of Japanese; some due to 'external injury,' causes of which were often not indicated; and some perished with 'unnatural deaths.' Based on these mysterious death records, members of SHRK concluded that those Korean workers were forced to work in the most dangerous portion of the coal mining tunnels and often suffered brutal violence from Japanese personnel. This inference was corroborated by the testimony of survivors of Hashima, as the group conducted a series of interviews with Koreans who used to work there during the war period.

One of the survivors confessed that '[due to scarce foods in addition to heavy labour] I had diarrhoea every day and my body was horribly debilitated. However, if I were to take a day off . . . I was beaten up [by Mitsubishi's foremen] until I say "I will go to work."'[33] Similar stories were also told by other survivors. In addition to their voice as evidence, the catastrophe of Hashima's underworld was also inscribed onto their bodies as visual traces. For instance, another survivor showed that his backbone was kept deformed due to the posture that he needed to keep during the mining work at Hashima. Furthermore, his leg still had a scar from an injury he received during his labour. Hence, excavating further down the historical ruin of this locale, the gaze of SHRK encountered various underground defacements, including human excrement and deformed bodies, all orchestrated by colonial power.

Swallowing those Koreans and turning them into undead slaves, 'the damp and clammy' subterranean world of Hashima during the war period was virtually the site of colonial pandemonium. In fact, the orifice, which penetrated a massive seawall and served as the only entrance into the premises of the islet, was named 'The Gate of Hell' by the Koreans because they realized, upon arriving on this site, that it was the place where 'once entering, no one can escape from it.'[34] And, they referred to Hashima as the 'Island of Hell' due to the nature of the aforementioned living conditions on this isolated place. By way of further situating this Hell within the regime of the grotesque realism (though not necessarily through laughter as Bakhtin intended), Hashima's historical abyss, its colonial past, should be further excavated, expanded, and illuminated by the downstream thrust. The next section looks at the way in which the island's colonial past is represented in the novel written by the Korean writer Han Susoon, further testing the potentiality of the downward gaze.

5. Pandemonium: Colonial Subterranean Monsters

Han elucidates Hashima's colonial pandemonium in his novel *Gunkanjima*, which was based upon his intensive research on the history of the Korean-Japanese in Nagasaki and wartime voluntary servitude on Hashima. In this book, he constructs literary spaces of multiple labourers who worked on this island. Those characters include Korean miners and prostitutes, Mitsubishi personnel, and Japanese doctors, among others. In order to bring forth the lived experience of the marginalized labourers, Han situates his narrative site within the realm of the grotesque, in which landscape and body manifest the transformative as well as the polymorphic characteristics of this locale, as expressed by the voices and bodies of survivors which were introduced in the previous section.

There are many scenes in Han's novel where Koreans, who lost their nationality and became de facto slaves for the Japanese empire, felt that they were no longer human, but were turning into creatures. Similar to the Schwartz family, Jewish émigré from the grave-like Nazi Germany, in Oates's *The Gravedigger's Daughter,* who, as Garrido argues in her essay in this volume, metamorphosed into identity-shifting 'beasts' alienated from the more civilized society of the US, those Koreans were ruthlessly dehumanized and not even allowed to feel anything, only transmogrifying further into monsters. The most vivid example of this 'becoming' was the imagined body of Chisung, one of the protagonists in the story, when he came back from his first day of labour in Hashima's mining tunnels:

> [H]e was not able to fall asleep and kept turning his positions. Although his body was worn out as tattered cloth, he sensed as if there were another body, independent from his own. As if he

> were standing naked, turning into a hairy creature, whose entire body was covered with long bodily hairs that exceeded ten centimetres. Although only a few days have passed, he has transformed so much. He almost could see himself crawling as if a worm.[35]

Here, the once-human Koreans metamorphosed into non-human creatures, or, following Franco Moretti's readings of Marx, they were reduced to 'alienated labour' from their previous social conditions.[36] The image of the 'crawling body' also plays a crucial role in Han's *Gunkanjima*. It not only hints at their bodily positions in the mining tunnels – the cavity of Hashima – but also shifts the spectator's gaze toward the ground of the island, the downward movement. In contrast to the soaring concrete high-rises, the life of marginalized labourers on the land surface was placed within the realm of the abyss, invisible from the towers. Han's narrative structure thereby incorporates the elevation dialectic of tower and abyss. In the following dialogue, looking up at those apartments at dawn, Myonguku, another protagonist, reflects back on the conversation he had with his workmate, Teboku:

> Teboku: What a height. What a skill. It is astonishing because it [structure] does not fall but it also hurts my neck when I look at them. Whoever built it, it is quite an accomplishment . . . .
> Myonguku: What makes them different if they live up high. We all eat three meals a day.
> Teboku: C'mon, man, get a grip. You are at the very bottom, like a worm. If someone spits on you, you receive it on your forehead. What I am saying is that those who live up there cannot see us as humans.[37]

Han again depicts Korean workers as dehumanized creatures and their habitats as 'bottom,' further transmogrifying the alienated labourer into the subterranean monster.

As Akui Takahiko claims, 'The living space for the island's residents was clearly defined based upon the job classification system.'[38] While Japanese and a handful of pro-Japanese Koreans occupied the upper floors of the apartment buildings, many foreign workers were placed at the lower levels of a concrete tower or in 2-to-3-story living quarters (*hanba*) that were built on the lowest part of the island. In other words, the elevation dialectic is the very embodiment of the island's colonialist power structure: demarcating the imperial-capitalists of the upper realm, the tower, from monsterized colonial subjects of the subterranean world, the abyss. Furthermore, unlike H. G. Wells's powerless and beautiful creatures, the Eloi of the future upper world, Hashima's tower people during the

1940s instead were portrayed by Han as a vampire-like species, sucking living labour out of the underworld monsters.

> A: Anyway, the people in the labour department hate dog's blood the most, and the second is human's.
> B: Isn't human blood the vampire's favourite? The people in the company [Mitsubishi] are the vampires themselves, aren't they? So, why don't they like human blood?
> A: I have no idea.[39]

Although the above conversation between two Korean workers takes place in the context of discussing how 'blood' is seen as an inauspicious object in mining, Han's metaphoric use of the vampire for Mitsubishi personnel through the words of subterranean monsters is striking – especially when immediately following this scene comes the description of Chisung 'definitely getting thinner.'[40]

Han's narrative structure thereby consists of two regimes: thinning monsters of subterranean labour, and blood-sucking vampires of superstratum imperial capital. This precisely enunciates the monster-vampire dialectic that is postulated in Moretti's readings on Marx's conception of capitalist production. Referring to Frankenstein's monster, Moretti suggests, '[capitalist production] forms by deforming, civilizes by barbarizing, enriches by impoverishing [living labour].'[41] He also claims, 'The stronger the vampire becomes, the weaker the living [labourers] become. . . . Like capital, Dracula is impelled towards a continuous growth.'[42] As Marx conceived capital as dead labour, or the dead itself, it further dehumanizes workers to become part of the dead, wherein '[o]nly vampires find anything sensuous in the dead'[43] turning the 'already-dead' labourers into undead slaves. The dialectic of monster and vampire thus constitutes that of wage labour and capital. Han, by rendering polymorphic monstrosity, awakens 'the dead' from Hashima's ruin of imperial capitalism.

Seen through Han's pandemonium, Hashima no longer appears as glorious as the memorialists attempted to portray. The physicality of the island, previously institutionalized through their use of UNESCO's framework, now internalizes multiplicity. The massive seawalls that protected the island from the waves are simultaneously the fortification that imprisoned and enslaved the dehumanized labour force. Furthermore, Japan's first reinforced concrete apartments, seen to represent a more universal value, are the towers that subsumed and subordinated the subterranean zone, connected via 'dung and urine,' where undead slaves were domesticated. Thus, the ruined topography of Hashima is indeed the expression of its grotesque past – it is the 'piles of debris' that Benjamin's angel sees. Unlike his debris, however, this grotesque landscape can still provide a potential site to 'awaken the dead, and make whole what has been smashed 'at every instance of 'now-time'. Otherwise, it will vanish in 'homogeneous, empty time' under the storm of progress.[44]

6. The Present: Spectral Labour in Ruins

Since all the subterranean monsters and capitalist vampires left the island in 1974, Hashima the battleship was abandoned almost overnight. Tossed out in the middle of ocean, structures on the site, including massive seawalls and buildings, were relentlessly exposed to waves and sea breezes without having proper maintenance. Consequently, those structures crumbled into decay and the ferroconcrete towers discoloured as the steel reinforcements were oxidized by the salty waves and winds. Various flora nestled within those structures and encroached the surface of Hashima that was once characterized as 'the island without greenery.' Through these endless magical frolics with nature, the islet turned into something more than a mere dead ship over time, producing a shape-shifting and colour-changing appearance.

The Japanese photographer Saiga Yuji reflects back on his second visit to this fantastic post-industrial ruin in the mid-1980s and describes it as an uncannily deserted and yet animated landscape. 'The strange atmosphere,' he writes, 'led me to wonder if the island had remained in a state of sleep ever since its inhabitants left. . . . The innumerable articles left behind, all shrouded in dust and rusted, at first seemed to be merely drifting toward death. Yet, after some time, they began to look vivid and beautiful.'[45] Through his photographs, Hashima appears, Michiko Kasahara claims, as the site of 'strange things,' which 'seem separated and freed from time and history.'[46] Hashima thereby gained a seemingly 'autonomous' aesthetic character, as captured in Saiga's series of photographs of Hashima.

It was Karl Marx who described a 'mysterious character of the commodity form' as 'a very strange thing, abounding in metaphysical subtleties and theological nicetie'.[47] Furthermore, anthropologist Michel Taussig portrays the commodity as 'a surreal object of . . . such self-transformative and shape shifting significance,'[48] whereas colour plays as a medium and 'gives a buzz' to the commodity. Likewise, the polymorphous and polychromatic landscape of Hashima not only appears but also 'acts' as a strange thing, subsumed into the post-industrial economy, becoming less autonomous.

Having lost its use-exchange values for a while, with the advent of the recent ruins boom, Hashima's spectacle of ruins has lured many spectators through its 4000-yen cruising tours, becoming a tourist commodity. The memorialists being the part of the sightseeing organization, their movement no doubt contributed to this (re)valorisation process, putting the island in a different social relation, or rather mode of production. In a sense, the memorialists, collaborating with UNESCO and the state, have become transformed into capitalist-vampires themselves: 'dead-labour … which lives only by sucking living labours.'[49] However, there are no bodily labours, as previously supported the island economy from below. There is only the vanishing ruin. These rather passive vampires, then, instead live by sucking 'spectral labours' out of this post-industrial locale, further fetishizing it into their lost home.

In *the Legacy of Gunkanjima*, there is a section entitled 'Eternal Home (*eien no kokyo*),' in which Sakamoto stresses the communal life as well as the pleasant living environment of his former home. Furthermore, in the last chapter of the book, he insists that the present Hashima is not a ruin but still their 'hometown (*kokyo*).' This move to extract an ideal home from the dilapidated site is uncannily similar to the way in which the home rhetoric was previously used in Japan. Theorizing what she coins as the discourse of vanishing, Marilyn Ivy shows that the Japanese folklorists of the 1920s, along with the recursive movement of their discourse in the 1960s which was largely induced by the tourist industry and mass media, placed the rural village in the realm of Japan's home or 'tradition.' In these villages, they claimed, Japan's national identity miraculously exists, unchanged for many centuries, having survived the periods of industrialization of the 1920s, of militarization and of post-war rapid economic growth. As Japan's modernization was believed to have been erasing national authenticity, these vanishing peripheral homes (*furusato*) insure a static identity and, ironically, became tourist attractions operating as phantasms within capitalism.

Further, Goto suggests that Hashima's distinctive community had a strong sense of neighbourhood and should become an ideal model for contemporary Japanese society in which this sense has collapsed. This rhetoric is almost identical to Ivy's 'vanishing' discourse; locating what had disappeared within post-industrial urbanity in the vanishing remote island. However, the significant difference is that, while their predecessors returned 'to modernity's before'[50] as a locus of the home, the memorialist, on the contrary, is drawing our gaze to 'modernity as past.'[51]

Amidst post-industrial capitalism, the once quintessentially symbolic locus of Japan's modernity has already been fossilized in the space of fifty years. As this chapter demonstrates above, Hashima has been fetishized into a vanished ideal home by erasing other forms of history and memory of the island. In some way, 'spectralization,' which Louise Katz in her essay of this volume, discusses operates here at multiple levels; the ghostly image of home conjured by the memorialists, and the erasure of the dead (the 'derealization of spectres,' so to speak). Before vampire-like capital entirely moulds the island into a homogenized body in empty (fossilized) time by further exploiting the spectral labour of the ruins, this site should be situated in the realm of the grotesque. Much like, as Garrido shows, Gothic-postmodernist texts that allow for grappling with 'the real,' always transforming and polymorphing, the grotesque, somewhat counter-intuitively, prevents Hashima from becoming an enchanted place where ghostly labourers are constantly working to construct the magically static image of the one and only vanished hometown. Just as the aforementioned Society of Human Rights for Koreans was able to bring to the surface the voices of ex-colonial slaves, injecting the grotesque downstream movement into the history of the island, the grotesque instead provides a means for visualizing its multiple bodies of monstrosity, which could possibly challenge the totalizing commodification. In fact, in a recent interview the author, Takazane Yasunori, the current representative of SHRK, mentions that one of the core members of the memorialists is now shifting his gaze to the island's colonial past due to the long-running effort made by SHRK. Thus, the Bakhtinian downward movement will never be in vain. Continuously following it allows for the disenchantment of this site of ruins by representing the islet as it is – a mixed breed of natural island and artificial battleship embodying its own catastrophe. Hashima is, after all, the habitat of countless historical, yet still-living monsters.

Notes

[1] Walter Benjamin, *Walter Benjamin Selected Writings, Vol 4*, 1938-1940, ed. Howard Eiland and Michael W. Jennings, trans. Edmund Jephcott and others (Cambridge: Harvard University Press, 2003), 392.
[2] Mikhail Bakhtin, *Rabelais and His World* (Indiana: Indiana University Press, 1984), 320.
[3] Keinosuke Goto and Doutoku Sakamoto, *Legacy of Gunkanjima* (Gunakanjima no Isan), 2nd ed. (Nagasaki: Nagasaki Shinbunsha, 2010), 33.
[4] Karl Marx, *Capital Volume 1* (Penguin Classics, 1990), 503.
[5] Brian Burke-Gaffney, 'Hashima: The Ghost Island,' Cabinet, Summer (2002): http:// www.cabinetmagazine.org/issues/7/hashima.php.
[6] Michiko Kasahara, 'Strange Things,' in *Gunkanjima: Awakening within Asleep* (Gunkanjima: Nemurino Nakano Kakusei), ed. Yuji Saiga, 4th ed. (Kyoto: Tankōsha), 143.
[7] Bakhtin, *Rabelais*, 318.
[8] The Hashima Shrine (*Hashima Jinja*), the only shrine on the island, enshrines the Mountain God (yama gami). In every spring, the Yamagami Festival was held on the island. See Goto, *Legacy of Gunkanjima*, 136.
[9] Yoshitaka Akui and Shiga Hideitsu, *Gunkanjima Land Survey Collection* (Gunkanjima Jissoku Chōsa Shiryōshū), 3rd ed. (Tokyo: Tokyo Denki Daigaku Shuppankyoku, 2010), 596.
[10] The original group was formed in 2002, as 'World Heritage Group (Sekai Isan no Kai).' See the timetable of the group in their website: http://www.gunkanjima-wh.com/npo/katudou.html.
[11] See Goto and Sakamoto, *Legacy of Gunkanjima*, 209.
[12] See Ministry of Economy, Trade and Industry, 'Propagation for Modern Industrial Heritage,'

http://www.meti.go.jp/policy/local_economy/nipponsaikoh/nipponsaikohsangyouisan.htm.
[13] See UNESCO World Heritage Convention, 'Criteria for Selection.' http//whc.unesco.org/en/criteria.
[14] Goto and Sakamoto, *Legacy of Gunkanjima*, 208-209.
[15] Ibid., 39.
[16] Ibid., 72.
[17] Minato Kawamura, 'Commentary on Gunkanjima (*Gunkanjima ni Tsuite*),' *Gunkanjima,* vol. 2, 4th ed. Han Soosan (Tokyo: Sakuhin-sha), 470.
[18] See Kawamura, 'Commentary on Gunkanjima,' 471.
[19] Goto, *Legacy of Gunkanjima*, 51.
[20] Eidai Hayashi, *Chikuho Gunkanjima; Korean Forced Labor and After* (Chikuhō Gunkanjima: Chōsenjin Kyōseirenkō, Sono Go), 2nd ed. (Tokyo: Genshobō, 2011), 62.
[21] The Society of Human Rights for Koreans, *Atomic Bomb and Koreans* (Genbaku to Chōsenjin), vol. 4 (Nagasaki: The Society of Human Rights for Koreans, 1986), 29.
[22]Hayashi, *Chikuho Gunkanjima,* 164.
[23] Goto and Sakamoto, *Legacy of Gunkanjima*, 51
[24] Bakhtin, *Rabelais*, 368-370.
[25] Gunkanjima for World Heritage Site, *Gunkanjima: Memory of Living* (Gunkanjima Sumikata no Kioku) (Nagasaki: Gunkanjima wo Sekai Isan ni Surukai, 2008), 1.
[26]Ibid., 18.
[27] Goto and Sakamoto, *Legacy of Gunkanjima*, 101-102.
[28] Ibid., 111. Sakamoto claims, 'Roof spaces of buildings on the island carries significant meanings with regards to Hashima's community formation.'
[29] Ibid., 107.
[30] Bakhtin, *Rabelais*, 336.
[31] See H.G. Wells, *The Time Machine*, (New York: First Signet Classic Printing, 2002), 72.
[32] The Society of Human Rights for Koreans, *Listening to Gunkanjima* (Gunkanjima ni Mimiwo Sumaseba) (Tokyo: Shakaihyōronsha, 2011), 116-117.
[33] The Society of Human Rights for Koreans, *Listening to Gunkanjima* (Gunkanjima ni Mimiwo Sumaseba) (Tokyo: Shakaihyōronsha, 2011), 28.
[34] Takeshi Ayai, *Remember Gunkanjima* (Kioku no 'Gunkanjima') (Japan: Rīburu Shuppan, 2006), 12.
[35] Soosan Han, *Gunkanjima*, vol. 1, 4th ed. (Tokyo: Sakuhin-sha, 2010), 206. The book was originally published in Korean in 2003. It was entitled 'Khamagui (Raven).'

[36] See Franco Moretti, *Signs Taken For Wonders*, Rev ed. (London: Verso, 1988), 91.
[37] Soosan, *Gunkanjima*, vol. 1, 248.
[38] Akui, *Gunkanjima Land Survey*, 636.
[39] Soosan, *Gunkanjima*, vol. 1, 217.
[40] Ibid., 217
[41] Moretti, *Signs Taken*, 87.
[42] Ibid., 91.
[43] Mark Neocleous, *The Monstrous and the Dead: Burke, Marx, Fascism* (Cardiff: University of Wales Press, 2005), 53.
[44] Walter Benjamin, *Walter Benjamin Selected Writings, Vol 4*, 395.
[45] Yoji Saiga, 'Gunkanjima, View of a Deserted Island,' in *Shrinking Cities, vol. 1* ed. Philipp Oswalt (Germany: Hatje Cantz Verlag, 2005), 124-125.
[46] Kasahara, *Strange Things*, 142.
[47] Marx, *Capital*, 163.
[48] Michael Taussig, *Benjamin's Grave* (Chicago: The University of Chicago Press, 2006), 109. Also, for colour, see Taussig, *What Color is the Sacred?* (Chicago: The University of Chicago Press, 2009), 234,
[49] Marx cited by Moretti. See Moretti, *Signs Taken*, 91.
[50] Marilyn Ivy, *Discourse of the Vanishing: Modernity Phantasm Japan* (Chicago, The University of Chicago Press, 1995), 15.
[51] Memorialist's tactic, locating 'Japan-ness' in their vanished home, may be placed within 'a double-structure' of modernity discourse. See Harry Harootunian, 'Japan's Long Post war,' in *Japan After Japan*, ed. Tomiko Yoda and Harry Harootunian (Durham: Duke University Press, 2006), 110-114.

Bibliography

Akui, Yoshitaka and Shiga Hideitsu. *Gunkanjima Land Survey Collection* (Gunkanjima Jissoku Chōsa Shiryōshū). 3rd ed. Tokyo: Tokyo Denki Daigaku Shuppankyoku, 2010.

Bakhtin, Mikhail. *Rabelais and His World*, translated by Hélène Iswolsky. Bloomington: Indiana University Press, 1984.

Benjamin, Walter. 'On the Concept of History.' In *Walter Benjamin Selected Writings, Vol 4, 1938-1940*. Translated by Edmund Jephcott and others, edited by Howard Eiland and Michael W. Jennings, 389-400. Cambridge: Harvard University Press, 2003.

Brian Burke-Gaffney. 'Hashima: The Ghost Island.' *Cabinet*. Summer (2002): http://www.cabinetmagazine .org/issues/7/hashima.php.

Goto, Keinosuke and Sakamoto Doutoku. *Legacy of Gunkanjima* (Gunakanjima no Isan). 2nd ed. Nagasaki: Nagasaki Shinbunsha, 2010.

Gunkanjima for World Heritage Site. *Gunkanjima: Memory of Living* (Gunkanjima Sumikata no Kioku). Nagasaki: Gunkanjima wo Sekai Isan ni Surukai, 2008.

Gunkanjima for World Heritage Site.
http://www.gunkanjima-wh.com/npo/katudou.html

Harootunian, Harry. 'Japan's Long Post War.' in *Japan After Japan*, edited by Tomiko Yoda and Harry Harootunian, 98-121. Durham: Duke University Press, 2006.

Hayashi, Eidai. *Chikuho Gunkanjima; Korean Forced Labor and After* (Chikuhō Gunkanjima: Chōsenjin Kyōseirenkō, Sono Go). 2nd ed. Tokyo: Genshobō, 2011.

Ivy, Marilyn. *Discourse of the Vanishing: Modernity Phantasm Japan*. Chicago: The University of Chicago Press, 1995.

Marx, Karl. *Capital: Volume 1*. Penguin Classics, 1990.

Moretti, Franco. *Signs Taken For Wonders*. Rev. ed. London: Verso, 1988.

Neocleous, Mark. *The Monstrous and the Dead: Burke, Marx, Fascism*. Cardiff: University of Wales Press, 2005.

Saiga, Yuji. *Gunkanjima: Awakening within Asleep* (Gunkanjima: Nemurino Nakano Kakusei). 4th ed. Kyoto: Tankōsha.

———. 'Gunkanjima, View of a Deserted Island.' In *Shrinking Cities, vol. 1*, edited by Philipp Oswalt, 122-128. Germany: Hatje Cantz Verlag, 2005.

Han, Soosan. *Gunkanjima*, vol. 1 and 2, 4th ed. Translated by Minato Kawamura and others. Tokyo: Sakuhin-sha, 2010.

Taussig, Michael. *Benjamin's Grave*. Chicago: The University of Chicago Press, 2006.

Taussig, Michael. *What Color is the Sacred?* Chicago: The University of Chicago Press, 2009.

The Society of Human Rights for Koreans. *Atomic Bomb and Koreans* (Genbaku to Chōsenjin). vol. 4, Nagasaki: The Society of Human Rights for Koreans, 1986.

The Society of Human Rights for Koreans. *Listening to Gunkanjima* (Gunkanjima ni Mimiwo Sumaseba). Tokyo: Shakaihyōronsha, 2011.

UNESCO World Heritage Convention,'Criteria for Selection.' http://whc.unesco.org/en/criteria.

Wells, H.G. *The Time Machine*, New York: First Signet Classic Printing, 2002.

Norihiko Tsuneishi is a PhD student at Graduate School of Architecture, Planning and Preservation, Columbia University, USA, studying architecture history and theory. His research looks at the socio-political implication of space in 20th century Japan.

Monsters and Survivors in Oates's Jewish American Saga

Maria Luisa Pascual-Garrido

Abstract
Joyce Carol Oates's thirty-sixth published novel, *The Gravedigger's Daughter* (2007), tells the story of the Schwarts, a family of Jew immigrants fleeing Nazi Germany in 1936 and their inability to adjust themselves to American society. In telling their story Oates shows that, far from vanishing, fears and monsters still activate our sense of the uncanny although the causes of terror might be difficult to ascertain due to the changes occurred since Gothic fiction first emerged. To that purpose, I contend, Oates draws on Gothic-postmodernist elements and strategies which expose some current sources of terror and the processes whereby marginal communities and hybrid individuals may be perceived as monstrous. In *The Gravedigger's Daughter* all the members of the Schwart family undergo a grotesque mutation becoming abject beings or otherwise ghostly creatures with a liminal existence. Yet, Rebecca, the seemingly successful female protagonist, surprisingly manages to survive. She is apparently able to escape the family's doom which necessarily entails their transmogrification and/or extinction. However, Rebecca's repressed fears and monsters haunt her existence as she grows into adulthood and enjoys the safety and comfort of a bourgeois life. Rebecca's pays a high price for integration in the community, which entails a process of self-alienation and the rejection of her past identity. Drawing on the analysis of Gothic-postmodernism (Beville 2009) and monster theory (Cohen 1996), I argue that monstrosity and monsters in Oates's novel originate from the inability of the dominant culture to cope with difference and hybridity. *The Gravedigger's Daughter* reveals the failure of a community to cope with 'otherness,' therefore making monsters out of those who do not conform to dominant cultural models or who resist easy categorization. Rebecca's strategies for survival and their implication are also taken into consideration in an effort to try to understand the nature of her accomplishment.

Key Words: Gothic-postmodernism, fear, monstrosity, survival, self-alienation, hybridity, identity, liminal existence, Oates.

*****

1. Introduction

Although Gothic literature emerged as a reaction against the excessive strictures of the Enlightenment reaching its peak just after the French Revolution, the postmodernist age shares with that historical period an awareness of terror and death. Gothic terror and anxiety generally relate to a fast changing reality defined by violence, confusion and meaninglessness. Consequently, many of the issues articulated in the tradition of Gothic and terror novels – the distrust of power, the dangers of science, godlessness, social anarchy and privation – together with a sense self-alienation still pervade contemporary artistic manifestations increasing their presence at crucial moments like our post-9/11 terrorised culture. Therefore, it could be argued that today's Gothic postmodernist narratives function as an 'artistic response' to the different kinds of terror that trouble our collective unconscious. It could also be added that Gothic postmodernist fiction of the sort provided by Joyce Carol Oates in *The Gravedigger's Daughter* (2007) also echoes a suppressed yearning to deal with the darker and indefinable regions of our observable reality.

In this chapter I will examine the construction of monstrous identities in Joyce Carol Oates's *The Gravedigger's Daughter*, a story of personal endurance and immigrant assimilation. As is well-known, identity and reinvention of the self have been major preoccupations in American literature, and Oates, who has consistently explored these issues, is probably one of the best contemporary commentators. Hence, violence, death and terror pervade Oates's production as this analysis of monstrosity in *The Gravedigger's Daughter* also aims to attest. In this novel, which Oates dedicates to her paternal grandmother, Blanche Woodside, the writer revisits themes of her earlier works—abuse, anti-Semitism, dysfunctional family life and women's struggle for independence—in a period that spans from 1936 to the late 1990s. I contend that in dealing with those topics Oates once again launches on a personal 'exploration of identity [that] involves both a perceived *lack* of identity and an assertion of identity that […] transcends the individual to become cultural.'[1] As Lee Siegel notes in a *New York Times* review of the novel: 'Oates's fiction courses around the twin poles of our national [American] existence: hybridity and fluidity.'[2] Indeed, Oates herself has declared that she is

> not only American, but a kind of cross-section of America – barring the real wealth and the real poverty. Which is more authentically myself I can´t know but would guess – judging from the odd jarring sympathies I feel even for monsters like Manson – that I place myself *psychologically* even below the decent respectable working-class background of my childhood.'[3]

The Gravedigger's Daughter tells the story of a family of Jew immigrants fleeing Nazi Germany and their failure to adapt themselves and be assimilated by American culture. Around the problematic issue of the hybrid identity in the mid and late 20th century, a number of apparently clear-cut oppositions (American/non-American, male/female, monstrous/natural, civilised/savage and human/inhuman) linked to the definition of the self rise prominently in this novel to question own their validity.

The Gravedigger's Daughter flashes back to 1936, when Rebecca's German-Jewish family arrives in New York where she 'is born' an 'American' in a putrid immigrant boat. Once settled in rural upstate New York Jacob Schwart descends from being Math teacher in his native Germany to a despicable gravedigger in America. The graveyard, at the outer edge of Milburn, signals their marginal position in the community, and hence symbolically highlights their being 'outside' civilisation and the 'human' species. Jacob and his family strive desperately to escape from their doomed existence in the damp and gloomy graveyard cottage where they are confined by the community. Yet, the Schwarts are continually ostracized and terrorized by prejudiced vandals who paint tar swastikas and resort to such contradictory labels as '*Gravedigger! Kraut! Nazi!, Jew!*' (59) to offend them. Their spatial displacement from the centre of the community is also linked to the prejudiced idea according to which the Jews as embodiment of 'otherness' are dangerous beings. Louise Katz's chapter in this volume on the monstrous and ghostly identities generated for marginalised Jews and Arabs – in longstanding historical and fictional narratives as well as in current accounts of the Middle East in newspapers and legal texts – also very clearly illustrates how the 'other' is culturally and ideologically reconstructed and defined as 'monstrous'.

As a consequence of the prejudice against their origin, the Schwarts subsist in extreme poverty and shrink grotesquely in the isolated and insalubrious cottage near the graveyard as the father gradually turns into an abject unforgiving being of deformed appearance. Humiliated by racial and cultural discrimination and his debased way of living, Jacob Schwart violently rejects American civilisation and starts tormenting his wife and children until he finally kills her and commits suicide in the face of their 13-year-old daughter. Although the event traumatises Rebecca, she endures. Later on, Rebecca also breaks away from the overprotective care of her obsessive Christian guard to end up in the hands of a sexually-appealing mobster, Niles Tignor, an absent husband/father-figure who brutally beats up her and their 3-year-old son. Yet, once again Rebecca Schwart is able to avoid her extinction as she does at 23, when she escapes death by Byron Hendricks, a terrifying serial killer whose monstrosity remains hidden under a mask of refined behaviour. Determined on survival, the 'gravedigger's daughter' progresses from traumatised orphan, hotel chambermaid, numbed factory worker and abused run-away wife, to the affluent wife of a media tycoon and mother of a promising pianist who goes by the name of Hazel Gallagher. On a shallow appraisal, this prodigious transformation of the protagonist could be read as the quintessential fulfilment of the American dream. I will argue, however, that Oates's focal point is not so much the prodigious outcome but the dangerous and mystifying process of self-alienation the protagonist undergoes as she repudiates her past. For, in order to survive, Rebecca has to assume several 'false' identities, starting with that of a 'true' American, Hazel Jones, one of Hendricks's innocent victims. Yet, the adoption of a new name does not bring about the birth of a 'brand new self' for

Rebecca Schwart; on the contrary, Rebecca's social success is accompanied by a deep sense of alienation of Rebecca's 'true self.'

The looping and fragmented narrative opens in 1959 when 23-year-old Rebecca Schwart – now Mrs Tignor – a wedded woman and loving mother hears a sentence that hovers in her mind since she was a child: *'In animal life the weak are quickly disposed of.'*[4] The words reverberate in her father's haunting voice as a nagging refrain at crucial moments in Rebecca's life, followed by '*So you must hide your weakness, Rebecca. We must.*' Jacob's faith in the crude Darwinian dogma will help Rebecca react when threatened and chased by her terror of death and extinction of the self. Certainly, persecution is a constant motif in the novel for it does not only bear relevance on the personal – Rebecca's running away from her abusing husband – and the historical – the Nazi genocide that forces their exile – levels of identity of the protagonist. Persecution also looms large at the symbolic level where the archetypal myth of the Wandering Jew, first voiced in the community's rejection of the Schwarts also emerges in Tignor's speech:

> 'Your race, Rebecca. You are wanderers.'
> 'Race? What race?'
> 'The race to which you were born.'[5]

In my view, to approach Oates's novel as a Gothic narrative allows a fuller appreciation of the problematic issue of identity of the 'alien' as 'other', and of the 'hybrid self' – neither purely German Jewish nor American – in a contemporary setting. In the following sections I will focus, first of all, on key aspects of Gothic postmodernism, and then on the stock devices of sublime terror – such as the presence of uncanny fragments of the self, the monstrous or the double – used by Oates in this Gothic-postmodernist piece.

2. Gothic Fiction in the Era of Postmodernism

The Gothic has long provided an outlet for the expression of fears relating to terror and terrorism while also playing a significant role in the creation of terror itself.[6] Fred Botting notes that from a historical perspective the Gothic is 'a writing of excess [...] which shadows the despairing ecstasies of Romantic idealism and individualism and the uncanny dualities of Victorian realism and decadence.'[7] For other critics like Robert Miles, the Gothic is neither a genre nor a style characterised by a set of well known conventions but 'a discursive site, a carnivalesque mode for representations of a fragmented subject.'[8]

Even if we must not overlook the presence of those devices traditionally associated to the Gothic, I personally agree with Beville that in dealing with Gothic-postmodernism 'it is necessary to look beyond traditional conventions and stereotypes and to recognise the discourses, themes and sublime excesses that maintain the relevance and value of the Gothic aspects of the genre.'[9] When considering what the value of Gothic writing might be today, Beville has identified a number of traits shared by a broad spectrum of the so-called Gothic-postmodernist fictions. Among these is the ability of Gothic-postmodernist texts to explore the subjective experience of terror allowing us to grasp what Baudrillard would call 'the real.' Secondly, these texts take the concept of objectified horror to the internal unstable core of the individual human subject. Thirdly, they work to destabilise conventional oppositions such as self/other, good/evil, normal/abnormal, civilised/uncivilised focusing the Gothic imaginary on the postmodernist approach to reality as boundless and immeasurable, and in so doing they unveil the gender, sexual and racially-based prejudices of our postmodern culture. And finally, in Gothic-postmodernism these prejudices are exposed by amalgamating Gothic and metafictional literary devices such as sensationalism, the supernatural, mystery, suspense and the fabulous.[10]

As Edmund Burke claimed in his *Philosophical Enquiry into the Origin of Our ideas of the Sublime and the Beautiful* (1757) 'terror is in all cases whatsoever, either more openly or latently, the ruling principle of the sublime.'[11] Indeed, the sublime had an essential role in the construction of Gothic aesthetics in the 18th century thereby directing the attention toward the dark side of human subjective experience. Therefore, it may be inferred that in any instance of the Gothic in literature the sublime experience must be present for it extends the domain of the perceptible, an assertion that has obvious implications on the role of terror in postmodernist literature. I will then follow Beville in the conviction that 'terror, in its deepest sense of experience is a fundamental preoccupation of Gothic-postmodernism, so much so, that it could be defined as a guiding principle.'[12]

Considered in this light, Oates's *The Gravedigger's Daughter* may be said to explore the experience of terror as it relates to the central problem of subjectivity and being. As I hope to demonstrate, the epistemology and ontology of the self are problematised in *The Gravedigger's Daughter*. The identified self of the heroine, Rebecca Schwart, is always 'an-*other*' as her father constantly reminds her – '*You are one of them. Born here.*'[13] Hence, as Rebecca changes names from Schwart to Tignor, and then from that to Hazel Jones and Hazel Gallagher, her social identity and status mutate but deep inside the conflict about the nature of her 'true' self (half German, half American, one of us, one of them) remains unresolved.

3. Monstrosity

Identity and reinvention of the self have been major American preoccupations, and Oates has consistently explored these issues from the beginning of her career. Violence and threat also pervade Oates's fiction as it is apparent from her early days as a writer. Indeed, her first short story – 'Where Are You Going, Where Have You Been?' published in 1966 – was based on the Tucson serial killer and she has not only written Gothic tales and novels but has compiled and edited *American Gothic Tales* (1996).

Monsters and monstrous identities emerge in Oates's novel not only as a result of an ongoing and never-ending process of renegotiation of the multifaceted self but also as a cultural and ideological construction of the marginal other. This double perspective on the monstrous implies a resistance to our common attempts to establish a rigid and straightforward categorization of experience, which is one of the key arguments proposed by Cohen (1996) in his 'Monster Culture: Seven Theses':

> The refusal to participate in the classificatory 'order of things' is true of monsters generally; they are disturbing hybrids whose externally incoherent bodies resist attempts to include them in any systematic structuration. And so the monster is dangerous, a form suspended between forms that threaten to smash distinction.[14]

Accordingly, monstrosity arises from the impossibility of identifying or even defining beings and entities according to unwavering categories. As Tsuneishi's examination of the monstrous topography of Hashima in this volume also attests, both the changing role of the locus as well as the shifting gaze of outer observers impose alternative and unstable identities on the same object.[15]

In *The Gravedigger's Daughter* the Gothic and grotesque elements are ubiquitous. They are manifest in the setting of the ruined, dark smelling cottage at the Christian graveyard but also in most other places where Rebecca's early life elapses – the putrid boat of her birth, the hell-hole of the assembly line at Niagara Tubbing factory where workers erupt as 'bats out of hell,' the falling house at Poor Farm Road where she is battered, or the desolate towpath by the canal where she is 'tracked' by Hendricks. In Oates's novel the gloomy castle is replaced by the cottage by the graveyard or the bleak house where Tignor has abandoned her, while the labyrinth has been transformed into a 'culvert opened into a fetid marsh', and in the path where 'the horizon was unnaturally close'.

But apart from the frightening setting, one of the most conspicuous Gothic traits in this novel is the presence of grotesque monsters. Following Stephen Asma, 'the label of monster [...] is usually reserved for a person whose actions have placed him outside the range of humanity.'[16] Indeed, a careful examination of all the members of the Schwart family reveals that they increasingly develop traits of inhumanity. Alienated by the community and confined to the social fringes of the graveyard, they gradually transform themselves into impulsive beasts unfit to live in a seemingly more civilised world than the one they physically belong to – the graveyard –, and back in the Old World, Nazi Germany. All except resilient Rebecca, who surprisingly manages to escape death by her maddened father in her childhood, seem to possess abject qualities. At first, monstrosity in *The Gravedigger's Daughter* comes to be associated to the low animal-like instincts built up in the male members of the Schwart family. Yet, this oversimplified analysis of the notion of monstrosity will be challenged by Oates as she depicts other characters whose 'rational' conduct and 'civilised' appearance conceal all sorts of deviations from humanity as Hendricks's actions clearly reveal.

Hence, Jacob Schwart, described as 'a troll-man', stands out as the most conspicuous case of grotesque monstrosity:

> Like a creature who has emerged from the earth, slightly bent, broken-backed and with his head carried at an awkward angle so that he seemed always to be peering at the world suspiciously, from the side. He'd torn ligament in his knee and now walked with a limp, one of his shoulders was carried higher than the other.[17]

Socially, Jacob is perceived as a proud outsider by the working-class community in Milburn. As Katz's chapter on the stereotyped portrayal of Jews and Arabs illustrates, xenophobic attitudes and anti-Semitic myths have traditionally cast the former as prototypical villains or devilish figures. Being by birth a Jew, he hates the Nazis but also the Americans who humiliate Jacob, 'the Jew', employing him as a sexton at Milburn's Christian cemetery. And in the privacy of his home, bitter Jacob is cruel and aloof. He is especially vicious to his wife, whom he despises for being a weak helpless female. The unexpected reversal of Jacob's fortune has altered his personality too and as a result he assumes the role of the monstrous villain. With a university degree, Jacob had had a comfortable living in Germany and had held an optimistic opinion of humanity. He had read Hegel and believed 'that there is "progress" in the history of human kind'[18]; he had studied Schopenhauer, without succumbing to his pessimism, Feuerbach's savage critique of religion, and Marx. Yet, once in Milburn as Jacob gradually metamorphoses into a beast his speech gives way to grunts, and eventually, to silence. In short, Jacob progressively loses all faith of redemption in humankind, and with it, his own humanity. He blames the Nazi Holocaust and believes in an American conspiracy against them:

> Among his enemies here in the Chautauqua Valley, Jacob Schwart would not be hypnotized. He would not be unarmed. History would not repeat itself.
>
> He blamed his enemies for this, too: that he Jacob Schwart, a refined and educated individual, formely a citizen of Germany, should be forced to behave in such a barbaric manner.

> He, a former math teacher at a prestigious boys' school. A former respected employee of a most distinguished Munich printing firm specializing in scientific publications
>
> Now, a gravedigger. A caretaker of these others, his enemies.[19]

Jacob's sons also grow up as ignorant, brutish and unadjusted children in a narrow-minded community. Herschel, the oldest, is an impulsive brawler who flees as a dangerous fugitive at 21. Being quite slow and sexually appealed by his little sister, August, the youngest, is humiliated and battered by his father, and also vanishes forever before Rebecca's traumatic orphanage.

Anna Schwart, Rebecca's mother, undergoes a slightly different process of dehumanisation: rather than turning into a threatening monster she recoils in horror at the grim prospects of being a destitute female Jew in America living with a resentful husband, who thinks of her as a curse. Anna Schwart steadily succumbs to her fears of being water-poisoned and attacked by members of their hostile neighbourhood. Anna also becomes the terrorised victim of her tyrant husband. The steady process of dehumanisation alters her psychologically as well as physically to the extent of turning her into a spectral figure. Frightened, silent and unobtrusive as a shadow, she never crosses the outer boundaries of the cemetery, which stands for the ghostly world of the dead. In fact, Anna virtually ceases to exist long before she is killed by her enraged husband-monster. Likewise, all of Anna's relatives, expected for months to join the Schwarts but denied entrance in US, share that liminal existence: 'Or, if these Morgenstern existed, they were but strangers in photographs, a man and a woman in a setting dried of all colour, beginning to fade like ghosts.'[20]

Yet Rebecca's case is slightly different. Under the cynical authority of the gravedigger, and by analogy with the male members of her family, Rebecca takes the rebellious manner after her father, and suffers an alienated childhood and youth. She behaves in a distrustful manner against the unusual civilities and niceties of neighbours or teachers. However, by reason of her birth in US and her education at Milburn school, Rebecca will be quite unlike the rest of the Schwarts in Jacob's eyes: '*You are one of them. Born here*'. Paradoxically, to her neighbours, acquaintances, and her first husband she is still a 'Jew', a 'Gypsy-girl', 'the gravedigger's daughter'. The divergence at cataloguing Rebecca as a member of different ethnic, national and social categories underscores both her hybrid nature as an American born to immigrant Jews, and society's inability to understand and accept her multifaceted self. Rebecca's sexual identity as a girl seems equally indefinable. She is not a very feminine young woman and adopts 'something of a man's stance, in confronting others.'[21]

The fact that as years go by Rebecca adopts new names and with them acquires new public identities could at first suggest that Rebecca escapes transmogrification. However, as it will be argued, Oates is merely deceiving readers into accepting Rebecca's survival and her social success as a grand narrative of redemption only to later expose her deep sense of uncanniness and self-alienation.

Apart from the Schwarts, Niles Tignor – Rebecca's first lover – is the most obvious source of macho mischief and terror in the novel. After leaving her guard, innocent Rebecca is seduced by this sinister businessman who makes her believe they have been married. Tignor's duplicity – for he is physically attractive and popular but also violently self-possessed – deceives inexperienced Rebecca to regard his exaggerated manly pride as a sign of love for her: 'Niles Tignor was her hero. He'd taken her from Milburn in his car, they'd eloped to Niagara Falls. Her girlfriends had been envious.'[22] It will be only after she becomes pregnant and is abused by her lover that she will realise being under the grip of a terrifying monster. On the other hand, a much less patent case of monstrous doubleness is that of Byron Hendricks, the seemingly harmless man who introduces himself as an honourable doctor but obstinately chases Rebecca on her way home on the pretext that he had mistaken her for Hazel Jones.

> As he was a young-old man, so he was a weak-strong man, too. A man you misjudge as weak, but in fact he is strong. [...] Long ago Rebecca's father Jacob Schwart the gravedigger of Milburn had been a weak-strong man, only his family had known of his terrible strength, his reptile will, beneath the meek-seeming exterior. Rebecca sensed a similar doubleness here, in this man. He was apologetic, yet not humble. Not a strain of humility in his soul. He thought well of himself obviously. He knew Hazel Jones, he'd followed Hazel Jones. He would not give up on Hazel Jones, not easily.[23]

Due to the fact the external signs of politeness and rationality as generally interpreted as symptoms of reliability and human kindness, Hendricks dangerous potential may be initially underestimated. However, Rebecca's instinct of survival saves her from this psychopathic killer, a sort of 'civilised' monster. As in most traditional Gothic literature, the motif of the *doppelganger* also emerges in Oates's novel as one of the fundamental strategies to disclose the existence of the hidden counter-currents that lie repressed under the neat surface of a well-ordered reality which is built upon clear-cut notions that oppose each other to become distinguishable, as is the case with the concepts of 'civilised/savage' or 'human/monstrous.'

Calling attention to the duplicity of these two characters increases the readers' awareness of the risks Rebecca puts herself into. The knowledge of such instability in human nature deflates the readers' convictions as to the suitability of resorting to inherited concepts which, arranged into binary oppositions and steady categories, have helped humankind to define and classify reality and eventually to understand human experience.

4. Strategies for Survival

As has been noted the confrontation with the possibility of extinction, forces Rebecca Schwart to opt for several survival strategies throughout her troubled existence. The first one is young Rebecca's process of defeminisation which allows her to avoid what she views as a sign of 'female weakness':

> In essence she despised the weakness of women, deep in her soul. She was ashamed, infuriated. For this was the ancient weakness of women, her mother Anna Schwart's weakness. The weakness of a defeated race.[24]

It is worth noting that in order to survive Rebecca ironically assumes the patriarchal and racial prejudice that victimises her in the 'civilised' culture of mid-20th century America, even if this done unconsciously as a self-defence mechanism. However, after fleeing her abusive lover, a more mature Rebecca realises the missed potential in not denying her more seductive and feminine side, which, she realises, is perceived as much more acceptable in a patriarchal culture of the 1950's and 1960's. It is in that new feminine role that she acquires the ability of attracting new admirers and eventually meets Gallagher, her second husband. The paradoxical nature of such shifting gender attitudes in the female protagonist exemplifies the power of patriarchal stereotypes to annihilate hybrid or unstable sexual identities in the temporal framework under consideration here.

A second strategy of survival may also be identified in Rebecca's eventual dehumanisation confirmed by her brutish reactions when kicking bullies like a hunted animal, or likewise when she runs away and hides from drunken Tignor as a frightened beast to protect her offspring. Yet, a much more dehumanising feature is revealed in Rebecca's extreme emotional detachment from her relatives. From the time of her harrowing orphanage, an unfeeling Rebecca severs family ties to the extent of concealing her true identity to her brother August, who recognises his sister in her new role as the 'all-American' Hazel Jones. A similar defence mechanism is ascertained in Rebecca's decision to hide her traumatic past as a destitute immigrant Jew from Gallagher, one of the few loving and trustworthy male figures in the novel, who finally persuades her into marriage and provides her with a comfortable living. This attitude renders Rebecca even more inhuman human and unsympathetic, since Gallagher stands for the safety she was denied as the 'gravedigger's daughter'.

Yet, I would argue that the fundamental survival strategy for the protagonist is the generation and adoption of new identity. The former is intimately related to the (mis)use of language and naming in the novel. In *The Gravedigger's Daughter* Rebecca conjures up a new personal identity by naming herself after a deceased woman, one of Hendricks's victims of a cold-blooded series of murders. In this respect it could be said that Rebecca 'vampirises' Hazel Jones, using her identity to go on living. Such parasitic existence finally exposes Rebecca's non-apparent monstrosity, which remains masked under her successful mature self as Hazel Gallagher, wife to an influential business man and mother of a promising pianist. As part of her scheme for survival, Rebecca also renames her son Niley Tignor and calls him Zach Jones, although in this case the change of name and identity is render unproblematic for the boy's self-identity, since he is not consciously hiding a shameful past. It can be clearly inferred from this strategy of naming and renaming that language generates reality instead of representing it as Derrida and deconstructionist would put it. Consequently, naming is a device for the creation of a new, safer identity, allowing Rebecca to survive as 'an-*other*', whereas not naming and silencing stands out as a tactic to make terror and its sources – domestic and commonplace monsters – disappear. Therefore, it is when Rebecca stars suspecting Tignor's betrayal that she speaks out aloud her new name – 'I am. I am Mrs. Niles Tignor. The wedding was real,'[25] – in an attempt to reassure herself of her status as a married woman. Similarly, not-naming creates the illusion of absence and non-existence. Accordingly, in her apprehensive wish to make tyrannical Tignor disappear from her harrowing existence Rebecca reflects: '*He, him* was the danger. His name unspoken he had become strangely powerful with the passage of time. [...] *He, him*. This was Daddy-must-not-be named.'[26]

Therefore, although it is only helpless Rebecca Schwart who manages to stay alive and apparently make the American dream come true, it could be argued that in order to survive the 'gravedigger's daughter' is forced to 'erase' her personal history and thereby undergoes a symbolic death. In adopting the name of Hazel Jones, someone who is actually dead, she avoids being physically killed by sadistic Niles Tignor but at the same time she rejects her origin and dies emotionally.

Yet, in the final months of her life, Rebecca/Hazel starts correspondence with her long-lost cousin, Fryeda Morgenstern, the only relative who unexpectedly survived the Holocaust and became a prestigious member of the American academic community. Fryeda Morgenstern, best-seller writer of the Holocaust memoir *Back from the Dead*, reluctantly receives Rebecca's tortured and emotive confession of her life and her childhood dreams of being reunited. It is 1998 and Rebecca has been diagnosed a cancer. Her correspondence with Fryeda reveals her unconscious shame for having rejected her origin as a destitute and wandering female Jew in a racially-prejudiced and patriarchal society, but also the survivor's guilt which she can only share with someone as 'monstrous' as herself – not purely American nor foreign, a hybrid being made up of the different fake identities she has assumed throughout her life. To a certain extent, Rebecca has developed a shifting, unstable, monstrous identity, which although indefinable and less obvious than that of her grotesque father is finally verbalised and acknowledged in her letters to her cousin Fryeda, her ultimate *alter-ego*.

5. Conclusion

In *The Gravedigger's Daughter* Joyce Carol Oates situates her protagonist in the recurrent working-class scenery of her childhood and youth and fictionalises on her paternal grandmother's biography to undertake an exploration of the complex nature of hybrid beings in our recent historical past. Nevertheless, the fact that the novelist pays as a special homage to her grandmother, to whom she dedicates the novel, does not necessarily entail that Oates's imaginary journey into her ancestral origins in the United States should exclusively be read as an instance of her family memoir. Quite on the contrary, what starts as a fictional rewriting of her grandmother's harsh beginnings in America as the abused child of Jewish immigrants turns into a Gothic-postmodernist narrative of communal dimension read against the intra-historical background of immigrants of the World War II generation who underwent and survived similar experiences of discrimination, privation and family abuse. In the face of poverty, social intolerance and domestic violence, Oates's account of endurance and seemingly personal achievement of a poor isolated immigrant female provokes a collapse of the American dream merely to highlight the darkest aspects of the American life. It could also be argued that eventually it is the contradictory image of the "civilised culture" that eventually appears as monstrous by forcing a complete transformation of the marginal subject in order to fulfil the dream of equality and social approval.

Simultaneously, by focusing on the life story of Rebecca Schwart as the female descendant of Jewish immigrants readers are confronted with the hard process of understanding one's own hybrid identity. The fact is that Rebecca Schwart does not fit into the stable categories available to define the self: from the historical point of view, she descends from educated German-Jewish parents but in the US she is the daughter of a unadjusted gravedigger; she is neither foreign nor purely American as she is raised by German parents who are unable to speak English fluently; socially she does not really fit into opposite extremes (ignorant-poor/ affluent bourgeois; subordinated/ independent daughter-wife-widow-mother) but instead transforms her 'self' as she changes her identity and her economic power. Finally, as for her self-identity, her alternative names (Rebecca Schwart-Tignor/Hazel Jones-Gallagher) also highlight the impossibility of sticking to a single identity. Faced with the impending presence of death, the protagonist undergoes an arduous process of negotiation with her multiple selves.

Oates compels readers to glimpse the complexity of hybridity and liminal existence – that of the reinvented self which fluctuates between the real and the unreal – which so typical characterises the postmodern condition. For Rebecca is neither a perfect embodiment of the 'other' nor completely American, and as a consequence her *alter-egos* switch endlessly in an excessive accumulation of multiple names, identities and alternate versions of herself. In this sense the novel explores a long-standing Gothic obsession: the unsteady nature of one's self. It is patent that Rebecca's tactics save her from physical extinction yet they prove a failure in her attempts to eradicate her sense of alienation and her fears of not-being.

Notes

[1] Gavin Cologne-Brookes, *Dark Eyes on America: The Novels of Joyce Carol Oates* (Baton Rouge: Louisiana State University Press, 2005), 237.
[2] Lee Siegel, 'A History of Violence' review of *The Gravedigger's Daughter*, by Joyce Carol Oates, *New York Times* 17 June 2007, Sunday Book Review.
[3] Quoted in Cologne-Brookes, *Dark Eyes on America*, 237.
[4] Joyce Carol Oates, *The Gravedigger's Daughter* (New York: Harper Perennial, 2008), 10.
[5] Oates, *The Gravedigger's Daughter*, 233.
[6] Maria Beville, *Gothic-Postmodernism: Voicing the Terrors of Postmodernity* (Amsterdam: Rodopi, 2009), 33.
[7] Fred Botting, *Gothic* (London: Routledge, 1996),1.
[8] Robert Miles, *Gothic Writing 1750-1820: A Genealogy* (Routledge: London, 1993), 28.
[9] Beville, *Gothic-Postmodernism*, 39.
[10] Ibid., 59.
[11] Edmund Burke, *Philosophical Enquiry into the Origin of our Ideas of the Sublime and the Beautifu*, (London: Penguin, 1998), 101.
[12] Beville, *Gothic-Postmodernism*, 34.
[13] Oates, *The Gravedigger's Daughter*, 49.
[14] Jeffrey J. Cohen, *Monster Theory: Reading Culture* (Minneapolis: University of Minnesota Press, 1996), 6.
[15] Tsuneishi's reflection on the monstrous topography of Hashima also reveals an interesting strategy of flattening or erasure of the past triggered by the ideological and economic interests of memorialists, which underlies their attempts at redefinition or re-categorization of the Hashima as a World Heritage Site. This strategy resembles Rebecca's denial of her family past in her endeavours to forge a new identity.
[16] Stephen T. Asma, *On Monsters: An Unnatural History of Our Worst Fears* (Oxford: Oxford University Press, 2009), 205.
[17] Oates, *The Gravedigger's Daughter*, 126.
[18] Ibid., 85.
[19] Ibid., 156.
[20] Ibid., 105.

[21] Ibid., 11.
[22] Ibid., 188.
[23] Ibid, 23.
[24] Ibid., 11.
[25] Ibid., 36.
[26] Ibid., 386-387.

Bibliography

Asma, Stephen T. *On Monsters: An Unnatural History of Our Worst Fears*. Oxford: Oxford University Press, 2009.

Beville, Maria. *Gothic-Postmodernism: Voicing the Terrors of Postmodernity*. Amsterdam: Rodopi, 2009.

Botting, Fred. *Gothic*. London: Routledge, 1996.

Burke, Edmund. *Philosophical Enquiry into the Origin of our Ideas of the Sublime and the Beautiful*, edited by David Womersley. London: Penguin, 1998.

Cohen, Jeffrey J. 'Monster Culture (Seven Theses).' In *Monster Theory: Reading Culture*, edited by Jeffrey Cohen, 3-25. Minneapolis: University of Minnesota Press, 1996.

Gavin Cologne-Brooks. *Dark Eyes on America: The Novels of Joyce Carol Oates*. Baton Rouge: Louisiana State University Press, 2005.

Miles, Robert. *Gothic Writing 1750-1820: A Genealogy*. Routledge: London, 1993.

Oates, Joyce Carol, ed. *American Gothic Tales*. New York: Plume, 1996.

———. *The Gravedigger's Daughter*. New York: Harper Perennial, 2008.

Maria Luisa Pascual Garrido is Lecturer of English at the University of Cordoba (Spain) and she is interested in the history of Gothic fiction. Her current research is now devoted to utopian literature and the feminist writings of Mary Astell.

Grave Tales, Monstrous Realities

Louise Katz

Abstract
Human beings are story-telling animals. This chapter is concerned with how characterisation of story subjects, whether places or people, depends on the narrator's cultural and political position – and also their preferred genre, again influenced by the social climate in which the narrative is created. 'Grave Tales' deals in part with characters illuminated with a lurid gothic light, who may come to be viewed as monstrous. It also examines the way in which misrecognition or a lack of acknowledgement can have the effect of leaching the substance of the subject so that it is rendered down to a spectral condition. That is, while being literally realised through narrative process, people or places are effectively 'de-realised' in actuality.[1] We begin with an examination of the traditional anti-Semitic imagining of the Jew as vampire, including reference to Maria Luisa Pascual-Garrido's 'Oates' Jewish American Saga.' From here, discussion of notions of misrecognition and alienation in the Jewish context lead into political debates surrounding Israel/Palestine and the people who inhabit it, focusing on the marginalisation and 'spectralisation' of the Palestinian people within the Jewish state, which is read in the context of Foucault's concept of the in-between site of the heterotopia, or transitional zone. This chapter then shifts its emphasis to another spectral site which may be read as a Foucauldian heterotopia, further illuminated with gothicism's dark radiance; that is, the de-realised or abstracted island, Hashima, off the coast of Nagasaki, Japan, as discussed by Norihiko Tsuneishi in his 'Spectres of Capitalism: Ghostly Labour and the Topography of Ruin in Post-Industrial Japan'. In each case – Middle-Eastern and Japanese – coloniser and colonised are implicated; indeed, at work here is a congeries of interrelationships, far more complex than the traditional self/other dichotomy. Here, we will see how narratival imperatives may compel places and people to be seen as more spectral than real, more monstrous than human.

Key Words: Monstrosity, Palestine, Israel, Jews, Arabs, Hashima, derealisation, Gothic, vampire, spectral, liminal.

*****

1. Introduction

We might think of consensual reality as a sort of blank template upon which we inscribe mythic/historic images accrued over time and stored in a kind of imaginarium, or cultural image database: what is real and what is imagined are linked by the stories we tell ourselves about each other. In other words, myth-making creates reality; reality gives rise to new stories. Some characters in our stories are cast as villains, transgressors who may or may not pose a real threat, yet are relegated to the social fringes. To be marginalised is to be consigned to a condition of only partial reality, making of a woman or a man a kind of ghostly trace of a person. By a further act of imagination, the marginal, already an object of fear, may become imbued with a nightmare aspect. One case in point is the historical anti-Semitic image of the Jew as aspirational monster, dying to become what you are, to take your blood and ultimately, to replace you: Jew as vampire. Another is the 'spectralisation' of Arab Israelis who have, in Judith Butler's words, 'fallen outside the human'.[2] Social and political exigencies – particularly limits posed on Israeli Arab citizenship – result in this group being simultaneously present yet absent within the Jewish state. Further instances of 'spectralisation' focus on sites that have become de-realised through the exigencies of historical and political processes and the repetition of myth-generating narratives.

It is through imaginative processes and storytelling that we continually create and recreate the realities we must then inhabit. For instance, Stephen Prothero points out the centrality of storytelling and mythmaking to Judaism and Jewish identity; Richard Devetak discusses how the American Gothic tradition found a political framework for its themes of horror and anxiety post 9/11, averring that Bush's rhetoric both expressed and assisted in the construction of fear within the populace and abroad;[3] and Ghassan Hage refers to the 'political imaginaries'[4] that create political actions in the context of Palestinian suicide bombers and marvels at 'the capacity of the human imagination to commit individuals along a path of an imagined enjoyable life following the cessation of physical life'.[5]

To 17th century philosopher Robert Fludd, the imagination is a shadow world inhabited by the likenesses of forms found in reality.[6] If *terra umbrae* is influenced by *terra firma*, then the opposite may also be applied: Fludd's shades extend their influence into reality.

2. Jew as Vampire

The vampire casts a shadow into our world of facts and solids that touches those whom society has agreed are separate from the mainstream, dangerous and probably evil. In his discussion of Gothic fiction in 'Terror's Abduction of Experience', Matthew Wickman accords the alarm inspired by rapid social and technological change a 'regenerative phenomenological value', claiming that it 'binds us to each other and reunites us with our past' in a kind of collective 'mourning'.[7] That is, the terror 'restores our sense of kinship with our fellow mourners … In essence, terror's shocking characteristics accommodate an image of collective experience uniting us across our differences.' This may indeed be so in consideration of the 'us', but in this chapter I attempt also to accommodate the experience of the 'them', so to speak.

Societies undergoing collective distress during or in the aftermath of massive confidence-shattering experiences may create images to contain and bear that anxiety, and these may be hyperbolic representations of the 'other'. Historically this role has been allocated to those within – yet separate from – the mainstream 'collective'. Thus we must consider the social function of the marginal as scapegoat. Having said that, in the case of the Jew-as-vampire to be discussed, the term 'scapegoat' is not quite sufficient to encapsulate, in Judith Halberstam's formulation, the 'construct[ion of] a monster out of the traits which ideologies of race, class, gender, sexuality, and capital want to disavow'[8] in that Dracula, 'with his peculiar physique, his parasitical desires, his aversion to the cross and all the trappings of Christianity, his blood-sucking attacks, and his avaricious relation to money, resemble[s] stereotypical anti-Semitic representations of the Jew'.[9] Here we find both Jew and his caricature as vampire personifying tyranny, depravity, a particularly base venality that associates blood and money, as well as the perceived menace of the foreign outsider. However, in the chapter, 'Technologies of Monstrosity' in *Skin Shows*, rather than leaving the image of Jew and vampire as mirror images of each other, Halberstam then asks questions about the construction and production of monstrosity itself as 'an aggregate of race, class and gender'.[10] She contends that monsters of the Gothic mode are aggregations of 'money, science, perversion, and imperialism'.[11] To this assessment one might also add that they often act from within a darkly radiant nimbus of disturbing allure.

Nineteenth century Gothic horror stories infuse with sinister glamour that particular minority group of immigrants, largely refugees from the modern Russian pogroms. The number of Jewish immigrants to England between 1891 and 1900 increased by 600%: 'The Jews [are] coming in like an army, *eating up* Christian gentiles' (italics mine).[12] Zanger also reminds us that Svengali, the Jewish hypnotist from George du Maurier's *Trilby*, was almost as popular a villain at the time as Bram Stoker's *Dracula.*[13] Svengali, along with Shakespeare's Shylock and Charles Dickens' Fagin, was an 'Oriental Israelite Hebrew' whose glamour and powers of suggestion enabled him to bend women to his irresistible will. Like Dracula, Jewish Svengali is tall, darkly handsome; yet both are also likened to creatures often invested with nightmarish qualities of bats, rats, and wolves. The horror of beasts with claws and fangs, the nightmares in which we are pursued, controlled, and ultimately devoured, combine with an attraction to the darkly alluring strangers who emerge from, in Du Maurier's words, '[t]he poisonous East – birthplace and home of an ill wind that blows nobody any good'.[14]

3. Colonialist Nightmares Aided by Viral Reproductivity

Dracula was written at a time when new technologies were proliferating at an unwonted pace. It was also a time of political transition. A parallel is often made between the aggressively potent reproductive capacity of the vampire and prolific image production – the apparently inexhaustible re-creativity enabled by communications technology that lent inspiration to the early Gothic horror writers, notably Bram Stoker. The sort of cultural anxiety referred to by Wickman would have already affected the British zeitgeist as, at this time in history they were witnessing the waning of the power and influence of their empire, creating fertile ground for the production of symbolic stories that represented fears of the possibility of the encroachment of the 'other' from the exotic, mysterious, uncivilised and dangerous East. Or, in Goya's terms, 'the dream of reason produces nightmares': the colonialist empire is shaken by the consequences of the very powers that once made it seem so secure. And, according to Stephen Arata, 'vampires are intimately linked to military conquest and to the rise and fall of empires'.[15] The 'irrational East' now pervades the dreams, and therefore the cultural artifacts produced by the 'rational' West' (an idea explored in depth by Arata in his essay on Dracula and the anxieties of reverse colonization; it is also highlighted in Francis Ford Coppola's version of Bram Stoker's *Dracula*).[16] Add to this the inventions of the telegraph, photograph and phonograph, recreating the voices and images of the dead as well as the living, anxiety is heightened further; people in the 19th century suddenly had to deal with a slew of new ghosts, what Walter Benjamin later referred to as 'phantasmagoria'.[17] Communications technology gave a new reality to the un-alive, raising questions in the 19th-century mind about the possibility of communication with the dead, one of the themes of Gothic horror. It is also a means by which Fludd's shadows of real forms could emerge from his 'other world' in this particular political and cultural climate.

The image of the vampire is that of a lethal yet sensual shadow being, a parasite whose desire is to propagate his own by feeding of real living people, (in the manner of the disensouling technology of photography as discussed, for example, in Janet Hoskins' 'The Camera as Global Vampire'[18]) thus becoming a threat to civilization. However, after having read various essays by Stoker on the degeneracy of writers who were not good Christians, and considering his friendship with Richard Burton whose *The Jew, the Gypsy and El Islam*, a tract reviving revived the blood libel, Halberstam sees Stoker's representation of the monster, Dracula as less an accidental parody or unconscious manifestation of a terror, than a more odious 'hidden agenda' at work.[19]

4. Jew as Vampire

Indeed, in Europe's tradition of anti-Semitism, the Ashkenazi Jew was seen as an alien and oily pariah, who, from within the dankest crevices of culture, works his sinister magic in a similar fashion to that of the vampire. Anti-Semitic images and literature identify the Jew, like the vampire, with parasitism, avarice, and aversion to Christianity and its symbols. Looking further back, we find that historically, Jewish blood was thought to be 'black and putrid':[20]

> There is no people more wicked, more impudent, more troublesome, more venomous, more wrathful, more deceptive and more ignominious', and Jews were 'often considered

> representatives of the devil – if not demons and devils themselves'. [21]

In 'Dracula's Legacy' the German Lacanian critic, Friedrich Kittler comments on the inclusion in *Dracula* of one Armenius Vambery, who is based on an actual professor whom Stoker had met at London's Lyceum Club. Vambery was an international sophisticate and a scholar who 'travelled the Orient in oriental disguise, gathering information'.[22] He was also a Jew who sought to expiate his Jewishness and through the exigencies of education, travel, and profession his Jewish identity was 'thoroughly dispersed'. He is present, yet in a sense also phantasmal, being perpetually camouflaged; in the East, a Westerner and in the West, an Oriental, depending on what was required of him. He was an effective agent in the world, though always through subterfuge, and he embodies characteristics invested in Gothic monsters: mobility, permeability and infinite interpretability.[23] These traits are also those which at that time in history, associate the caricature of the Diaspora Jew – whose corrupting influence infiltrates the social body – with the parasite or the vampire. In his article, Kittler identifies Vambery, with his 'combination of espionage, Orientalism and disguise' as '*actually…some sort of a vampire*' (my italics).[24] Here we are reminded of Halberstam's warning against 'essentialising Jewishness' by 'stabilis[ing] the relationship between [monster and Jew] as mirroring'.[25]

This characterization of Vambery is reminiscent in some regards to that Maria Luisa Pascual-Garrido provides of Rebecca Schwart in her chapter, 'Oates' Jewish American Saga'. Garrido speaks of Rebecca as the only one in her family who is not transformed by their immigrant experience into a monster. Indeed, after their escape from Nazi persecution followed by extreme poverty and alienation suffered in America, the brothers, the father, and the mother ('delirious, muttering and raving'[26], characterized by her husband as a *dybbuk*, which is a parasitic ghoul from Yiddish mythology) do become monstrous. However, perhaps Rebecca may also be read as different kind of monster, one of the same ilk as Vambery, a version of the Wandering Jew.

That is, haunted by her father's admonition to 'hide your weakness' because 'in animal life the weak are quickly disposed of',[27] Rebecca learns to live in perpetual motion so as to stay ahead of her oppressors. She is born neither in Europe nor in America, but in a harbour after arrival but before disembarkation – on the threshold, so to speak – in a transitional waiting space that might be conceived of as a Foucauldian heterotopia, a real space which is also mythic in its nature and functions, reserved for people in transit from one condition to another.[28] She is not entirely German or quite American; and if, as Richard Devetak proposes, monsters are 'liminal creatures who "defy borders" as well as perceived "normality"'[29] then Rebecca may also be read as a liminal monster. As a refugee she is already a trespasser with regard to geographical boundaries, and as Oates' story progresses she also comes to transgress the bounds of personality. Her character resists absolute classification. As with Vambery, it is her race and her history that impels her to enlist this 'keeping-going' as a survival strategy, as is her adoption of a series of identities.[30] Ironically, it is Vambery's facility for mimicry and his perceived lack of essential identity, 'that reminds him that he is, still, a Jew'.[31] This might also be said of Rebecca's character.

Rebecca's 'alter-egos switch endlessly in an excessive accumulation of multiple names, identities and alternative versions of herself'.[32] Her hybridity and mobility reflect notions of Jewishness that link Vambery with the vampire and are consistent with the anti-Semitic portrayal of the Jew, who although corporeal is associated with ghostly Wanderers. Such instability and interpretability are precisely the attributes that had Kittler characterize Vambery as monstrous and a cultural or moral threat, for although an inability to belong is a mark of vulnerability, it also has the ability to fill those who *do* 'belong' with apprehension.

5. *It's an ill wind…*Prodigies, Villains and Scapegoats

It is worth considering at this point the confluence of the fear of change or social disruption and fear of monsters, and particularly the vampire. The vampire is the menace from beyond the pale who has contrived to enter the city, the trespasser whose foreign presence alters the status quo, a bacterial invader infecting the host. The implication here is that the host is an integrated entity, functioning adequately until the invasion. Yet as discussed, Gothic horror stories (whether Victorian tales or post 9/11 Gothic-postmodern narratives reflecting a 'terrified' awareness[33]) emerge at times of insecurity in response to unstable social and political conditions, which belies the assumption that the host was healthy before it was contaminated by the intruder. So, the vampire, whose home is the twilight zone between the poles of life and death, might then be revisioned as a messenger or harbinger of change rather than of doom, even an agent of progression.

The monster is able to act with facility on unstable ground and in times of transition – conditions that terrify human beings unused to incorporating opposites without experiencing a profound sense of unease. This would also account in part for the allure of the vampire previously discussed, and also 'vampire envy', if you will: in uncertain times the innately ambivalent (alive/dead, human/bestial, corporeal/immortal) nature of the vampire is an advantage. Thus, from Bram Stoker's Dracula and George du Maurier's Svengali, to Charlaine Harris' Eric Northman and Stephenie Meyers' Edward Cullen, vampires are portrayed with a kind of corrupt grace that is both human and inhuman. They are prodigiously attractive, aspirational monsters who are doomed to perpetual suffering, but also capable of ecstasies unattainable by mere human beings. A part *of* yet apart *from* nature, more than natural – supernatural and beautiful. And, as Rennie Sparks from the 'country gothic' duo, The Handsome Family, phrases it with eloquently macabre irony: 'But darling, don't you know it's only human/To want to kill a beautiful thing'.[34]

If monsters are, as Halberstam has phrased it, 'meaning machines',[35] then we are encouraged to interrogate those meanings through the literature of horror. Gothic and gothic-postmodern stories can be seen not only as exposing cultural insecurities which provide the ground for the generation of monsters, but for promoting change in an organism which might be considered disaffected rather than infected, or to return to my earlier bacterial metaphor: they may be a probiotic agent of health.

Thus we have gothicism as means of expressing fear, of revealing anxiety and, as Maria Garrido highlights in her essay, playing 'a significant role in the creation of terror itself'.[36] And clearly, the consequences of attributing monstrous attributes to actual people – the Vambery/Vampire problem, if you will – are dire. Thus, we return to the scapegoat: once disenfranchised and marginalized and 'monsterfied', a human being may also be transformed into that indispensible sacrificial victim, the blood-spattered fall-guy for the perceived ills and sins of the dominant social body. Stories of such transformations owe their potency in part to their age, for their antecedents are mythic. In stories from traditional mythology it is so arranged that transgressors become so because they are perceived to have disobeyed (whether the god, the collective aesthetic, or consensual morality). Roles are designated: hero in the right corner, villain in the left, and occupying the in-between territory is the scapegoat.

Simone Weil has considered the concept of *malheur* as a condition which 'stamps the soul to its very depths with the scorn, the disgust and even the self-hatred and guilt defilement…Everybody despises the afflicted'.[37] Yet she insisted that it is those least deserving of affliction that come to endure it, because they are the ones who come closest to enlightenment.[38] Weil was probably thinking of saintly people rather than mythologised others who figure as monsters in the cultural imagination and who, having been indicted, now exist in a kind of non-space like the static between channels. Unaligned and ostracised, they may be used to represent whatever the group desires them to represent. Perhaps this is the mechanism by which certain of Weil's 'afflicted' become martyrs. It may also be the mechanism by which people are transformed into monsters. But in the latter case and unlike Weil's saintly person, for whom suffering is no punishment, but 'God holding his hand and pressing it rather hard',[39] the monsters are the abandoned ones, those whose hands God dropped. So they fell. And in the traditional stories that inform reality this is the point as which the roles of monstrous villain and scapegoat may merge.

For example, these roles combine in the legend of the fall of Lucifer without whom God would lack an adversary (as necessary as his own left – sinister – hand) through which to define himself. The 'traitor' Judas supplies another instance wherein villain and scapegoat merge, for without his betrayal there would be no Christian sacrifice or redemption for humankind. The villain/scapegoat role is echoed also in the disobedience of Lilith (Adam's first wife, who was banished from the Garden for her refusal to assume the subordinate position during sex), without whom carnal desire would lack that gamy, asafoetidal whiff of corruption and there would be no opposite, evil woman for misogynists to blame for their transgressions. She is probably the oldest of mythical transgressors, cast out for her wanton behaviour, playing out her role – like Lucifer – as adversary, spawning manifold monsters and forcing herself upon innumerable men, returning after her banishment to seduce Adam (now married to Eve) and later, the blameless Cain and all those irreproachable men that followed. She is the prototype of feminine evil, the scapegoat who carries the burden of guilt associated with male desire. She is also considered to belong to the succubi or vampire class of demon[40] and by some, as Queen of all vampires.[41]

Such mythic violators are cast out from the group, yet remain central symbols to the culture that produced them, perhaps contributing to the formation of cultural mores and attitudes towards those readily 'othered' – minorities and women. They are the 'chosen ones' who endure the interminable desolation of what George K. Anderson refers to in *The Legend of the Wandering Jew* – whose crime was held to be one of blasphemy – as 'tedious punishment'. As victims of ongoing cultural sacrifice, they suffer for others' social, sexual, and political crimes.

6. Jew as Vampire (iii)

Returning now to European anti-Semitism and the burden of guilt for the troubles of nations falling upon the Jewish villain/scapegoat. Like Halberstam, Kittler, Oates and others, in his study of fascism and anti-Semitism, Mark Neocleous too focuses on the Jew's apparent elusiveness and mimetic facility which allows him or her access 'into every culture, state and social grouping' and to live 'a life parasitic upon these' by virtue of their ability to apparently 'slip from being a race, a religion, a culture of a nation…and back again'. 'The enemy is a formless entity transgressing all borders.' Neocleous refers to the fascist notion of the Jew's contradictory nature which is 'both superhuman and subhuman'. Unsurprisingly, he infers from such descriptions that 'the real monster for fascism is none other than the vampire'.[42]

In order to understand the Jew-as-vampire concept, Neocleous places modern anti-Semitism 'in the context of nationalism and "race-thinking"' that emerged in the 19th century, and focuses on the Jewish people's homelessness being behind the notion of Jew as parasitic entity menacing the existence of nations. Thus we return to the 'foreign body' invading the 'corporate body' metaphor making it possible, by the end of the nineteenth century in Germany, for the term *schadlinge* to be used by Wilhelm Marr to characterize Jews. *Shadlinge*, Alex Bein informs us in 'The Jewish Parasite' are '…creatures which damage the objects of man in agriculture … breeding stock …the human body itself'. The Jew dehumanized and envisioned as parasite may, like vampires, viruses or white-ants, may be 'more or less systematically attacked and destroyed'.[43] So that by the 1930s in Germany, the 'Jewish parasite', simultaneous exotic and lethal, was seen to have once again reached plague proportions, ready again to invade 'like an army, eating up Christian gentiles'. Neocleous avers that by now, 'for fascism generally, the sexual vampire and the racial vampire both overlap with the economic vampire, all of which are encoded within the vampire's *foreignness*.'[44]

7. A Different Story

> Judaism begins and ends with a story.... Judaism is about narrative. This story has everything you could ever want in a good read. It has sex, deceit, love, murder, transgression, and tragedy of biblical proportions...The Jewish narrative is a story of slavery and freedom, of covenants made and broken and made anew. But above all it is about a people banished and then called home – a story of exile and return.[45]

With the creation of the state of Israel in 1948, the East/West, parasite/victim, coloniser/colonised, foreign/indigenous paradigms find new forms on the world stage at a time when imperialism is at last becoming a dirty word. Stephen Arata saw Bram Stoker as 'probing the heart of a culture's sense of itself...in its hour of perceived decline'. [46] A parallel may be drawn between Stoker's representation of cultural anxiety in nineteenth-century Britain, and the particular fears and prejudices that beleaguer modern Israel in what may be seen as that nation state's 'hour of perceived decline'. 'Decline' in this case refers less to imperial failure but to the Israeli loss of their original post-war idealism and sense of righteousness, the validity of the nation's *raison d'être* being criticised from within as well as from external commentators. Both Israel's self-image and its international image are now foundering; its story out of control. It is, as journalist Paul McGeough phrased it in 2010, 'losing the battle for the Middle-East narrative'.[47]

The original Hebraic tale of exile and return is at last consolidated with the creation of Israel as a Jewish state. This story is one of David and Goliath-like heroism, and it sustained the new nation for more than half a century. But in its most recent history, the freedom fighter narrative has loss its glow. A simplified time line illustrates this point: the Jewish state is ratified in 1948; the kibbutz movement begins establishing settlements; the pre-emptive strike against Egypt, Jordan and Syria in the Six Day War in 1967 is magnificently successful, as is the Yom Kippur War in 1973; the 1976 rescue of hostages from Entebbe further casts Israelis as defenders of righteousness... However, world sympathies begin to shift with the Lebanon War in the 1980s, presenting Israel in the role of oppressor; ongoing settlements in the occupied territories; the invasion of Gaza in 2008 where Israel is accused of war crimes; the abuse in Dubai of other countries' passports by the Israeli Special operations team; and the interception of the Gaza flotilla in May 2010, which was judged by the UN as unlawful. In 'The Battle for the Middle East Narrative', McGeough, discussing the territorial conflict with Palestinians, describes how the one-time 'settlers' (conjuring images of valour and discovery) are now seen as 'colonisers', (read dispossession and loss).[48] Israel is falling behind in the contest for narratival authority, but more than losing a propaganda fight for the moral high-ground – which is about appearances rather than substance – Israel is literally losing its self and at the same time, participating in a new story – a horror story. It may also be said to be generating a new kind of ghost.

8. Palestinian as Spectre

The setting: the unstable terrain of Israel/Palestine, a zone that may be described by way of the Foucauldian formulation of the 'heterotopia', or utopian counter-site. Unlike a utopia, which is an imagined world, heterotopias exist within 'the real space of society'.[49]Israel occupies geographical space and historical time, but is also liminal; that is, both mythic and actual, sacred and profane, illuminated with representations of incompatible realities that function in relation to the oppositional poles of the imaginary and the real. Its actual materiality is undermined by its massive load of connotative meaning, and Israel's inhabitants, both Palestinian and Jew, must deal with the apparently insoluble paradox of belonging to two separate countries that inhabit the same physical space. They appear to be failing.

In 'Settler Nationalism' Joyce Dalsheim discusses the stories leftist Israeli liberals tell themselves in order to deal with the apparent contradictions of being socially democratic in politics and compassionate in outlook while also being nationalistic. What she refers to as 'nationalist imagining' manages a trick of perception so that the ethics of Jewish settlement is not compromised. The stories exhibit a certain carefully constructed ambivalence and denial of the other. Through narrative, what is imagined is perceived as real by means of utopian or wishful thinking.[50]

Dalsheim describes a school trip she accompanied to the Palmach museum, whose elaborate audio-visual presentations tell the story of the making of the state of Israel. The teachers, from backgrounds in the left-wing kibbutz movement, expressed an intention to refine their student's ability to think critically about history, yet ironically failed to consider including in the excursion a visit to any sites that had once been Arab, or to extant Palestinian towns. The author also notes that once at the museum, rather than a story being told which disparaged or in any way denigrated the original inhabitants, she found instead that 'that the enemy [was] surrealistically almost entirely absent from this narrative…it was as though they had somehow been wished away'.[51]

Dalsheim compares this wishful notion exemplified in the Zionist slogan, 'a land without a people for a people without a land' with the Australian misnomer, 'terra nullius'. But the glib dismissal of the Aboriginal population of Australia occurred at a time in history when 'Empire' was associated with glory, whereas the newer nation of Israel came into being long after colonialism had slipped to the moral 'low ground'. In imperial Britain there was hardly a need to find ethical justification for colonialist ambitions, but if Zionists are capable of absorbing and sustaining a similar belief as late as the 21st century, this act of mental gymnastics is now becoming increasingly difficult to exercise for the modern liberal humanists within the Israeli hegemony. Living in a postcolonial world, such convenient fabrications are morally insupportable, and so guilt and history meet and cross over and a form of ethical doublethink now comes into play.

Thus, precisely because it is recognised that Palestine was not without a people before 1948 (any more than Australia was not empty before 1770), new stories, formed with the aid of an imaginative disconnect based on an impossible paradox of recognising and simultaneously failing to recognise a whole nation with whom one coexists, creates a weird slippage between reality and make-believe into liminal space. In a fantastical psychic manoeuvre, people become, in Dalsheim's phrase, an 'uncanny absence'… *yesterday upon the stair/I met a man who wasn't there/he wasn't there again today/Oh how I wish he'd go away…*[52]

This poetic characterisation of the 'villains [who are] somehow not quite there'[53] reflects the official term used to describe the Palestinians who remained in Israel after 1950: 'present absentees'. Thus, 15% of the Israeli population[54] fell victim to the new 'Law of Absentee Property'. According to Joseph Schechla's 'The Invisible People Come to Light', the law 'retroactively and prospectively provided for the State of Israel to confiscate properties from anyone identified as an "absentee"'– even though some of those included in this category were, in fact, categorically present.[55] Schechla provides an example of a particularly ironic case of what we might think of as 'uncannily absent presence' or 'spectralisation' of a group of human beings with the case of the villages of Iqrit, Mansura and Kaf'r Birim, whose inhabitants' 'homes and lands were expropriated by the state under the Absentee Property Law even as they continued to press their case in the courts'.[56] Such dispossession, and thus invisibility, is illustrated further by Israeli scholar Hillel Cohen: ' 'Israel did not mention the origins of the internal refugees in the formal statistics. They were not included in the UNRWA registry, and the abandoned villages did not appear on maps.'[57]

In 'Violence, Mourning, Politics', rather than asking if Arabs have suffered dehumanisation, Judith Butler asks us to consider '*to what extent* have [they]… fallen outside the "human"?' (my italics). The derealisation of the "Other" means that it is neither alive nor dead, but interminably spectral'.[58]

In 'The Architecture of Erasure' Saree Makdisi discusses how, because Israel recognises only Jewish nationality, Muslims (plus Christians, Druze and other minorities) may be citizens of their country without being nationals.[59] Such narratives of misrecognition and alienation, according to Bourdieu, cut one off from 'access to a socially recognised social being ... to humanity'.[60] Like the Jewish 'vampires' discussed previously in this chapter, Arabs are simultaneously a part, yet *apart* from the mainstream. They form a real, yet not real, ghostly presence in a city which already labours under a burden of history so heavy that it seems composed as much of myth as of stone.

But regarding Arab 'erasure': A controversial case in point is that of The Centre for Human Dignity in Jerusalem, an offshoot of Los Angeles' Museum of Tolerance, designed by the internationally acclaimed architect Frank Gehry. It is now included within the Custodianship of Absentee Property. Makdisi writes of the museum's launch, where it was described as 'a unique institution that will focus on issues of human dignity and responsibility'. It emerges, however, that this site includes an important Muslim cemetery that had been in continual use since the Crusades until 1948.[61]

Built in the 7th century, the boundaries of the Ma'man Allah cemetery were formally delineated in the 19th, and mapped in detail during the Mandate period before it became 'absentee property'. Proponents of the museum argue that any new structures built in 3,000 year old city are bound to be built on graves, and that correct consultative procedures were followed; instances where Muslims have built roads and structures on other cemeteries are also cited, but legal and moral objections were raised by both Jewish and Muslim groups, locally and overseas. Many see the construction of a institution dedicated to tolerance and human dignity built on this particular site as a bleak irony, quite unlikely to deserve the accolade, "a great landmark promoting the principles of mutual respect"'.[62] Nevertheless, after a hiatus in 2006 when construction was halted for two years – after the excavators struck bones – the project continues.

Stories based on denial, misrecognition and invalidation of another may result in 'spectralisation' of that other, which has cultural ramifications for all concerned, and clear political implications for both colonist and colonised. That having been said, it is also important to note that to construct Palestinians and Israelis as one-dimensional heroes and villains overlooks the ongoing political machinations of both Middle Eastern and Western powerbrokers as well as the ancient and complex narratival palimpsest that is Israel/Palestine. Israeli author Amoz Oz speaks of the 'interdependence' of 'torturer and victim'[63] and Lebanese Australian anthropologist Ghassan Hage discusses how the 'dehumanising gaze' that sees 'Them as a non- differentiated entity ... is often accompanied by an equally self-dehumanising, abstracted version of Us'.[64] In the Jewish case, while the secular nationalist narrative (with embedded biblical aspects) and concomitant self-image is failing, a new Jewish Israeli 'Us' has yet to emerge. In the Arab case, if one continues to suffer 'the violence of derealization',[65] one's voice being repeatedly ignored, one is likely to start shouting. In 2002, Hage emailed 'Arab, Jewish and other concerned friends', attempting to think through the violence of Israel's reinvasion of the West Bank.[66] He found himself accused by colleagues of moral collusion. Apparently the affect of military actions, no matter how extreme, cannot match the existential horror provoked by acts of terrorism. 'They' must remain, in the mainstream consciousness, as inhuman, 'nondifferentiated', abstracted and evil.

In 'Terror's Abduction of Experience', Matthew Wickman tells us that terror is provoked by the spectacle of some awful and inexplicable fright and 'a turbid moodiness lingers … whereas with horror these conventions swell into monstrosities'.[67] Perhaps then, whether associating human beings with phantasmagoric bloodsuckers, or as in the case of suicide bombers, *failing* to associate humanity with those 'beyond the pale' in quite another sense, we are dealing less with terror than with horror? In the latter case, perhaps it is that the pedestrian nature of tanks and guns – their very legality – cannot match the trauma of entering a kind of mythic space that opens up when the quotidian world is ruptured by an act of terror – or horror – which is where 'the sublime and the grotesque meet, often in a panoply of kitsch imagery … characterised by a hyperbolic combination of visceral disgust and psychic anxiety'.[68] Wickman is discussing literature, but I think the analysis may be extended to the world of objects and people: Horror plunges the mind into what Bataille calls 'a strange world where anguish and ecstasy coexist'.[69]Thus, the 'horrorist', brings into the world a spiritual dimension of fright that culminates in an ontological dreadfulness that could only be perpetrated by those whom we choose no longer to identify as human, but as monsters.

9. Spectralised People and Liminal Spaces

At this point I would like to draw a parallel between Palestinian 'erasure' or spectralisation with particular reference to the Ma'man Allah Cemetery, and that of a people and a site that at first may seem quite unrelated; but in fact the two demonstrate certain commonalities. One might make a comparison between treatment of Ma'man Allah and Norihiko Tsuneishi's analysis of Hashima, a small island off the coast of Nagasaki, nicknamed 'Gunkanjima' for the form of its silhouette, that of a battleship.

The 2005 UNESCO publication, *The Legacy of Gukanjima* provides what Tsuneishi concedes is a valid depiction of the island when focusing on its culture of coal-mining; but he points out that other cultures are underplayed or ignored. Tsuneishi claims that this portrayal represents 'a strategic build-up to mold its history into the framework of UNESCO. It forms a sanitised, flattened history'.[70] Arguably, this is also the case with Jerusalem's Centre for Human Dignity. Ma'man Allah and Gukanjima have both suffered from the attempt on the part of different kinds of memorialists to re-submerge the already-dead – in one case Palestinians; in the other, colonial workers whose labour has 'shaped Hashima into deeply scarred physical space as well as a phantasmagoric site'.[71] This rather gothic description finds resonance in many a benighted site within war-ravaged Israel/Palestine; not only in echoing the scarred and disfigured landcapes and cityscapes, but also in the surreal nature of the Israeli/Palestinian heterotopia. That is, both Gukanjima and Ma'man, though occupying real space and time, exhibit qualities which are at once mythic and real, characterised by incongruous juxtapositions that lend to both sites a phantasmagoric air.

Tsuneishi also makes reference to the novel *Gunkanjima* by Han Soosan, which 'elucidates the deadly working conditions of Korean labour at Hashima [and for whom] the island's topography of abyss and tower becomes the embodiment of a colonial hierarchy'. Tsuneishi states that 'there are many scenes in Han's novel where Korean workers felt they had metamorphosed into dehumanized creatures'.[72] Indeed, Tsuneishi's description of the industrial complex's towers of the privileged and dungeons of the doomed is reminiscent of the fantastical and macabre city of New Crobuzon, in new weird author China Mieville's invented world of Bas Lag,[73] or Gormenghast Castle as imagined by gothic fantasy author, Mervyn Peake.[74]

Given that the Gothic aesthetic has changed over time 'from the haunted castle to the haunted metropolis and from the supernatural to the surreal',[75] Gunkanjima may be read as a ghostly and ghost-ridden wasteland imbued with a gothic-postmodern sensibility. The wasteland motif is echoed by the fact that very limited aspects of either Ma'man and Gukanjima are formally recognized, and these decisions were made according to the exigencies of particular political and cultural requirements. Indeed, both exhibit, in Tsuneishi's phrasing, 'a rather light touch' regarding history. Many argue that The Centre for Human Dignity denies the dead and defies a large number of the living. The superscription of both sites with tourist attractions disregards in Ma'man Allah's case the sacrosanct nature of a burial place and more broadly speaking, the palimpsestic history of ancient city of Jerusalem; and in Gukanjima, it denigrates through oversight the 'subterranean labours [which] have been forcibly buried under the 'universal' history.[76] Both Gunkanjima and Ma'man are commemorative sites whose histories have been myopically reduced.

The structures remain, though hollowed of their original meaning and function; Gukanjima's history is sterilized – or exorcised – and the stories of the people who once worked there largely undocumented. Similarly, Jerusalem's Centre for Human Dignity may be read as both an edifice of denial and a monument to the Gothic – built on a grave, the voices of the dead muted – as well as many of those of the living. In both Gunkanjima and in Jerusalem we see a kind of 'double-ghosting' in operation: places are cleansed of the contamination of history and the dead are denied remembrance. As memorial sites and tourist attractions both sites are markers in on-going colonialist narratives of denial.

10. Conclusion

Failure of acknowledgment or misrecognition of another may contribute to the other being seen as monstrous, or becoming, effectively, a shade. But those who are 'derealized', have, according to Judith Butler, 'a strange way of remaining animated and so must be negated again (and again)...they seem to live on, stubbornly, [vampire-like] in this state of deadness...[77] This analysis applies not only to human beings but to places like those discussed in this essay, Israel/Palestine and specifically the Museum of Tolerance in Jerusalem, and Gunkanjima Island. Gukanjima's memorialists see its historical significance only as industrial and architectural, denying us 'the much larger "human history"' when, Tsuneishi argues, the site had the potential to contribute to a broad understanding of colonialism, war and culture. Such an understanding is possible only with a more sympathetic analysis of the site and the people who once constituted its population.[78]

One might say that these places are invested with monstrous aspects in the sense of being ambiguous, permeable and manifestly interpretable, in contrast to being completed and 'strictly limited'.[79] Gunkanjima, a body in a state of becoming, being transformed during Japan's industrialization from a rocky little island until it resembles nothing less than a battleship – from the natural entity Hashima into the grotesque amalgam of the organic and the synthetic, Gunkanjima – is at this stage of history a kind of mechanical monster. If interpreted sympathetically, this artificial creation, like Frankenstein's monster, could relate a complex narrative, yet UNESCO'S story is seen by Tsuneishi as insufficient to the task, underplaying its 'its intrinsically transformative and polymorphic character'.[80]

Similarly, Jerusalem's Centre for Human Dignity overlooks – literally and metaphorically – a vital aspect of its positioning. Here, future and past converge – as elsewhere in this nation state – in a grotesque contemporary landscape in continual and agonizing flux, where the dead and the living converse in a the liminal twilight of the Israel/Palestine heterotopia. The debates involved in the construction of the museum on a grave further aggravate an already impossible political horror story, and contributes to the spectralisation of a percentage of the population still above the ground.

But a human being is not a monster, not a ghost; indeed, as Bourdieu writes in *Pascalian Meditations*, 'there is no worse dispossession, no worse privation, perhaps, than that of the losers in the symbolic struggle for recognition'.[81] Such monstrous images are based on old stories from a bank of cultural imagery, or a *terra umbrae* inhabited by 'shadows' of real forms, or by dreams and symbols, perpetuated through narrative. We might say that each culture has its image stock, built up over centuries of remembering and storytelling, available to feed into new contexts, which in turn may enter the cultural imaginarium, perhaps to be used again later on in history: an ongoing, two-way exchange between reality and imagination.

Notes

[1] Judith Butler, 'Violence, Mourning, Politics', *Studies in Gender and Sexuality* 41 (2003).
[2] Ibid., 21.
[3] Richard Devetak, 'The Gothic Scene of International Relations: Ghosts, Monsters, Terror and the Sublime after September 11', *Review of International Studies* (2005): 621-643.
[4] Ghassan Hage, '"Comes a Time We Are All Enthusiasm": Understanding Palestinian Suicide Bombers in Times of Exighophobia', *Public Culture* 15.1 (2003): 65-85, 66.
[5] Ibid., 89.
[6] Cited in Marina Warner, *Fantastic Metamorphoses, Other Worlds* (Oxford: Oxford University Press, 2002), 172.
[7] Matthew Wickman, 'Terror's Abduction of Experience: A Gothic History', *The Yale Journal of Criticism* 18.1 (2005): 180.
[8] Judith Halberstam, *Skin Shows: Gothic Horror and the Technology of Monsters* (Durham and London: Duke University Press, 1995), 102.
[9] Ibid., 86.
[10] Ibid., 88.
[11] Ibid., 21.
[12] Paul Johnson cited in Jules Zanger, 'A Sympathetic Vibration: Dracula and the Jews', *English Literature in Transition* 2 (1991): 33-34.
[13] Jules Zanger, 'A Sympathetic Vibration: Dracula and the Jews', *English Literature in Transition* 2 (1991): 35.
[14] Du Maurier, cited in Zanger, 35.
[15] Arata in Gelder, *Horror Reader*, 165.
[16] S. D. Arata, 'The Occidental Tourist: *Dracula* and the Anxiety of Reverse Colonization' (extract) in *The Horror Reader* (London and New York: Routledge, 2000), 162.
[17] M. Cohen, 'Benjamin's Phantasmagoria', cited in*The Cambridge Companion to Walter Benjamin*, ed. D.S. Ferris (Cambridge University Press, Cambridge Collections Online, 2004), viewed December 2008, http://cco.cambridge.org/extract?id=ccol0521793297.
[18] Janet Hoskins, 'The Camera as Global Vampire: The Distorted Mirror of Photography in Remote Indonesia and Elsewhere,' in *The Framed World: Tourism, Tourists and Photography*, eds. Mike Robinson and David Picard (Ashgate: Leeds Metropolitan University, 2009).
[19] Halberstam, *Skin Shows*, 86.

[20] Eric Zafran, 'Saturn and the Jews', *Journal of The Warburg and Courtauld Institutes* 34 (1972): 17
[21] Ibid.
[22] Arata in Gelder, *Horror Reader*, 9.
[23] Halberstam, *Skin Shows*, 21.
[24] Arata in Gelder, *Horror Reader*, 8-9
[25] Halberstam, *Skin Shows*, 88.
[26] Joyce Carol Oates, *The Gravedigger's Daughter* (London: Harper Perennial, 2008), 162.
[27] Ibid., 1-2.
[28] Michel Foucault, *Of Other Spaces*, 1967, viewed January 2007, http://foucault.info/documents/heteroTopia/foucault.heteroTopia.en.html
[29] Devetak, 'Gothic Scene', 724.
[30] Oates, *The Gravedigger's Daughter*, 386.
[31] Ibid., 11.
[32] Maria Luisa Pascual Garrido, 'Fear Monstrosity and Survival: A Gothic Reading of *The Gravedigger's Daughter*', in this volume.
[33] Maria Beville, *Gothic-Postmodernism* (Amsterdam and New York: Rodopi, 2009), 27.
[34] The Handsome Family, 'A Beautiful Thing', *In the Air* (Chicago, Carrot Top Records, 2000).
[35] Halberstam, *Skin Shows*, 21.
[36] Garrido, 'Fear Monstrosity and Survival'.
[37] Simone Weil, *On Science, Necessity and The Love of God*, trans. Richard Lees, (Oxford University Press: London, 1968): 170.
[38] Simone Weil, *Gravity and Grace* (London and New York: Routledge, 2002).
[39] Weil, *The Simone Weil Reader*.
[40] Simone Yehuda, 'Lilith, the Original Bad Girl or The Genesis of Genesis, transcript of paper for National Association of Women's Studies Conference, St. Louis (1997).
[41] Zacheryadam Quinn Collins, 'Lilith: Lie, Lore or Hard Core?' proceedings for Stephen F. Austin State University, Association for the Scientific Study of Religion, South West (2009), viewed February 2012, http://www.envirecon.com/ASSRProceedings2009.pdf#page=106
[42] Mark Neocleous, *The Monstrous and the Dead: Burke, Marx, Fascism* (Cardiff: University of Wales Press, 2005), 75-76.
[43] Alex Bein, 'The Jewish Parasite', *Leo Baeck Institute Yearbook* 9 (1964): 6-7.
[44] Neocleous, *The Monstrous and the Dead*, 87.
[45] Stephen Prothero, *God is Not One* (Melbourne: Black Inc., 2010), 244.
[46] Arata in Gelder, *Horror Reader*, 162.

[47] Paul McGeough, 'The Battle for the Middle East Narrative', *Sydney Morning Herald*, October 2, 2010, http://www.smh.com.au/world/the-battle-for-the-middle-east-narrative-20101001-1610u.html viewed October, 2010.
[48] Ibid., McGeough.
[49] Foucault, *Of Other Spaces*.
[50] Joyce Dalsheim, 'Settler Nationalism, Collective Memories of Violence and the "Uncanny Other"', *Social Identities* 10 (2004).
[51] Ibid., 160.
[52] William Mearns. 'Antigonish'. Cited in the FPA Column 'The Conning Tower', *New York World*, New York (1922)
[53] Ibid., 152.
[54] Danny Yee, 'Danny Yee's Book Reviews' Review of *Catastrophe Remembered: Palestine, Israel and the Internal Refugees* by Nur Masalha, London: Zed Books 2008, viewed May 2010,
http://dannyreviews.com/h/Catastrophe_Remembered.html
[55] Joseph Schechla, 'The Invisible People Come to Light: Israel's "Internally Displaced and "Unrecognised Villages"', *Journal of Palestine Studies* 31 (2001): 21.
[56] Ibid., 22.
[57] H. Cohen, 'The State of Israel *versus* the Internal Palestinian Refugees'. In *Catastrophe Remembered, Palestine, Israel, and the Internal Refugees: Essays in Memory of Edward W Said*, ed. Nur Masalha (London: Zed Books, 2005), 64.
[58] Judith Butler, 'Violence, Mourning, Politics', *Studies in Gender and Sexuality* 41 (2003): 21-22.
[59] Saree Makdisi, 'The Architecture of Erasure', *Critical Enquiry* 36 (2010):6
[60] Ghassan Hage, '"Comes a Time We Are All Enthusiasm", Understanding Palestinian Suicide Bombers in Times of Exigophobia', *Public Culture* 15 (2003): 78.
[61] Makdisi, *Architecture of Erasure*, 1-2.
[62] Ibid., 2.
[63] Amos Oz, *Black Box* (London: Vintage, 2002), 146.
[64] Ghassan Hage, '"Comes a Time We Are All Enthusiasm", Understanding Palestinian Suicide Bombers in Times of Exigophobia', *Public Culture* 15 (2003): 65-66.
[65] Judith Butler, 'Violence, Mourning, Politics', *Studies in Gender and Sexuality* 41 (2003): 22.
[66] Hage, '"Comes a Time We Are All Enthusiasm"', 65.
[67] Matthew Wickman, 'Terror's Abduction of Experience: A Gothic History', *The Yale Journal of Criticism* 18 (2005): 188.
[68] Wickman, *Terror's Abduction of Experience*, 188.

[69] Georges Bataille, *Inner Experience* trans. Leslie Anne Boldt (Albany: State University of New York Press: 1988), pxxxii.
[70] Norihiko Tsuneishi, 'Spectres of Capitalism: Ghostly Labour and the Topogaphy of Ruin in Post-Industrial Japan', in this volume.
[71] Ibid.
[72] Ibid.
[73] China Mieville, *Perdido Street Station* (London: Macmillan, 2000).
[74] Mervyn Peake, *Titus Groan* (London: Vintage, 1998).
[75] Maria Beville, *Gothic Post-modernism*, 38.
[76] Tsuneishi, 'Spectres of Capitalism', 4.
[77] Butler, 'Violence, Mourning, Politics', 22.
[78] Tsuneishi, 'Spectres of Capitalism', 4.
[79] Ibid., 2.
[80] Ibid., 3.
[81] Bourdieu cited in Hage, '"Comes a Time we are all Enthusiasm", 78.

Bibliogaphy

Arata, Stephen D. 'The Occidental Tourist: *Dracula* and the Anxiety of Reverse Colonization'. In *The Horror Reader*, edited by Ken Gelder, 81-97. London and New York: Routledge, 2000.

Bataille, George. *Inner Experience.* Translated by Leslie Anne Boldt. Albany: State University of New York Press, 1988.

Beville, Maria. *Gothic-Postmodernism.* Amsterdam and New York: Rodopi, 2009.

Butler, Judith 'Violence, Mourning, Politics'. *Studies in Gender and Sexuality* 41 (2003): 9-37.

Cohen, H. 'The State of Israel *versus* the Internal Palestinian Refugees'. In *Catastrophe Remembered, Palestine, Israel, and the Internal Refugees: Essays in Memory of Edward W Said*, edited by Nur Masalha, 56-73. London: Zed Books, 2005.

Cohen, M. 'Benjamin's Phantasmagoria'. In *The Cambridge Companion to Walter Benjamin*, edited by D. S. Ferris, Cambridge University Press, Cambridge Collections Online, 2004. Viewed 11 June 2008.
http://cco.cambridge.org/extract?id=ccol0521793297_CCOL0521793297A012.

Collins, Zacheryadam Quinn. 'Lilith: Lie, Lore or Hard Core?' Proceedings for Stephen F. Austin State University, Association for the Scientific Study of Religion South West, 2000. Viewed 10 February 2012.
http://www.envirecon.com/ASSRProceedings2009.pdf#page=106.

Dalsheim, Joyce. 'Settler Nationalism, Collective Memories of Violence and the "Uncanny Other"'. *Social Identities* 10 (2004): 151-170.

Devetak, Richard, 'The Gothic Scene of International Relations: Ghosts, Monsters, Terror and the Sublime after September 11'. *Review of International Studies* (2005): 621-643.

Foucault, Michel, *Of Other Spaces. Diacritics16*. Viewed 10 January 2007.
ttp://foucault.info/documents/heteroTopia/foucault.heteroTopia.en.html.

Hage, Ghassan, '"Comes a Time We Are All Enthusiasm": Understanding Palestinian Suicide Bombers in Times of Exigophobia'. *Public Culture* 15 (2003): 65-89.

Halberstam, Judith. *Skin Shows: Gothic Horror and the Technology of Monsters*. Durham and London: Duke University Press, 1995.

Hoskins, Janet, 'The Camera as Global Vampire: The Distorted Mirror of Photography in Remote Indonesia and Elsewhere'. *The Framed World: Tourism, Tourists and Photography*, edited by Mike Robinson and David Picard. Ashgate: Leeds Metropolitan University, 2009.

McGeough, Paul, 'The Battle for the Middle East Narrative', *Sydney Morning Herald*, October 2, 2010. Viewed 2 October, 2010.
http://www.smh.com.au/world/the-battle-for-the-middle-east-narrative-20101001-1610u.html.

Makdisi, Saree, 'The Architecture of Erasure'. *Critical Enquiry* 36 (2010): 519-559.

Mieville, China. *Perdido Street Station*. London: Macmillan, 2000.

Neocleous, Mark. *The Monstrous and the Dead: Burke, Marx, Fascism*. Cardiff: University of Wales Press, 2005.

Oates, Joyce Carol, *The Gravedigger's Daughter*. London: Harper Perennial, 2008.

Oz, Amos, *Black Box*. London: Vintage, 2002.

Peake, Mervyn. *Titus Groan*. London: Vintage, 1998.

Prothero, Stephen. *God is Not One*. Melbourne: Black Inc., 2010.

Schechla, Joseph, 'The Invisible People Come to Light: Israel's "Internally Displaced" and "Unrecognised Villages"'. *Journal of Palestine Studies* 31 (2001): 20-31.

Warner, Marina, *Fantastic Metamorphoses, Other Worlds*. Oxford: Oxford University Press, 2002.

Weil, Simone. *On Science, Necessity and The Love of God.* Translated by Richard Lees. Oxford University Press: London, 1968.

———. *Gravity and Grace*. London and New York: Routledge, 2002.

———. In *The Simone Weil Reader*, edited by George Andrew Panichas. New York: David McKay Company, 1977.

Wickman, Matthew. 'Terror's Abduction of Experience: A Gothic History'. *The Yale Journal of Criticism* 18 (2005): 170-207.

Yee, Danny, 'Danny Yee's Book Reviews'. Review of *Catastrophe Remembered: Palestine, Israel and the Internal Refugees*, by Nur Masalha. London: Zed Books, 2008. Viewed 28 May 2010.
http://dannyreviews.com/h/Catastrophe_Remembered.html.

Yehuda, Simone. 'Lilith, the Original Bad Girl or The Genesis of Genesis'. Transcript of paper for The National Association of Women's Studies Conference, St Louis, 1997.

Zafran, Eris, 'Saturn and the Jews'. *Journal of The Warburg and Courtauld Institutes* 34 (1972): 16-27.

Zanger, Jules, 'A Sympathetic Vibration: Dracula and the Jews'. *English Literature in Transition* 2 (1991): 33-44.

Louise Katz works at the University of Sydney as a lecturer in writing, and has published several fantasy novels and stories.